Standard for Automatic Exchange of Financial Account Information in Tax Matters

OECD

BETTER POLICIES FOR BETTER LIVES

This document and any map included herein are without prejudice to the status of or sovereignty over any territory, to the delimitation of international frontiers and boundaries and to the name of any territory, city or area.

Please cite this publication as:
OECD (2014), *Standard for Automatic Exchange of Financial Account Information in Tax Matters*, OECD Publishing.
http://dx.doi.org/10.1787/9789264216525-en

ISBN 978-92-64-21651-8 (print)
ISBN 978-92-64-21652-5 (PDF)

Foreword

This is the first edition of the publication entitled *Standard for Automatic Exchange of Financial Account Information in Tax Matters.*

This edition includes the text of the Model Competent Authority Agreement and the Common Reporting Standard, and the Commentaries thereon, as they read on 15 July 2014 after the approval of the Standard for Automatic Exchange of Financial Account Information in Tax Matters by the Council of the OECD.

Abbreviations and acronyms

AEOI	Automatic Exchange of Information
CRS	Common Reporting Standard
EU	European Union
FATCA	Foreign Account Tax Compliance Act
FATF	Financial Action Task Force
FI	Financial Institution
IT	Information Technology
Model CAA	Model Competent Authority Agreement
OECD	Organisation for Economic Co-operation and Development
TIEA	Tax Information Exchange Agreement

I. Introduction

A. Background

1.   As the world has become increasingly globalised it is easier for all taxpayers to make, hold and manage investments through financial institutions outside of their country of residence. Vast amounts of money are kept offshore and go untaxed to the extent that taxpayers fail to comply with tax obligations in their home jurisdiction. Offshore tax evasion is a serious problem for jurisdictions all over the world, OECD and non-OECD, small and large, developing and developed. Countries have a shared interest in maintaining the integrity of their tax systems. Co-operation between tax administrations is critical in the fight against tax evasion and in protecting the integrity of tax systems. A key aspect of that co-operation is exchange of information.

2.   The OECD has a long history of working on all forms of exchange of information – on request, spontaneous, and automatic – and the Multilateral Convention on Mutual Administrative Assistance in Tax Matters and Article 26 of the OECD Model Tax Convention provide a basis for all forms of information exchange. In particular, since 2009 much progress was made by the OECD, EU and the Global Forum on Transparency and Exchange of Information for Tax Purposes in improving transparency and exchange of information on request.

3.   Starting in 2012 political interest also focused on the opportunities provided by automatic exchange of information. On 19 April 2013 the G20 Finance Ministers and Central Bank Governors endorsed automatic exchange as the expected new standard. The G20 decision followed earlier announcements by five European countries of their intention to develop and pilot multilateral tax information exchange based on the Model Intergovernmental Agreement to Improve International Tax Compliance and to Implement FATCA, developed between these countries (France, Germany, Italy, Spain and the United Kingdom) and the United States (the "Model 1 IGA"). On 22 May 2013, the European Council unanimously agreed to give priority efforts to extend automatic exchange at EU and

global level and welcomed on-going efforts made in the G8, G20 and OECD to develop a global standard. On 12 June 2013 the European Commission adopted a legislative proposal to extend the scope of automatic exchange of information in its directive on administrative co-operation. On 19 June 2013 the G8 leaders welcomed the OECD Secretary General report "A Step Change in Tax Transparency" which set out the concrete steps that need to be undertaken to put a global model of automatic exchange into practice. G8 leaders agreed to work together with the OECD and in the G20 to implement its recommendations urgently. On 6 September 2013 the G20 Leaders committed to automatic exchange of information as the new global standard and fully supported the OECD work, with G20 countries, aimed at presenting such a single global standard in 2014. In February 2014, the G20 Finance Ministers and Central Bank Governors endorsed the Common Reporting Standard for automatic exchange of tax information contained in Part II of this document. By May 2014 over 60 jurisdictions had committed to swiftly implement the Common Reporting Standard, including translating it into domestic law. Further, 44 jurisdictions have agreed to a common timetable for the implementation of the Standard.

4.   The global model of automatic exchange is drafted with respect to financial account information. Many jurisdictions – OECD and non-OECD – already exchange information automatically with their exchange partners and also regionally (e.g. within the EU) on various categories of income and also transmit other types of information such as changes of residence, the purchase or disposition of immovable property, value added tax refunds, tax withheld at source, etc. The new global standard does not, nor is it intended to, restrict the other types or categories of automatic exchange of information. It sets out a minimum standard for the information to be exchanged. Jurisdictions may choose to exchange information beyond the minimum standard set out in this document.

5.   The Common Reporting Standard, with a view to maximising efficiency and reducing cost for financial institutions, draws extensively on the intergovernmental approach to implementing FATCA. While the intergovernmental approach to FATCA reporting does deviate in certain aspects from the CRS, the differences are driven by the multilateral nature of the CRS system and other US specific aspects, in particular the concept of taxation on the basis of citizenship and the presence of a significant and comprehensive FATCA withholding tax. Given these features, that the intergovernmental approach to FATCA is a pre-existing system with close similarities to the CRS, and the anticipated progress towards widespread participation in the CRS, it is compatible and consistent with the CRS for the United States to not require the look through treatment for investment entities in Non-Participating Jurisdictions.

B. Key features of a global model of automatic exchange of financial account information

6.   For a model of automatic exchange of financial account information to be effective it must be specifically designed with residence jurisdictions' tax compliance in mind rather than be a by-product of domestic reporting. Further, it needs to be standardised so as to benefit the maximum number of residence jurisdictions and financial institutions while recognising that certain issues remain to be decided by local implementation. The advantage of standardisation is process simplification, higher effectiveness and lower costs for all stakeholders concerned. A proliferation of different and inconsistent models would potentially impose significant costs on both government and business to collect the necessary information and operate the different models. It could lead to a fragmentation of standards, which may introduce conflicting requirements, further increasing the costs of compliance and reducing effectiveness. Finally, because tax evasion is a global issue, the model needs to have a global reach so that it addresses the issue of offshore tax evasion and does not merely relocate the problem rather than solving it. Mechanisms to encourage compliance may be also required to achieve this aim.

7.   In 2012 the OECD delivered to the G20 the report "Automatic Exchange of Information: What it is, How it works, Benefits, What remains to be done",[1] which summarises the key features of an effective model for automatic exchange. The main success factors for effective automatic exchange of financial information are: *(1)* a common standard on information reporting, due diligence and exchange of information, *(2)* a legal and operational basis for the exchange of information; and *(3)* common or compatible technical solutions.

1. Common standard on reporting, due diligence and exchange of information

8.   An effective model for automatic exchange of information requires a common standard on the information to be reported by financial institutions and exchanged with residence jurisdictions. This will ensure that the reporting by financial institutions is aligned with the interests of the residence country. It will also increase the quality and predictability of the information that is being exchanged. The result will be significant opportunities for the residence country to enhance compliance and make

---

1.   OECD (2012), *Automatic exchange of information: What it is, how it works, benefits, what remains to be done*, OECD, Paris, available on www.oecd.org/ctp/ exchange-of-tax-information/automatic-exchange-of-information-report.pdf.

optimal use of the information (e.g. through automatic matching with domestic compliance information and data analysis).

9.　　In order to limit the opportunities for taxpayers to circumvent the model by shifting assets to institutions or investing in products that are not covered by the model, a reporting regime requires a broad scope across three dimensions:

- **The scope of financial information reported:** A comprehensive reporting regime covers different types of investment income including interest, dividends and similar types of income, and also address situations where a taxpayer seeks to hide capital that itself represents income or assets on which tax has been evaded (e.g. by requiring information on account balances).

- **The scope of account holders subject to reporting:** A comprehensive reporting regime requires reporting not only with respect to individuals, but should also limit the opportunities for taxpayers to circumvent reporting by using interposed legal entities or arrangements. This means requiring financial institutions to look through shell companies, trusts or similar arrangements, including taxable entities to cover situations where a taxpayer seeks to hide the principal but is willing to pay tax on the income.

- **The scope of financial institutions required to report:** A comprehensive reporting regime covers not only banks but also other financial institutions such as brokers, certain collective investment vehicles and certain insurance companies.

10.　　In addition to a common standard on the scope of the information to be collected and exchanged, an effective model of automatic exchange of financial information also requires a common standard on a robust set of due diligence procedures to be followed by financial institutions to identify reportable accounts and obtain the accountholder identifying information that is required to be reported for such accounts. The due diligence procedures are critical as they help to ensure the quality of the information that is reported and exchanged. Finally feedback by the receiving jurisdiction to the sending jurisdiction regarding any errors in the information received can also be an important aspect of an effective automatic exchange model. Such feedback may take place in the form of spontaneous exchange of information, another important aspect of co-operation between tax authorities in itself.

2. Legal and operational basis for exchange of information

11.   Different legal basis for automatic exchange of information already exist. Whilst bilateral treaties such as those based on Article 26 of the OECD Model Tax Convention permit such exchanges, it may be more efficient to establish automatic exchange relationships on the basis of a multilateral exchange instrument. The Multilateral Convention on Mutual Administrative Assistance in Tax Matters (the "Convention"),[2] as amended in 2011, is such an instrument. It provides for all forms of administrative co-operation, contains strict rules on confidentiality and proper use of information, and permits automatic exchange of information. One of its main advantages is its global reach.[3] Automatic exchange under the Convention requires a separate agreement between the competent authorities of the parties, which can be entered into by two or more parties thus allowing for a single agreement with either two or more parties (with actual automatic exchange always taking place on a bilateral basis). Such a competent authority agreement then activates and "operationalises" automatic exchange between the participants. Where jurisdictions rely on other information exchange instruments, such as bilateral treaties, a competent authority agreement can serve the same function.

12.   All treaties and exchange of information instruments contain strict provisions that require information exchanged to be kept confidential and limit the persons to whom the information can be disclosed and the purposes for which the information may be used. The OECD released a Guide on Confidentiality,[4] which sets out best practices related to confidentiality and provides practical guidance on how to ensure an adequate level of protection. Before entering into an agreement to exchange information automatically with another jurisdiction, it is essential that the receiving jurisdiction has the legal framework and administrative capacity and processes in place to ensure the confidentiality of the information received and that such information is used only for the purposes specified in the instrument.

---

2.   The Multilateral Convention was developed jointly by the Council of Europe and the OECD and opened for signature by the member states of both organisations on 25 January 1988. The Convention was amended to respond to the call of the G20 at its April 2009 London Summit to align it to the international standard on exchange and to open it to all countries, in particular to ensure that developing countries could benefit from the new more transparent environment. It was opened for signature on 1 June 2011.

3.   For information on jurisdictions covered by the Convention, signatories and ratifications see www.oecd.org/tax/exchange-of-tax-information/status_of_convention.pdf.

4.   OECD (2012), *Keeping it Safe: The OECD Guide on the Protection of Confidentiality of Information Exchanged for Tax Purposes*, OECD, Paris, available on www.oecd.org/ctp/exchange-of-tax-information/keeping-it-safe-report.pdf.

3. Common or compatible technical solutions

13.   Common or compatible technical solutions for reporting and exchanging information are a critical element in a standardised automatic exchange system – especially one that will be used by a large number of jurisdictions and financial institutions. Standardisation will reduce costs for all parties concerned.

14.   The technical reporting format must be standardised so that information can be captured, exchanged and processed quickly and efficiently in a cost effective manner and secure and compatible methods of transmission and encryption of data must be in place.

C. Overview of the standard on automatic exchange of financial account information

15.   Part II of this document contains (A) a model competent authority agreement/arrangement ("Model CAA") and (B) the common standard on reporting and due diligence for financial account information (CRS). Together they constitute the common standard on reporting, due diligence and exchange of information on financial account information.

16.   Implementation of the standard will require translating the CRS into domestic law. Signing a competent authority agreement based on the model then allows putting in place the information exchange based on existing legal instruments, such as the Convention or bilateral income tax conventions. The exchange of information could also be implemented on the basis of a multilateral competent authority agreement/arrangement, or jurisdictions could enter into a multilateral intergovernmental agreement or multiple intergovernmental agreements that would be international treaties in their own right covering both the reporting obligations and due diligence procedures coupled with a more limited competent authority agreement. The legal basis could also be EU legislation that would cover the elements of the CRS.

1. Summary of the Model Competent Authority Agreement

17.   The Model CAA links the CRS and the legal basis for the exchange (such as the Convention or a bilateral tax treaty) allowing the financial account information to be exchanged. The Model CAA consists of a number of whereas clauses and seven sections, and provides for the modalities of the exchange to ensure the appropriate flows of information. The whereas clauses contain representations on the domestic reporting and due diligence rules that underpin the exchange of information pursuant to the competent authority agreement. They also contain representations on confidentiality, safeguards

and the existence of the necessary infrastructure for an effective exchange relationship.

18.   It contains a section dealing with definitions (Section 1), covers the type of information to be exchanged (Section 2), the time and manner of exchange (Section 3) and the confidentiality and data safeguards that must be respected (Section 5). Consultations between the competent authorities, collaboration on compliance and enforcement, amendments to the agreement and the term of the agreement, including suspension and termination, are dealt with in Sections 4, 6 and 7.

2. Summary of the Common Reporting Standard

19.   The CRS contains the reporting and due diligence standard that underpins the automatic exchange of financial account information. A jurisdiction implementing the CRS must have rules in place that require financial institutions to report information consistent with the scope of reporting set out in Section I and to follow due diligence procedures consistent with the procedures contained in Section II through VII. Capitalised terms used in the CRS are defined in Section VIII.

20.   The financial institutions covered by the standard include custodial institutions, depository institutions, investment entities and specified insurance companies, unless they present a low risk of being used for evading tax and are excluded from reporting. The financial information to be reported with respect to reportable accounts includes interest, dividends, account balance or value, income from certain insurance products, sales proceeds from financial assets and other income generated with respect to assets held in the account or payments made with respect to the account. Reportable accounts include accounts held by individuals and entities (which includes trusts and foundations), and the standard includes a requirement to look through passive entities to report on the relevant controlling persons.

21.   The due diligence procedures to be performed by reporting financial institutions for the identification of reportable accounts are described in Sections II through VII. They distinguish between individual accounts and entity accounts. They also make a distinction between pre-existing and new accounts, recognising that it is more difficult and costly for financial institutions to obtain information from existing account holders rather than requesting such information upon account opening.

- For **Preexisting Individual Accounts** financial institutions are required to review accounts without application of any de minimis threshold. The rules distinguish between Higher and Lower Value Accounts. For Lower Value Accounts they provide for a permanent residence address test based on documentary evidence or the FI would need to determine the residence on the basis of an indicia search. A self-certification (and/or documentary evidence) would be needed in case of conflicting indicia, in the absence of which reporting would be done to all reportable jurisdictions for which indicia have been found. For Higher Value Accounts enhanced due diligence procedures apply, including a paper record search and an actual knowledge test by the relationship manager.

- For **New Individual Accounts** the CRS requires a self-certification (and the confirmation of its reasonableness) without de minimis threshold.

- For **Preexisting Entity Accounts**, financial institutions are required to determine: a) whether the Entity itself is a Reportable Person, which can generally be done on the basis of available information (AML/KYC Procedures) and if not, a self-certification would be needed; and b) whether the Entity is a Passive NFE and, if so, the residency of Controlling Persons. For a number of account holders the active/passive assessment is rather straight forward and can be made on the basis of available information, for others this may require self-certification. Jurisdictions may choose to allow financial institutions to apply a threshold such that Preexisting Entity Accounts below USD 250 000 (or local currency equivalent) are not subject to review.

- For **New Entity Accounts**, the same assessments need to be made as for Pre-existing Accounts. However, as it is easier to obtain self-certifications for New Accounts, the USD 250 000 (or local currency equivalent) threshold does not apply.

22.   Section IX of the CRS describes the rules and administrative procedures an implementing jurisdiction is expected to have in place to ensure effective implementation of, and compliance with, the CRS.

3. Commentaries on the Model CAA and CRS

23.   For each section of the Model CAA and the CRS, there is a detailed Commentary that is intended to illustrate or interpret its provisions. The Commentaries are contained in Part III of the Report. Given that implementation will be based on domestic law, it is important to ensure consistency in application across jurisdictions to avoid creating unnecessary costs and complexity for financial institutions in particular those with operations in more than one jurisdiction. For certain limited situations alternatives are provided for in the Commentaries.

4. Technical Solutions

24.   Finally, this document also contains guidance on relevant technical solutions. It includes a schema to be used for exchanging the information and provides a standard in relation to the IT aspects of data safeguards and confidentiality, and transmission and encryption for the secure transmission of information under the CRS. Annex 3 contains a diagrammatic representation of the CRS schema and its user guide. As provided in the Model Competent Authority Agreement, Competent Authorities will use the CRS schema for purposes of exchanging the information to be reported. The schema may also be used by Reporting Financial Institutions for purposes of reporting the information (as permitted by domestic law). The IT aspects of data safeguards and confidentiality and the transmission and encryption standards are contained in the Commentary on Sections 3 and 5 of the Model CAA.

II. Model Competent Authority Agreement and Common Reporting Standard

A. Model Competent Authority Agreement

MODEL AGREEMENT BETWEEN THE COMPETENT AUTHORITIES OF [JURISDICTION A] AND [JURISDICTION B] ON THE AUTOMATIC EXCHANGE OF FINANCIAL ACCOUNT INFORMATION TO IMPROVE INTERNATIONAL TAX COMPLIANCE

Whereas, the Government of [Jurisdiction A] and the Government of [Jurisdiction B] have a longstanding and close relationship with respect to mutual assistance in tax matters and desire to improve international tax compliance by further building on that relationship;

Whereas, the laws of their respective jurisdictions [are expected to require]/[require]/[require or are expected to require] financial institutions to report information regarding certain accounts and follow related due diligence procedures, consistent with the scope of exchange contemplated by Section 2 of this Agreement and the reporting and due diligence procedures contained in the Common Reporting Standard;

Whereas, [Article [...] of the Income Tax Convention between [Jurisdiction A] and [Jurisdiction B]/[Article 6 of the Convention on Mutual Administrative Assistance in Tax Matters] (the "Convention")]/[other applicable legal instrument (the "Instrument")], authorises the exchange of information for tax purposes, including the exchange of information on an automatic basis, and allows the competent authorities of [Jurisdiction A] and [Jurisdiction B] (the "Competent Authorities") to agree the scope and modalities of such automatic exchanges;

Whereas, [Jurisdiction A] and [Jurisdiction B] have in place *(i)* appropriate safeguards to ensure that the information received pursuant to this Agreement remains confidential and is used solely for the purposes set out in the [Convention]/[Instrument], and *(ii)* the infrastructure for an effective exchange relationship (including established processes for ensuring timely, accurate, and confidential information exchanges, effective and reliable communications, and capabilities to promptly resolve questions and concerns about exchanges or requests for exchanges and to administer the provisions of Section 4 of this Agreement);

Whereas, the Competent Authorities desire to conclude an agreement to improve international tax compliance based on reciprocal automatic exchange pursuant to the [Convention]/[Instrument], and subject to the confidentiality and other protections provided for therein, including the provisions limiting the use of the information exchanged under the [Convention]/[Instrument];

Now, therefore, the Competent Authorities have agreed as follows:

SECTION 1

Definitions

1.   For the purposes of this agreement ("Agreement"), the following terms have the following meanings:

a) the term **"[Jurisdiction A]"** means […].

b) the term **"[Jurisdiction B]"** means […].

c) the term **"Competent Authority"** means:

   (1) in the case of [Jurisdiction A], […]; and

   (2) in the case of [Jurisdiction B], […].

d) the term **"[Jurisdiction A] Financial Institution"** means *(i)* any Financial Institution that is resident in [Jurisdiction A], but excludes any branch of that Financial Institution that is located outside [Jurisdiction A], and *(ii)* any branch of a Financial Institution that is not resident in [Jurisdiction A], if that branch is located in [Jurisdiction A].

e) the term **"[Jurisdiction B] Financial Institution"** means *(i)* any Financial Institution that is resident in [Jurisdiction B], but excludes any branch of that Financial Institution that is located outside [Jurisdiction B], and *(ii)* any branch of a Financial Institution that is not resident in [Jurisdiction B], if that branch is located in [Jurisdiction B].

f) the term **"Reporting Financial Institution"** means any [Jurisdiction A] Financial Institution or [Jurisdiction B] Financial Institution, as the context requires, that is not a Non-Reporting Financial Institution.

g) the term **"Reportable Account"** means a [Jurisdiction A] Reportable Account or a [Jurisdiction B] Reportable Account, as the context requires, provided it has been identified as such pursuant to due diligence procedures, consistent with the Common Reporting Standard, in place in [Jurisdiction A] or [Jurisdiction B].

h) the term **"[Jurisdiction A] Reportable Account"** means a Financial Account that is maintained by a [Jurisdiction B] Reporting Financial Institution and held by one or more [Jurisdiction A] Persons that are Reportable Persons or by a Passive NFE with one or more Controlling Persons that is a [Jurisdiction A] Reportable Person.

i) the term **"[Jurisdiction B] Reportable Account"** means a Financial Account that is maintained by a [Jurisdiction A] Reporting Financial Institution and held by one or more [Jurisdiction B] Persons that are Reportable Persons or by a Passive NFE with one or more Controlling Persons that is a [Jurisdiction B] Reportable Person.

j) the term **"[Jurisdiction A] Person"** means an individual or Entity that is identified by a [Jurisdiction B] Reporting Financial Institution as resident in [Jurisdiction A] pursuant to due diligence procedures consistent with the Common Reporting Standard, or an estate of a decedent that was a resident of [Jurisdiction A].

k) the term **"[Jurisdiction B] Person"** means an individual or Entity that is identified by a [Jurisdiction A] Reporting Financial Institution as resident in [Jurisdiction B] pursuant to due diligence procedures consistent with the Common Reporting Standard, or an estate of a decedent that was a resident of [Jurisdiction B].

l) the term **"TIN"** means a [Jurisdiction A] TIN or a [Jurisdiction B] TIN, as the context requires.

m) the term **"[Jurisdiction A] TIN"** means a […].

n) the term **"[Jurisdiction B] TIN"** means a […].

2.   Any capitalised term not otherwise defined in this Agreement will have the meaning that it has at that time under the law of the jurisdiction applying the Agreement, such meaning being consistent with the meaning set forth in the Common Reporting Standard. Any term not otherwise defined in this Agreement or in the Common Reporting Standard will, unless the context otherwise requires or the Competent Authorities agree to a common meaning (as permitted by domestic law), have the meaning that it has at that time under the law of the jurisdiction applying this Agreement, any meaning under the applicable tax laws of that jurisdiction prevailing over a meaning given to the term under other laws of that jurisdiction.

SECTION 2

Exchange of Information with Respect to Reportable Accounts

1.   Pursuant to the provisions of Article [...] of the [Convention]/ [Instrument] and subject to the applicable reporting and due diligence rules consistent with the Common Reporting Standard, each Competent Authority will annually exchange with the other Competent Authority on an automatic basis the information obtained pursuant to such rules and specified in paragraph 2.

2.   The information to be exchanged is, in the case of [Jurisdiction A] with respect to each [Jurisdiction B] Reportable Account, and in the case of [Jurisdiction B] with respect to each [Jurisdiction A] Reportable Account:

  a)   the name, address, TIN(s) and date and place of birth (in the case of an individual) of each Reportable Person that is an Account Holder of the account and, in the case of any Entity that is an Account Holder and that, after application of due diligence procedures consistent with the Common Reporting Standard, is identified as having one or more Controlling Persons that is a Reportable Person, the name, address, and TIN(s) of the Entity and the name, address, TIN(s) and date and place of birth of each Reportable Person;

  b)   the account number (or functional equivalent in the absence of an account number);

  c)   the name and identifying number (if any) of the Reporting Financial Institution;

  d)   the account balance or value (including, in the case of a Cash Value Insurance Contract or Annuity Contract, the Cash Value or surrender value) as of the end of the relevant calendar year or other appropriate reporting period or, if the account was closed during such year or period, the closure of the account;

  e)   in the case of any Custodial Account:

    (1)   the total gross amount of interest, the total gross amount of dividends, and the total gross amount of other income generated with respect to the assets held in the account, in each case paid or credited to the account (or with respect to the account) during the calendar year or other appropriate reporting period; and

    (2)   the total gross proceeds from the sale or redemption of Financial Assets paid or credited to the account during the calendar year or other appropriate reporting period with respect to which the

Reporting Financial Institution acted as a custodian, broker, nominee, or otherwise as an agent for the Account Holder;

f) in the case of any Depository Account, the total gross amount of interest paid or credited to the account during the calendar year or other appropriate reporting period; and

g) in the case of any account not described in subparagraph 2(e) or (f), the total gross amount paid or credited to the Account Holder with respect to the account during the calendar year or other appropriate reporting period with respect to which the Reporting Financial Institution is the obligor or debtor, including the aggregate amount of any redemption payments made to the Account Holder during the calendar year or other appropriate reporting period.

SECTION 3

Time and Manner of Exchange of Information

1. For the purposes of the exchange of information in Section 2, the amount and characterisation of payments made with respect to a Reportable Account may be determined in accordance with the principles of the tax laws of the jurisdiction exchanging the information.

2. For the purposes of the exchange of information in Section 2, the information exchanged will identify the currency in which each relevant amount is denominated.

3. With respect to paragraph 2 of Section 2, information is to be exchanged with respect to [xxxx] and all subsequent years and will be exchanged within nine months after the end of the calendar year to which the information relates. Notwithstanding the foregoing sentence information is only required to be exchanged with respect to a calendar year if both jurisdictions have in effect legislation that requires reporting with respect to such calendar year that is consistent with the scope of exchange provided for in Section 2 and the reporting and due diligence procedures contained in the Common Reporting Standard.

4. Notwithstanding paragraph 3, the information to be exchanged with respect to [xxxx] is the information described in paragraph 2 of Section 2, except for gross proceeds described in subparagraph 2(e)(2) of Section 2.

5. The Competent Authorities will automatically exchange the information described in Section 2 in a common reporting standard schema in Extensible Markup Language.

6.   The Competent Authorities will agree on one or more methods for data transmission including encryption standards.

SECTION 4

Collaboration on Compliance and Enforcement

A Competent Authority will notify the other Competent Authority when the first-mentioned Competent Authority has reason to believe that an error may have led to incorrect or incomplete information reporting or there is non-compliance by a Reporting Financial Institution with the applicable reporting requirements and due diligence procedures consistent with the Common Reporting Standard. The notified Competent Authority will take all appropriate measures available under its domestic law to address the errors or non-compliance described in the notice.

SECTION 5

Confidentiality and Data Safeguards

1.   All information exchanged is subject to the confidentiality rules and other safeguards provided for in the [Convention]/[Instrument], including the provisions limiting the use of the information exchanged and, to the extent needed to ensure the necessary level of protection of personal data, in accordance with the safeguards which may be specified by the supplying Competent Authority as required under its domestic law.

2.   Each Competent Authority will notify the other Competent Authority immediately regarding any breach of confidentiality or failure of safeguards and any sanctions and remedial actions consequently imposed.

SECTION 6

Consultations and Amendments

1.   If any difficulties in the implementation or interpretation of this Agreement arise, either Competent Authority may request consultations to develop appropriate measures to ensure that this Agreement is fulfilled.

2.   This Agreement may be amended by written agreement of the Competent Authorities. Unless otherwise agreed upon, such an amendment is effective on the first day of the month following the expiration of a period of one month after the date of the later of the signatures of such written

agreement or the date of the later of the notifications exchanged for purposes of such written agreement.

SECTION 7

Term of Agreement

1.   This Agreement will come into effect […]/[on the date of the later of the notifications provided by each Competent Authority that its jurisdiction has the necessary laws in place to implement the Agreement].

2.   A Competent Authority may suspend the exchange of information under this Agreement by giving notice in writing to the other Competent Authority that it has determined that there is or has been significant non-compliance by the other Competent Authority with this Agreement. Such suspension will have immediate effect. For the purposes of this paragraph, significant non-compliance includes, but is not limited to, non-compliance with the confidentiality and data safeguard provisions of this Agreement and the [Convention]/[Instrument], a failure by the Competent Authority to provide timely or adequate information as required under this Agreement or defining the status of Entities or accounts as Non-Reporting Financial Institutions and Excluded Accounts in a manner that frustrates the purposes of the Common Reporting Standard.

3.   Either Competent Authority may terminate this Agreement by giving notice of termination in writing to the other Competent Authority. Such termination will become effective on the first day of the month following the expiration of a period of 12 months after the date of the notice of termination. In the event of termination, all information previously received under this Agreement will remain confidential and subject to the terms of the [Convention/Instrument].

Signed in duplicate in […] on […].

Competent Authority for
[Jurisdiction A]

Competent Authority for
[Jurisdiction B]

B. Common Reporting Standard

COMMON STANDARD ON REPORTING AND DUE DILIGENCE FOR FINANCIAL ACCOUNT INFORMATION

Section I: General Reporting Requirements

A. Subject to paragraphs C through F, each Reporting Financial Institution must report the following information with respect to each Reportable Account of such Reporting Financial Institution:

1. the name, address, jurisdiction(s) of residence, TIN(s) and date and place of birth (in the case of an individual) of each Reportable Person that is an Account Holder of the account and, in the case of any Entity that is an Account Holder and that, after application of the due diligence procedures consistent with Sections V, VI and VII, is identified as having one or more Controlling Persons that is a Reportable Person, the name, address, jurisdiction(s) of residence and TIN(s) of the Entity and the name, address, jurisdiction(s) of residence, TIN(s) and date and place of birth of each Reportable Person;

2. the account number (or functional equivalent in the absence of an account number);

3. the name and identifying number (if any) of the Reporting Financial Institution;

4. the account balance or value (including, in the case of a Cash Value Insurance Contract or Annuity Contract, the Cash Value or surrender value) as of the end of the relevant calendar year or other appropriate reporting period or, if the account was closed during such year or period, the closure of the account;

5. in the case of any Custodial Account:

   a) the total gross amount of interest, the total gross amount of dividends, and the total gross amount of other income generated with respect to the assets held in the account, in each case paid or credited to the account (or with respect to the account) during the calendar year or other appropriate reporting period; and

   b) the total gross proceeds from the sale or redemption of Financial Assets paid or credited to the account during the calendar year or other appropriate reporting period with respect to which the Reporting Financial Institution acted as a custodian, broker, nominee, or otherwise as an agent for the Account Holder;

6. in the case of any Depository Account, the total gross amount of interest paid or credited to the account during the calendar year or other appropriate reporting period; and

7. in the case of any account not described in subparagraph A(5) or (6), the total gross amount paid or credited to the Account Holder with respect to the account during the calendar year or other appropriate reporting period with respect to which the Reporting Financial Institution is the obligor or debtor, including the aggregate amount of any redemption payments made to the Account Holder during the calendar year or other appropriate reporting period.

B. The information reported must identify the currency in which each amount is denominated.

C. Notwithstanding subparagraph A(1), with respect to each Reportable Account that is a Preexisting Account, the TIN(s) or date of birth is not required to be reported if such TIN(s) or date of birth is not in the records of the Reporting Financial Institution and is not otherwise required to be collected by such Reporting Financial Institution under domestic law. However, a Reporting Financial Institution is required to use reasonable efforts to obtain the TIN(s) and date of birth with respect to Preexisting Accounts by the end of the second calendar year following the year in which such Accounts were identified as Reportable Accounts.

D. Notwithstanding subparagraph A(1), the TIN is not required to be reported if (i) a TIN is not issued by the relevant Reportable Jurisdiction or (ii) the domestic law of the relevant Reportable Jurisdiction does not require the collection of the TIN issued by such Reportable Jurisdiction.

E. Notwithstanding subparagraph A(1), the place of birth is not required to be reported unless the Reporting Financial Institution is otherwise required to obtain and report it under domestic law and it is available in the electronically searchable data maintained by the Reporting Financial Institution.

F. Notwithstanding paragraph A, the information to be reported with respect to [xxxx] is the information described in such paragraph, except for gross proceeds described in subparagraph A(5)(b).

Section II: General Due Diligence Requirements

A. An account is treated as a Reportable Account beginning as of the date it is identified as such pursuant to the due diligence procedures in Sections II through VII and, unless otherwise provided, information with respect to a Reportable Account must be reported annually in the calendar year following the year to which the information relates.

B. The balance or value of an account is determined as of the last day of the calendar year or other appropriate reporting period.

C. Where a balance or value threshold is to be determined as of the last day of a calendar year, the relevant balance or value must be determined as of the last day of the reporting period that ends with or within that calendar year.

D. Each Jurisdiction may allow Reporting Financial Institutions to use service providers to fulfil the reporting and due diligence obligations imposed on such Reporting Financial Institutions, as contemplated in domestic law, but these obligations shall remain the responsibility of the Reporting Financial Institutions.

E. Each Jurisdiction may allow Reporting Financial Institutions to apply the due diligence procedures for New Accounts to Preexisting Accounts, and the due diligence procedures for High Value Accounts to Lower Value Accounts. Where a Jurisdiction allows New Account due diligence procedures to be used for Preexisting Accounts, the rules otherwise applicable to Preexisting Accounts continue to apply.

Section III: Due Diligence for Preexisting Individual Accounts

The following procedures apply for purposes of identifying Reportable Accounts among Preexisting Individual Accounts.

A. **Accounts Not Required to be Reviewed, Identified, or Reported.** A Preexisting Individual Account that is a Cash Value Insurance

[handwritten annotations at top: "eg Can sell his contract to USA but needs a licence to do so + who not opt out = 'effectively prevented'"]

[handwritten annotation left margin: "Sep 11 ∂"]

Contract or an Annuity Contract is not required to be reviewed, identified or reported, provided the Reporting Financial Institution is effectively prevented by law from selling such Contract to residents of a Reportable Jurisdiction.

B. **Lower Value Accounts.** The following procedures apply with respect to Lower Value Accounts.

1. **Residence Address.** If the Reporting Financial Institution has in its records a current residence address for the individual Account Holder based on Documentary Evidence, the Reporting Financial Institution may treat the individual Account Holder as being a resident for tax purposes of the jurisdiction in which the address is located for purposes of determining whether such individual Account Holder is a Reportable Person.

2. **Electronic Record Search.** If the Reporting Financial Institution does not rely on a current residence address for the individual Account Holder based on Documentary Evidence as set forth in subparagraph B(1), the Reporting Financial Institution must review electronically searchable data maintained by the Reporting Financial Institution for any of the following indicia and apply subparagraphs B(3) through (6):

   a) identification of the Account Holder as a resident of a Reportable Jurisdiction;

   b) current mailing or residence address (including a post office box) in a Reportable Jurisdiction;

   c) one or more telephone numbers in a Reportable Jurisdiction and no telephone number in the jurisdiction of the Reporting Financial Institution;

   d) standing instructions (other than with respect to a Depository Account) to transfer funds to an account maintained in a Reportable Jurisdiction;

   e) currently effective power of attorney or signatory authority granted to a person with an address in a Reportable Jurisdiction; or

   f) a "hold mail" instruction or "in-care-of" address in a Reportable Jurisdiction if the Reporting Financial Institution does not have any other address on file for the Account Holder.

3. If none of the indicia listed in subparagraph B(2) are discovered in the electronic search, then no further action is required

until there is a change in circumstances that results in one or more indicia being associated with the account, or the account becomes a High Value Account.

4. If any of the indicia listed in subparagraph B(2)(a) through (e) are discovered in the electronic search, or if there is a change in circumstances that results in one or more indicia being associated with the account, then the Reporting Financial Institution must treat the Account Holder as a resident for tax purposes of each Reportable Jurisdiction for which an indicium is identified, unless it elects to apply subparagraph B(6) and one of the exceptions in such subparagraph applies with respect to that account.

5. If a "hold mail" instruction or "in-care-of" address is discovered in the electronic search and no other address and none of the other indicia listed in subparagraph B(2)(a) through (e) are identified for the Account Holder, the Reporting Financial Institution must, in the order most appropriate to the circumstances, apply the paper record search described in subparagraph C(2), or seek to obtain from the Account Holder a self-certification or Documentary Evidence to establish the residence(s) for tax purposes of such Account Holder. If the paper search fails to establish an indicium and the attempt to obtain the self-certification or Documentary Evidence is not successful, the Reporting Financial Institution must report the account as an undocumented account.

6. Notwithstanding a finding of indicia under subparagraph B(2), a Reporting Financial Institution is not required to treat an Account Holder as a resident of a Reportable Jurisdiction if:

   a) the Account Holder information contains a current mailing or residence address in the Reportable Jurisdiction, one or more telephone numbers in the Reportable Jurisdiction (and no telephone number in the jurisdiction of the Reporting Financial Institution) or standing instructions (with respect to Financial Accounts other than Depository Accounts) to transfer funds to an account maintained in a Reportable Jurisdiction, the Reporting Financial Institution obtains, or has previously reviewed and maintains a record of:

      i) a self-certification from the Account Holder of the jurisdiction(s) of residence of such Account Holder that does not include such Reportable Jurisdiction; and

      ii) Documentary Evidence establishing the Account Holder's non-reportable status.

b) the Account Holder information contains a currently effective power of attorney or signatory authority granted to a person with an address in the Reportable Jurisdiction, the Reporting Financial Institution obtains, or has previously reviewed and maintains a record of:

   i) a self-certification from the Account Holder of the jurisdiction(s) of residence of such Account Holder that does not include such Reportable Jurisdiction; or

   ii) Documentary Evidence establishing the Account Holder's non-reportable status.

C. **Enhanced Review Procedures for High Value Accounts.** The following enhanced review procedures apply with respect to High Value Accounts.

   1. **Electronic Record Search.** With respect to High Value Accounts, the Reporting Financial Institution must review electronically searchable data maintained by the Reporting Financial Institution for any of the indicia described in subparagraph B(2).

   2. **Paper Record Search.** If the Reporting Financial Institution's electronically searchable databases include fields for, and capture all of the information described in, subparagraph C(3), then a further paper record search is not required. If the electronic databases do not capture all of this information, then with respect to a High Value Account, the Reporting Financial Institution must also review the current customer master file and, to the extent not contained in the current customer master file, the following documents associated with the account and obtained by the Reporting Financial Institution within the last five years for any of the indicia described in subparagraph B(2):

      a) the most recent Documentary Evidence collected with respect to the account;

      b) the most recent account opening contract or documentation;

      c) the most recent documentation obtained by the Reporting Financial Institution pursuant to AML/KYC Procedures or for other regulatory purposes;

      d) any power of attorney or signature authority forms currently in effect; and

      e) any standing instructions (other than with respect to a Depository Account) to transfer funds currently in effect.

3. **Exception To The Extent Databases Contain Sufficient Information.** A Reporting Financial Institution is not required to perform the paper record search described in subparagraph C(2) to the extent the Reporting Financial Institution's electronically searchable information includes the following:

   a) the Account Holder's residence status;

   b) the Account Holder's residence address and mailing address currently on file with the Reporting Financial Institution;

   c) the Account Holder's telephone number(s) currently on file, if any, with the Reporting Financial Institution;

   d) in the case of Financial Accounts other than Depository Accounts, whether there are standing instructions to transfer funds in the account to another account (including an account at another branch of the Reporting Financial Institution or another Financial Institution);

   e) whether there is a current "in-care-of" address or "hold mail" instruction for the Account Holder; and

   f) whether there is any power of attorney or signatory authority for the account.

4. **Relationship Manager Inquiry for Actual Knowledge.** In addition to the electronic and paper record searches described above, the Reporting Financial Institution must treat as a Reportable Account any High Value Account assigned to a relationship manager (including any Financial Accounts aggregated with that High Value Account) if the relationship manager has actual knowledge that the Account Holder is a Reportable Person.

5. **Effect of Finding Indicia.**

   a) If none of the indicia listed in subparagraph B(2) are discovered in the enhanced review of High Value Accounts described above, and the account is not identified as held by a Reportable Person in subparagraph C(4), then further action is not required until there is a change in circumstances that results in one or more indicia being associated with the account.

   b) If any of the indicia listed in subparagraph B(2)(a) through (e) are discovered in the enhanced review of High Value Accounts described above, or if there is a subsequent change in circumstances that results in one or more indicia being associated with the account, then the Reporting Financial Institution must treat the account as a Reportable Account with respect to each Reportable Jurisdiction for which an indicium is identified unless it elects to apply subparagraph B(6) and one of the exceptions in such subparagraph applies with respect to that account.

c) If a "hold mail" instruction or "in-care-of" address is discovered in the enhanced review of High Value Accounts described above, and no other address and none of the other indicia listed in subparagraph B(2)(a) through (e) are identified for the Account Holder, the Reporting Financial Institution must obtain from such Account Holder a self-certification or Documentary Evidence to establish the residence(s) for tax purposes of the Account Holder. If the Reporting Financial Institution cannot obtain such self-certification or Documentary Evidence, it must report the account as an undocumented account.

6. If a Preexisting Individual Account is not a High Value Account as of 31 December [xxxx], but becomes a High Value Account as of the last day of a subsequent calendar year, the Reporting Financial Institution must complete the enhanced review procedures described in paragraph C with respect to such account within the calendar year following the year in which the account becomes a High Value Account. If based on this review such account is identified as a Reportable Account, the Reporting Financial Institution must report the required information about such account with respect to the year in which it is identified as a Reportable Account and subsequent years on an annual basis, unless the Account Holder ceases to be a Reportable Person.

7. Once a Reporting Financial Institution applies the enhanced review procedures described in paragraph C to a High Value Account, the Reporting Financial Institution is not required to re-apply such procedures, other than the relationship manager inquiry described in subparagraph C(4), to the same High Value Account in any subsequent year unless the account is undocumented where the Reporting Financial Institution should re-apply them annually until such account ceases to be undocumented.

8. If there is a change of circumstances with respect to a High Value Account that results in one or more indicia described in subparagraph B(2) being associated with the account, then the Reporting Financial Institution must treat the account as a Reportable Account with respect to each Reportable Jurisdiction for which an indicium is identified unless it elects

to apply subparagraph B(6) and one of the exceptions in such subparagraph applies with respect to that account.

9. A Reporting Financial Institution must implement procedures to ensure that a relationship manager identifies any change in circumstances of an account. For example, if a relationship manager is notified that the Account Holder has a new mailing address in a Reportable Jurisdiction, the Reporting Financial Institution is required to treat the new address as a change in circumstances and, if it elects to apply subparagraph B(6), is required to obtain the appropriate documentation from the Account Holder.

D. Review of Preexisting Individual Accounts must be completed by [xx/xx/xxxx].

E. Any Preexisting Individual Account that has been identified as a Reportable Account under this Section must be treated as a Reportable Account in all subsequent years, unless the Account Holder ceases to be a Reportable Person.

Section IV: Due Diligence for New Individual Accounts

The following procedures apply for purposes of identifying Reportable Accounts among New Individual Accounts.

A. With respect to New Individual Accounts, upon account opening, the Reporting Financial Institution must obtain a self-certification, which may be part of the account opening documentation, that allows the Reporting Financial Institution to determine the Account Holder's residence(s) for tax purposes and confirm the reasonableness of such self-certification based on the information obtained by the Reporting Financial Institution in connection with the opening of the account, including any documentation collected pursuant to AML/KYC Procedures.

B. If the self-certification establishes that the Account Holder is resident for tax purposes in a Reportable Jurisdiction, the Reporting Financial Institution must treat the account as a Reportable Account and the self-certification must also include the Account Holder's TIN with respect to such Reportable Jurisdiction (subject to paragraph D of Section I) and date of birth.

C. If there is a change of circumstances with respect to a New Individual Account that causes the Reporting Financial Institution to know, or have reason to know, that the original self-certification is incorrect or unreliable, the Reporting Financial Institution cannot rely on the original self-certification and must obtain a valid self-certification that establishes the residence(s) for tax purposes of the Account Holder.

Section V: Due Diligence for Preexisting Entity Accounts

The following procedures apply for purposes of identifying Reportable Accounts among Preexisting Entity Accounts.

A. **Entity Accounts Not Required to Be Reviewed, Identified or Reported.** Unless the Reporting Financial Institution elects otherwise, either with respect to all Preexisting Entity Accounts or, separately, with respect to any clearly identified group of such accounts, a Preexisting Entity Account with an aggregate account balance or value that does not exceed USD 250 000 as of 31 December [xxxx], is not required to be reviewed, identified, or reported as a Reportable Account until the aggregate account balance or value exceeds USD 250 000 as of the last day of any subsequent calendar year.

B. **Entity Accounts Subject to Review.** A Preexisting Entity Account that has an aggregate account balance or value that exceeds USD 250 000 as of 31 December [xxxx], and a Preexisting Entity Account that does not exceed USD 250 000 as of 31 December [xxxx] but the aggregate account balance or value of which exceeds USD 250 000 as of the last day of any subsequent calendar year, must be reviewed in accordance with the procedures set forth in paragraph D.

C. **Entity Accounts With Respect to Which Reporting Is Required.** With respect to Preexisting Entity Accounts described in paragraph B, only accounts that are held by one or more Entities that are Reportable Persons, or by Passive NFEs with one or more Controlling Persons who are Reportable Persons, shall be treated as Reportable Accounts.

D. **Review Procedures for Identifying Entity Accounts With Respect to Which Reporting Is Required.** For Preexisting Entity Accounts described in paragraph B, a Reporting Financial Institution must apply the following review procedures to determine whether the account is held by one or more Reportable Persons, or by Passive NFEs with one or more Controlling Persons who are Reportable Persons:

1. **Determine Whether the Entity Is a Reportable Person.**

   a) Review information maintained for regulatory or customer relationship purposes (including information collected pursuant to AML/KYC Procedures) to determine whether the information indicates that the Account Holder is resident in a Reportable Jurisdiction. For this purpose, information indicating that the Account Holder is resident in a Reportable Jurisdiction includes a place of incorporation or organisation, or an address in a Reportable Jurisdiction.

b) If the information indicates that the Account Holder is resident in a Reportable Jurisdiction, the Reporting Financial Institution must treat the account as a Reportable Account unless it obtains a self-certification from the Account Holder, or reasonably determines based on information in its possession or that is publicly available, that the Account Holder is not a Reportable Person.

2. **Determine Whether the Entity is a Passive NFE with One or More Controlling Persons Who Are Reportable Persons.** With respect to an Account Holder of a Preexisting Entity Account (including an Entity that is a Reportable Person), the Reporting Financial Institution must determine whether the Account Holder is a Passive NFE with one or more Controlling Persons who are Reportable Persons. If any of the Controlling Persons of a Passive NFE is a Reportable Person, then the account must be treated as a Reportable Account. In making these determinations the Reporting Financial Institution must follow the guidance in subparagraphs D(2)(a) through (c) in the order most appropriate under the circumstances.

a) **Determining whether the Account Holder is a Passive NFE.** For purposes of determining whether the Account Holder is a Passive NFE, the Reporting Financial Institution must obtain a self-certification from the Account Holder to establish its status, unless it has information in its possession or that is publicly available, based on which it can reasonably determine that the Account Holder is an Active NFE or a Financial Institution other than an Investment Entity described in subparagraph A(6)(b) of Section VIII that is not a Participating Jurisdiction Financial Institution.

b) **Determining the Controlling Persons of an Account Holder.** For the purposes of determining the Controlling Persons of an Account Holder, a Reporting Financial Institution may rely on information collected and maintained pursuant to AML/KYC Procedures.

c) **Determining whether a Controlling Person of a Passive NFE is a Reportable Person.** For the purposes of determining whether a Controlling Person of a Passive NFE is a Reportable Person, a Reporting Financial Institution may rely on:

i) information collected and maintained pursuant to AML/KYC Procedures in the case of a Preexisting Entity Account held by one or more NFEs with an aggregate account balance or value that does not exceed USD 1 000 000; or

ii) a self-certification from the Account Holder or such Controlling Person of the jurisdiction(s) in which the Controlling Person is resident for tax purposes.

E. **Timing of Review and Additional Procedures Applicable to Preexisting Entity Accounts.**

1. Review of Preexisting Entity Accounts with an aggregate account balance or value that exceeds USD 250 000 as of 31 December [xxxx] must be completed by 31 December [xxxx].

2. Review of Preexisting Entity Accounts with an aggregate account balance or value that does not exceed USD 250 000 as of 31 December [xxxx], but exceeds USD 250 000 as of 31 December of a subsequent year, must be completed within the calendar year following the year in which the aggregate account balance or value exceeds USD 250 000.

3. If there is a change of circumstances with respect to a Preexisting Entity Account that causes the Reporting Financial Institution to know, or have reason to know, that the self-certification or other documentation associated with an account is incorrect or unreliable, the Reporting Financial Institution must re-determine the status of the account in accordance with the procedures set forth in paragraph D.

Section VI: Due Diligence for New Entity Accounts

The following procedures apply for purposes of identifying Reportable Accounts among New Entity Accounts.

A. **Review Procedures for Identifying Entity Accounts With Respect to Which Reporting Is Required.** For New Entity Accounts, a Reporting Financial Institution must apply the following review procedures to determine whether the account is held by one or more Reportable Persons, or by Passive NFEs with one or more Controlling Persons who are Reportable Persons:

1. **Determine Whether the Entity Is a Reportable Person.**

   a) Obtain a self-certification, which may be part of the account opening documentation, that allows the Reporting Financial Institution to determine the Account Holder's residence(s) for tax purposes and confirm the reasonableness of such self-certification based on the information obtained by the Reporting Financial Institution in connection with the opening of the account, including any documentation collected pursuant to AML/KYC Procedures. If the Entity certifies that it has no residence for tax purposes, the Reporting Financial Institution may rely on the address of the principal office of the Entity to determine the residence of the Account Holder.

   b) If the self-certification indicates that the Account Holder is resident in a Reportable Jurisdiction, the Reporting Financial Institution must treat the account as a Reportable Account unless it reasonably determines based on information in its possession or that is publicly available, that the Account Holder is not a Reportable Person with respect to such Reportable Jurisdiction.

2. **Determine Whether the Entity is a Passive NFE with One or More Controlling Persons Who Are Reportable Persons.** With respect to an Account Holder of a New Entity Account (including an Entity that is a Reportable Person), the Reporting Financial Institution must determine whether the Account Holder is a Passive NFE with one or more Controlling Persons who are Reportable Persons. If any of the Controlling Persons of a Passive NFE is a Reportable Person, then the account must be treated as a Reportable Account. In making these determinations the Reporting Financial Institution must follow the guidance in subparagraphs A(2)(a) through (c) in the order most appropriate under the circumstances.

   a) **Determining whether the Account Holder is a Passive NFE.** For purposes of determining whether the Account Holder is a Passive NFE, the Reporting Financial Institution must rely on a self-certification from the Account Holder to establish its status, unless it has information in its possession or that is publicly available, based on which it can reasonably determine that the Account Holder is an Active NFE or a Financial Institution other than an Investment Entity described in subparagraph A(6)(b) of Section VIII that is not a Participating Jurisdiction Financial Institution.

b) **Determining the Controlling Persons of an Account Holder.** For purposes of determining the Controlling Persons of an Account Holder, a Reporting Financial Institution may rely on information collected and maintained pursuant to AML/KYC Procedures.

c) **Determining whether a Controlling Person of a Passive NFE is a Reportable Person.** For purposes of determining whether a Controlling Person of a Passive NFE is a Reportable Person, a Reporting Financial Institution may rely on a self-certification from the Account Holder or such Controlling Person.

Section VII: Special Due Diligence Rules

The following additional rules apply in implementing the due diligence procedures described above:

A. **Reliance on Self-Certifications and Documentary Evidence.** A Reporting Financial Institution may not rely on a self-certification or Documentary Evidence if the Reporting Financial Institution knows or has reason to know that the self-certification or Documentary Evidence is incorrect or unreliable.

B. **Alternative Procedures for Financial Accounts Held by Individual Beneficiaries of a Cash Value Insurance Contract or an Annuity Contract.** A Reporting Financial Institution may presume that an individual beneficiary (other than the owner) of a Cash Value Insurance Contract or an Annuity Contract receiving a death benefit is not a Reportable Person and may treat such Financial Account as other than a Reportable Account unless the Reporting Financial Institution has actual knowledge, or reason to know, that the beneficiary is a Reportable Person. A Reporting Financial Institution has reason to know that a beneficiary of a Cash Value Insurance Contract or an Annuity Contract is a Reportable Person if the information collected by the Reporting Financial Institution and associated with the beneficiary contains indicia as described in paragraph B of Section III. If a Reporting Financial Institution has actual knowledge, or reason to know, that the beneficiary is a Reportable Person, the Reporting Financial Institution must follow the procedures in paragraph B of Section III.

C. **Account Balance Aggregation and Currency Rules.**

1. **Aggregation of Individual Accounts.** For purposes of determining the aggregate balance or value of Financial Accounts held by an individual, a Reporting Financial Institution is required to

aggregate all Financial Accounts maintained by the Reporting Financial Institution, or by a Related Entity, but only to the extent that the Reporting Financial Institution's computerised systems link the Financial Accounts by reference to a data element such as client number or TIN, and allow account balances or values to be aggregated. Each holder of a jointly held Financial Account shall be attributed the entire balance or value of the jointly held Financial Account for purposes of applying the aggregation requirements described in this subparagraph.

2. **Aggregation of Entity Accounts.** For purposes of determining the aggregate balance or value of Financial Accounts held by an Entity, a Reporting Financial Institution is required to take into account all Financial Accounts that are maintained by the Reporting Financial Institution, or by a Related Entity, but only to the extent that the Reporting Financial Institution's computerised systems link the Financial Accounts by reference to a data element such as client number or TIN, and allow account balances or values to be aggregated. Each holder of a jointly held Financial Account shall be attributed the entire balance or value of the jointly held Financial Account for purposes of applying the aggregation requirements described in this subparagraph.

3. **Special Aggregation Rule Applicable to Relationship Managers.** For purposes of determining the aggregate balance or value of Financial Accounts held by a person to determine whether a Financial Account is a High Value Account, a Reporting Financial Institution is also required, in the case of any Financial Accounts that a relationship manager knows, or has reason to know, are directly or indirectly owned, controlled, or established (other than in a fiduciary capacity) by the same person, to aggregate all such accounts.

4. **Amounts Read to Include Equivalent in Other Currencies.** All dollar amounts are in US dollars and shall be read to include equivalent amounts in other currencies, as determined by domestic law.

Section VIII: Defined Terms

The following terms have the meanings set forth below:

A. Reporting Financial Institution

1. The term **"Reporting Financial Institution"** means any Participating Jurisdiction Financial Institution that is not a Non-Reporting Financial Institution.

2. The term **"Participating Jurisdiction Financial Institution"** means *(i)* any Financial Institution that is resident in a Participating Jurisdiction, but excludes any branch of that Financial Institution that is located outside such Participating Jurisdiction, and *(ii)* any branch of a Financial Institution that is not resident in a Participating Jurisdiction, if that branch is located in such Participating Jurisdiction.

3. The term **"Financial Institution"** means a Custodial Institution, a Depository Institution, an Investment Entity, or a Specified Insurance Company.

4. The term **"Custodial Institution"** means any Entity that holds, as a substantial portion of its business, Financial Assets for the account of others. An Entity holds Financial Assets for the account of others as a substantial portion of its business if the Entity's gross income attributable to the holding of Financial Assets and related financial services equals or exceeds 20% of the Entity's gross income during the shorter of: *(i)* the three-year period that ends on 31 December (or the final day of a non-calendar year accounting period) prior to the year in which the determination is being made; or *(ii)* the period during which the Entity has been in existence.

5. The term **"Depository Institution"** means any Entity that accepts deposits in the ordinary course of a banking or similar business.

6. The term **"Investment Entity"** means any Entity:

    a) that primarily conducts as a business one or more of the following activities or operations for or on behalf of a customer:

        i) trading in money market instruments (cheques, bills, certificates of deposit, derivatives, etc.); foreign exchange; exchange, interest rate and index instruments; transferable securities; or commodity futures trading;

        ii) individual and collective portfolio management; or

        iii) otherwise investing, administering, or managing Financial Assets or money on behalf of other persons; or

    b) the gross income of which is primarily attributable to investing, reinvesting, or trading in Financial Assets, if the Entity is managed by another Entity that is a Depository Institution, a Custodial Institution, a Specified Insurance Company, or an Investment Entity described in subparagraph A(6)(a).

An Entity is treated as primarily conducting as a business one or more of the activities described in subparagraph A(6)(a), or an Entity's gross income is primarily attributable to investing, reinvesting, or trading in Financial Assets for purposes of subparagraph A(6)(b), if the Entity's gross income attributable to the relevant activities equals or exceeds 50% of the Entity's gross income during the shorter of: *(i)* the three-year period ending on 31 December of the year preceding the year in which the determination is made; or *(ii)* the period during which the Entity has been in existence. The term "Investment Entity" does not include an Entity that is an Active NFE because it meets any of the criteria in subparagraphs D(9)(d) through (g).

This paragraph shall be interpreted in a manner consistent with similar language set forth in the definition of "financial institution" in the Financial Action Task Force Recommendations.

7. The term **"Financial Asset"** includes a security (for example, a share of stock in a corporation; partnership or beneficial ownership interest in a widely held or publicly traded partnership or trust; note, bond, debenture, or other evidence of indebtedness), partnership interest, commodity, swap (for example, interest rate swaps, currency swaps, basis swaps, interest rate caps, interest rate floors, commodity swaps, equity swaps, equity index swaps, and similar agreements), Insurance Contract or Annuity Contract, or any interest (including a futures or forward contract or option) in a security, partnership interest, commodity, swap, Insurance Contract, or Annuity Contract. The term "Financial Asset" does not include a non-debt, direct interest in real property.

8. The term **"Specified Insurance Company"** means any Entity that is an insurance company (or the holding company of an insurance company) that issues, or is obligated to make payments with respect to, a Cash Value Insurance Contract or an Annuity Contract.

B. **Non-Reporting Financial Institution**

1. The term **"Non-Reporting Financial Institution"** means any Financial Institution that is:

   a) a Governmental Entity, International Organisation or Central Bank, other than with respect to a payment that is derived from an obligation held in connection with a commercial financial activity of a type engaged in by a Specified Insurance Company, Custodial Institution, or Depository Institution;

b) a Broad Participation Retirement Fund; a Narrow Participation Retirement Fund; a Pension Fund of a Governmental Entity, International Organisation or Central Bank; or a Qualified Credit Card Issuer;

c) any other Entity that presents a low risk of being used to evade tax, has substantially similar characteristics to any of the Entities described in subparagraphs B(1)(a) and (b), and is defined in domestic law as a Non-Reporting Financial Institution, provided that the status of such Entity as a Non-Reporting Financial Institution does not frustrate the purposes of the Common Reporting Standard;

d) an Exempt Collective Investment Vehicle; or

e) a trust to the extent that the trustee of the trust is a Reporting Financial Institution and reports all information required to be reported pursuant to Section I with respect to all Reportable Accounts of the trust.

2. The term **"Governmental Entity"** means the government of a jurisdiction, any political subdivision of a jurisdiction (which, for the avoidance of doubt, includes a state, province, county, or municipality), or any wholly owned agency or instrumentality of a jurisdiction or of any one or more of the foregoing (each, a "Governmental Entity"). This category is comprised of the integral parts, controlled entities, and political subdivisions of a jurisdiction.

a) An "integral part" of a jurisdiction means any person, organisation, agency, bureau, fund, instrumentality, or other body, however designated, that constitutes a governing authority of a jurisdiction. The net earnings of the governing authority must be credited to its own account or to other accounts of the jurisdiction, with no portion inuring to the benefit of any private person. An integral part does not include any individual who is a sovereign, official, or administrator acting in a private or personal capacity.

b) A controlled entity means an Entity that is separate in form from the jurisdiction or that otherwise constitutes a separate juridical entity, provided that:

i) the Entity is wholly owned and controlled by one or more Governmental Entities directly or through one or more controlled entities;

ii) the Entity's net earnings are credited to its own account or to the accounts of one or more Governmental Entities, with no portion of its income inuring to the benefit of any private person; and

iii) the Entity's assets vest in one or more Governmental Entities upon dissolution.

c) Income does not inure to the benefit of private persons if such persons are the intended beneficiaries of a governmental programme, and the programme activities are performed for the general public with respect to the common welfare or relate to the administration of some phase of government. Notwithstanding the foregoing, however, income is considered to inure to the benefit of private persons if the income is derived from the use of a governmental entity to conduct a commercial business, such as a commercial banking business, that provides financial services to private persons.

3. The term **"International Organisation"** means any international organisation or wholly owned agency or instrumentality thereof. This category includes any intergovernmental organisation (including a supranational organisation) *(1)* that is comprised primarily of governments; *(2)* that has in effect a headquarters or substantially similar agreement with the jurisdiction; and *(3)* the income of which does not inure to the benefit of private persons.

4. The term **"Central Bank"** means an institution that is by law or government sanction the principal authority, other than the government of the jurisdiction itself, issuing instruments intended to circulate as currency. Such an institution may include an instrumentality that is separate from the government of the jurisdiction, whether or not owned in whole or in part by the jurisdiction.

5. The term **"Broad Participation Retirement Fund"** means a fund established to provide retirement, disability, or death benefits, or any combination thereof, to beneficiaries that are current or former employees (or persons designated by such employees) of one or more employers in consideration for services rendered, provided that the fund:

a) does not have a single beneficiary with a right to more than five per cent of the fund's assets;

b) is subject to government regulation and provides information reporting to the tax authorities; and *c)* satisfies at least one of the following requirements:

    i) the fund is generally exempt from tax on investment income, or taxation of such income is deferred or taxed at a reduced rate, due to its status as a retirement or pension plan;

    ii) the fund receives at least 50% of its total contributions (other than transfers of assets from other plans described in subparagraphs B(5) through (7) or from retirement and pension accounts described in subparagraph C(17)(a)) from the sponsoring employers;

    iii) distributions or withdrawals from the fund are allowed only upon the occurrence of specified events related to retirement, disability, or death (except rollover distributions to other retirement funds described in subparagraphs B(5) through (7) or retirement and pension accounts described in subparagraph C(17)(a)), or penalties apply to distributions or withdrawals made before such specified events; or

    iv) contributions (other than certain permitted make-up contributions) by employees to the fund are limited by reference to earned income of the employee or may not exceed USD 50 000 annually, applying the rules set forth in paragraph C of Section VII for account aggregation and currency translation.

6. The term **"Narrow Participation Retirement Fund"** means a fund established to provide retirement, disability, or death benefits to beneficiaries that are current or former employees (or persons designated by such employees) of one or more employers in consideration for services rendered, provided that:

  a) the fund has fewer than 50 participants;

  b) the fund is sponsored by one or more employers that are not Investment Entities or Passive NFEs;

  c) the employee and employer contributions to the fund (other than transfers of assets from retirement and pension accounts described in subparagraph C(17)(a)) are limited by reference to earned income and compensation of the employee, respectively;

d) participants that are not residents of the jurisdiction in which the fund is established are not entitled to more than 20% of the fund's assets; and

e) the fund is subject to government regulation and provides information reporting to the tax authorities.

7. The term **"Pension Fund of a Governmental Entity, International Organisation or Central Bank"** means a fund established by a Governmental Entity, International Organisation or Central Bank to provide retirement, disability, or death benefits to beneficiaries or participants that are current or former employees (or persons designated by such employees), or that are not current or former employees, if the benefits provided to such beneficiaries or participants are in consideration of personal services performed for the Governmental Entity, International Organisation or Central Bank.

8. The term **"Qualified Credit Card Issuer"** means a Financial Institution satisfying the following requirements:

a) the Financial Institution is a Financial Institution solely because it is an issuer of credit cards that accepts deposits only when a customer makes a payment in excess of a balance due with respect to the card and the overpayment is not immediately returned to the customer; and

b) beginning on or before [xx/xx/xxxx], the Financial Institution implements policies and procedures either to prevent a customer from making an overpayment in excess of USD 50 000, or to ensure that any customer overpayment in excess of USD 50 000 is refunded to the customer within 60 days, in each case applying the rules set forth in paragraph C of Section VII for account aggregation and currency translation. For this purpose, a customer overpayment does not refer to credit balances to the extent of disputed charges but does include credit balances resulting from merchandise returns.

9. The term **"Exempt Collective Investment Vehicle"** means an Investment Entity that is regulated as a collective investment vehicle, provided that all of the interests in the collective investment vehicle are held by or through individuals or Entities that are not Reportable Persons, except a Passive NFE with Controlling Persons who are Reportable Persons.

An Investment Entity that is regulated as a collective investment vehicle does not fail to qualify under subparagraph B(9) as an Exempt Collective Investment Vehicle, solely because the collective investment vehicle has issued physical shares in bearer form, provided that:

 a) the collective investment vehicle has not issued, and does not issue, any physical shares in bearer form after [xx/xx/xxxx];

 b) the collective investment vehicle retires all such shares upon surrender;

 c) the collective investment vehicle performs the due diligence procedures set forth in Sections II through VII and reports any information required to be reported with respect to any such shares when such shares are presented for redemption or other payment; and

 d) the collective investment vehicle has in place policies and procedures to ensure that such shares are redeemed or immobilised as soon as possible, and in any event prior to [xx/xx/xxxx].

C. **Financial Account**

1. The term **"Financial Account"** means an account maintained by a Financial Institution, and includes a Depository Account, a Custodial Account and:

 a) in the case of an Investment Entity, any equity or debt interest in the Financial Institution. Notwithstanding the foregoing, the term "Financial Account" does not include any equity or debt interest in an Entity that is an Investment Entity solely because it *(i)* renders investment advice to, and acts on behalf of, or *(ii)* manages portfolios for, and acts on behalf of, a customer for the purpose of investing, managing, or administering Financial Assets deposited in the name of the customer with a Financial Institution other than such Entity;

 b) in the case of a Financial Institution not described in subparagraph C(1)(a), any equity or debt interest in the Financial Institution, if the class of interests was established with a purpose of avoiding reporting in accordance with Section I; and

 c) any Cash Value Insurance Contract and any Annuity Contract issued or maintained by a Financial Institution, other than a noninvestment-linked, non-transferable immediate life annuity that is issued to an individual and monetises a pension or disability benefit provided under an account that is an Excluded Account.

The term "Financial Account" does not include any account that is an Excluded Account.

2. The term **"Depository Account"** includes any commercial, checking, savings, time, or thrift account, or an account that is evidenced by a certificate of deposit, thrift certificate, investment certificate, certificate of indebtedness, or other similar instrument maintained by a Financial Institution in the ordinary course of a banking or similar business. A Depository Account also includes an amount held by an insurance company pursuant to a guaranteed investment contract or similar agreement to pay or credit interest thereon.

3. The term **"Custodial Account"** means an account (other than an Insurance Contract or Annuity Contract) that holds one or more Financial Assets for the benefit of another person.

4. The term **"Equity Interest"** means, in the case of a partnership that is a Financial Institution, either a capital or profits interest in the partnership. In the case of a trust that is a Financial Institution, an Equity Interest is considered to be held by any person treated as a settlor or beneficiary of all or a portion of the trust, or any other natural person exercising ultimate effective control over the trust. A Reportable Person will be treated as being a beneficiary of a trust if such Reportable Person has the right to receive directly or indirectly (for example, through a nominee) a mandatory distribution or may receive, directly or indirectly, a discretionary distribution from the trust.

5. The term **"Insurance Contract"** means a contract (other than an Annuity Contract) under which the issuer agrees to pay an amount upon the occurrence of a specified contingency involving mortality, morbidity, accident, liability, or property risk.

6. The term **"Annuity Contract"** means a contract under which the issuer agrees to make payments for a period of time determined in whole or in part by reference to the life expectancy of one or more individuals. The term also includes a contract that is considered to be an Annuity Contract in accordance with the law, regulation, or practice of the jurisdiction in which the contract was issued, and under which the issuer agrees to make payments for a term of years.

7. The term **"Cash Value Insurance Contract"** means an Insurance Contract (other than an indemnity reinsurance contract between two insurance companies) that has a Cash Value.

8. The term **"Cash Value"** means the greater of *(i)* the amount that the policyholder is entitled to receive upon surrender or termination of the contract (determined without reduction for any surrender charge or policy loan), and *(ii)* the amount the policyholder can borrow under or with regard to the contract. Notwithstanding the foregoing, the term "Cash Value" does not include an amount payable under an Insurance Contract:

a) solely by reason of the death of an individual insured under a life insurance contract;

b) as a personal injury or sickness benefit or other benefit providing indemnification of an economic loss incurred upon the occurrence of the event insured against;

c) as a refund of a previously paid premium (less cost of insurance charges whether or not actually imposed) under an Insurance Contract (other than an investment-linked life insurance or annuity contract) due to cancellation or termination of the contract, decrease in risk exposure during the effective period of the contract, or arising from the correction of a posting or similar error with regard to the premium for the contract;

d) as a policyholder dividend (other than a termination dividend) provided that the dividend relates to an Insurance Contract under which the only benefits payable are described in subparagraph C(8)(b); or

e) as a return of an advance premium or premium deposit for an Insurance Contract for which the premium is payable at least annually if the amount of the advance premium or premium deposit does not exceed the next annual premium that will be payable under the contract.

9. The term **"Preexisting Account"** means a Financial Account maintained by a Reporting Financial Institution as of [xx/xx/xxxx].

10. The term **"New Account"** means a Financial Account maintained by a Reporting Financial Institution opened on or after [xx/xx/xxxx].

11. The term **"Preexisting Individual Account"** means a Preexisting Account held by one or more individuals.

12. The term **"New Individual Account"** means a New Account held by one or more individuals.

13. The term **"Preexisting Entity Account"** means a Preexisting Account held by one or more Entities.

14. The term **"Lower Value Account"** means a Preexisting Individual Account with an aggregate balance or value as of 31 December [xxxx] that does not exceed USD 1 000 000.

15. The term **"High Value Account"** means a Preexisting Individual Account with an aggregate balance or value that exceeds USD 1 000 000 as of 31 December [xxxx] or 31 December of any subsequent year.

16. The term **"New Entity Account"** means a New Account held by one or more Entities.

17. The term **"Excluded Account"** means any of the following accounts:

    a) a retirement or pension account that satisfies the following requirements:

    i) the account is subject to regulation as a personal retirement account or is part of a registered or regulated retirement or pension plan for the provision of retirement or pension benefits (including disability or death benefits);

    ii) the account is tax-favoured (i.e. contributions to the account that would otherwise be subject to tax are deductible or excluded from the gross income of the account holder or taxed at a reduced rate, or taxation of investment income from the account is deferred or taxed at a reduced rate);

    iii) information reporting is required to the tax authorities with respect to the account;

    iv) withdrawals are conditioned on reaching a specified retirement age, disability, or death, or penalties apply to withdrawals made before such specified events; and

    v) either *(i)* annual contributions are limited to USD 50 000 or less, or *(ii)* there is a maximum lifetime contribution limit to the account of USD 1 000 000 or less, in each case applying the rules set forth in paragraph C of Section VII for account aggregation and currency translation.

    A Financial Account that otherwise satisfies the requirement of subparagraph C(17)(a)(v) will not fail to satisfy such requirement solely because such Financial Account may receive assets or funds transferred from one or more Financial Accounts that meet the requirements of subparagraph C(17)(a) or (b) or from one or more retirement or pension funds that meet the requirements of any of subparagraphs B(5) through (7).

b) an account that satisfies the following requirements:

   i)   the account is subject to regulation as an investment vehicle for purposes other than for retirement and is regularly traded on an established securities market, or the account is subject to regulation as a savings vehicle for purposes other than for retirement;

   ii) the account is tax-favoured (i.e. contributions to the account that would otherwise be subject to tax are deductible or excluded from the gross income of the account holder or taxed at a reduced rate, or taxation of investment income from the account is deferred or taxed at a reduced rate);

   iii) withdrawals are conditioned on meeting specific criteria related to the purpose of the investment or savings account (for example, the provision of educational or medical benefits), or penalties apply to withdrawals made before such criteria are met; and

   iv) annual contributions are limited to USD 50 000 or less, applying the rules set forth in paragraph C of Section VII for account aggregation and currency translation.

   A Financial Account that otherwise satisfies the requirement of subparagraph C(17)(b)(iv) will not fail to satisfy such requirement solely because such Financial Account may receive assets or funds transferred from one or more Financial Accounts that meet the requirements of subparagraph C(17)(a) or (b) or from one or more retirement or pension funds that meet the requirements of any of subparagraphs B(5) through (7).

c) a life insurance contract with a coverage period that will end before the insured individual attains age 90, provided that the contract satisfies the following requirements:

   i)   periodic premiums, which do not decrease over time, are payable at least annually during the period the contract is in existence or until the insured attains age 90, whichever is shorter;

ii) the contract has no contract value that any person can access (by withdrawal, loan, or otherwise) without terminating the contract;

iii) the amount (other than a death benefit) payable upon cancellation or termination of the contract cannot exceed the aggregate premiums paid for the contract, less the sum of mortality, morbidity, and expense charges (whether or not actually imposed) for the period or periods of the contract's existence and any amounts paid prior to the cancellation or termination of the contract; and

iv) the contract is not held by a transferee for value.

d) an account that is held solely by an estate if the documentation for such account includes a copy of the deceased's will or death certificate.

e) an account established in connection with any of the following:

i) a court order or judgment.

ii) a sale, exchange, or lease of real or personal property, provided that the account satisfies the following requirements:

i) the account is funded solely with a down payment, earnest money, deposit in an amount appropriate to secure an obligation directly related to the transaction, or a similar payment, or is funded with a Financial Asset that is deposited in the account in connection with the sale, exchange, or lease of the property;

ii) the account is established and used solely to secure the obligation of the purchaser to pay the purchase price for the property, the seller to pay any contingent liability, or the lessor or lessee to pay for any damages relating to the leased property as agreed under the lease;

iii) the assets of the account, including the income earned thereon, will be paid or otherwise distributed for the benefit of the purchaser, seller, lessor, or lessee (including to satisfy such person's obligation) when the property is sold, exchanged, or surrendered, or the lease terminates;

iv) the account is not a margin or similar account established in connection with a sale or exchange of a Financial Asset; and

v) the account is not associated with an account described in subparagraph C(17)(f).

iii) an obligation of a Financial Institution servicing a loan secured by real property to set aside a portion of a payment solely to facilitate the payment of taxes or insurance related to the real property at a later time.

iv) an obligation of a Financial Institution solely to facilitate the payment of taxes at a later time.

f) a Depository Account that satisfies the following requirements:

i) the account exists solely because a customer makes a payment in excess of a balance due with respect to a credit card or other revolving credit facility and the overpayment is not immediately returned to the customer; and

ii) beginning on or before [xx/xx/xxxx], the Financial Institution implements policies and procedures either to prevent a customer from making an overpayment in excess of USD 50 000, or to ensure that any customer overpayment in excess of USD 50 000 is refunded to the customer within 60 days, in each case applying the rules set forth in paragraph C of Section VII for currency translation. For this purpose, a customer overpayment does not refer to credit balances to the extent of disputed charges but does include credit balances resulting from merchandise returns.

g) any other account that presents a low risk of being used to evade tax, has substantially similar characteristics to any of the accounts described in subparagraphs C(17)(a) through (f), and is defined in domestic law as an Excluded Account, provided that the status of such account as an Excluded Account does not frustrate the purposes of the Common Reporting Standard.

D. **Reportable Account**

1. The term **"Reportable Account"** means an account held by one or more Reportable Persons or by a Passive NFE with one or more Controlling Persons that is a Reportable Person, provided it has been identified as such pursuant to the due diligence procedures described in Sections II through VII.

2. The term **"Reportable Person"** means a Reportable Jurisdiction Person other than: *(i)* a corporation the stock of which is regularly traded on one or more established securities markets; *(ii)* any corporation that is a Related Entity of a corporation described in clause (i); *(iii)* a Governmental Entity; *(iv)* an International Organisation; *(v)* a Central Bank; or *(vi)* a Financial Institution.

3. The term **"Reportable Jurisdiction Person"** means an individual or Entity that is resident in a Reportable Jurisdiction under the tax laws of such jurisdiction, or an estate of a decedent that was a resident of a Reportable Jurisdiction. For this purpose, an Entity such as a partnership, limited liability partnership or similar legal arrangement that has no residence for tax purposes shall be treated as resident in the jurisdiction in which its place of effective management is situated.

4. The term **"Reportable Jurisdiction"** means a jurisdiction *(i)* with which an agreement is in place pursuant to which there is an obligation in place to provide the information specified in Section I, and *(ii)* which is identified in a published list.

5. The term **"Participating Jurisdiction"** means a jurisdiction *(i)* with which an agreement is in place pursuant to which it will provide the information specified in Section I, and *(ii)* which is identified in a published list.

6. The term **"Controlling Persons"** means the natural persons who exercise control over an Entity. In the case of a trust, such term means the settlor(s), the trustee(s), the protector(s) (if any), the beneficiary(ies) or class(es) of beneficiaries, and any other natural person(s) exercising ultimate effective control over the trust, and in the case of a legal arrangement other than a trust, such term means persons in equivalent or similar positions. The term "Controlling Persons" must be interpreted in a manner consistent with the Financial Action Task Force Recommendations.

7. The term **"NFE"** means any Entity that is not a Financial Institution.

8. The term **"Passive NFE"** means any: *(i)* NFE that is not an Active NFE; or *(ii)* an Investment Entity described in subparagraph A(6)(b) that is not a Participating Jurisdiction Financial Institution.

9. The term **"Active NFE"** means any NFE that meets any of the following criteria:

   a) less than 50% of the NFE's gross income for the preceding calendar year or other appropriate reporting period is passive income and less than 50% of the assets held by the NFE during the preceding calendar year or other appropriate reporting period are assets that produce or are held for the production of passive income;

   b) the stock of the NFE is regularly traded on an established securities market or the NFE is a Related Entity of an Entity the stock of which is regularly traded on an established securities market;

   c) the NFE is a Governmental Entity, an International Organisation, a Central Bank, or an Entity wholly owned by one or more of the foregoing;

   d) substantially all of the activities of the NFE consist of holding (in whole or in part) the outstanding stock of, or providing financing and services to, one or more subsidiaries that engage in trades or businesses other than the business of a Financial Institution, except that an Entity does not qualify for this status if the Entity functions (or holds itself out) as an investment fund, such as a private equity fund, venture capital fund, leveraged buyout fund, or any investment vehicle whose purpose is to acquire or fund companies and then hold interests in those companies as capital assets for investment purposes;

   e) the NFE is not yet operating a business and has no prior operating history, but is investing capital into assets with the intent to operate a business other than that of a Financial Institution, provided that the NFE does not qualify for this exception after the date that is 24 months after the date of the initial organisation of the NFE;

   f) the NFE was not a Financial Institution in the past five years, and is in the process of liquidating its assets or is reorganising with the intent to continue or recommence operations in a business other than that of a Financial Institution;

g) the NFE primarily engages in financing and hedging transactions with, or for, Related Entities that are not Financial Institutions, and does not provide financing or hedging services to any Entity that is not a Related Entity, provided that the group of any such Related Entities is primarily engaged in a business other than that of a Financial Institution; or

h) the NFE meets all of the following requirements:

i) it is established and operated in its jurisdiction of residence exclusively for religious, charitable, scientific, artistic, cultural, athletic, or educational purposes; or it is established and operated in its jurisdiction of residence and it is a professional organisation, business league, chamber of commerce, labour organisation, agricultural or horticultural organisation, civic league or an organisation operated exclusively for the promotion of social welfare;

ii) it is exempt from income tax in its jurisdiction of residence;

iii) it has no shareholders or members who have a proprietary or beneficial interest in its income or assets;

iv) the applicable laws of the NFE's jurisdiction of residence or the NFE's formation documents do not permit any income or assets of the NFE to be distributed to, or applied for the benefit of, a private person or non-charitable Entity other than pursuant to the conduct of the NFE's charitable activities, or as payment of reasonable compensation for services rendered, or as payment representing the fair market value of property which the NFE has purchased; and

v) the applicable laws of the NFE's jurisdiction of residence or the NFE's formation documents require that, upon the NFE's liquidation or dissolution, all of its assets be distributed to a Governmental Entity or other non-profit organisation, or escheat to the government of the NFE's jurisdiction of residence or any political subdivision thereof.

E. **Miscellaneous**

1. The term **"Account Holder"** means the person listed or identified as the holder of a Financial Account by the Financial Institution that maintains the account. A person, other than a Financial Institution, holding a Financial Account for the benefit or account of another person as agent, custodian, nominee, signatory, investment advisor, or intermediary, is not treated as holding the account for purposes of the Common Reporting Standard, and such other person is treated as holding the account. In the case of a Cash Value Insurance Contract or an Annuity Contract, the Account Holder is any person entitled to access the Cash Value or change the beneficiary of the contract. If no person can access the Cash Value or change the beneficiary, the Account Holder is any person named as the owner in the contract and any person with a vested entitlement to payment under the terms of the contract. Upon the maturity of a Cash Value Insurance Contract or an Annuity Contract, each person entitled to receive a payment under the contract is treated as an Account Holder.

2. The term **"AML/KYC Procedures"** means the customer due diligence procedures of a Reporting Financial Institution pursuant to the anti-money laundering or similar requirements to which such Reporting Financial Institution is subject.

3. The term **"Entity"** means a legal person or a legal arrangement, such as a corporation, partnership, trust, or foundation.

4. An Entity is a **"Related Entity"** of another Entity if either Entity controls the other Entity, or the two Entities are under common control. For this purpose control includes direct or indirect ownership of more than 50% of the vote and value in an Entity.

5. The term **"TIN"** means Taxpayer Identification Number (or functional equivalent in the absence of a Taxpayer Identification Number).

6. The term **"Documentary Evidence"** includes any of the following:

   a) a certificate of residence issued by an authorised government body (for example, a government or agency thereof, or a municipality) of the jurisdiction in which the payee claims to be a resident.

   b) with respect to an individual, any valid identification issued by an authorised government body (for example, a government or agency thereof, or a municipality), that includes the individual's name and is typically used for identification purposes.

c) with respect to an Entity, any official documentation issued by an authorised government body (for example, a government or agency thereof, or a municipality) that includes the name of the Entity and either the address of its principal office in the jurisdiction in which it claims to be a resident or the jurisdiction in which the Entity was incorporated or organised.

d) any audited financial statement, third-party credit report, bankruptcy filing, or securities regulator's report.

Section IX: Effective Implementation

A. A jurisdiction must have rules and administrative procedures in place to ensure effective implementation of, and compliance with, the reporting and due diligence procedures set out above including:

1. rules to prevent any Financial Institutions, persons or intermediaries from adopting practices intended to circumvent the reporting and due diligence procedures;

2. rules requiring Reporting Financial Institutions to keep records of the steps undertaken and any evidence relied upon for the performance of the above procedures and adequate measures to obtain those records;

3. administrative procedures to verify Reporting Financial Institutions' compliance with the reporting and due diligence procedures; administrative procedures to follow up with a Reporting Financial Institution when undocumented accounts are reported;

4. administrative procedures to ensure that the Entities and accounts defined in domestic law as Non-Reporting Financial Institutions and Excluded Accounts continue to have a low risk of being used to evade tax; and

5. effective enforcement provisions to address non-compliance.

III. Commentaries on the Model Competent Authority Agreement and the Common Reporting Standard

A. Commentaries on
the Model Competent Authority Agreement

Introduction

1.   The Model CAA links the CRS and the legal basis for the exchange (such as the Convention on Mutual Administrative Assistance in Tax Matters or a bilateral tax treaty). The Model CAA consists of a preamble and seven sections and provides for the modalities of the exchange to ensure the appropriate flows of the information. The preamble contains representations on domestic reporting and due diligence rules that underpin the exchange of information pursuant to the Model CAA. It also contains representations on confidentiality, safeguards and the existence of the necessary infrastructure for an effective exchange relationship.

2.   The Model CAA contains a section dealing with definitions (Section 1), covers the type of information to be exchanged (Section 2), the time and manner of the exchange (Section 3) ,collaboration on compliance and enforcement (Section 4) and the confidentiality and data safeguards that must be respected (Section 5). Consultations between the Competent Authorities, amendments to the Agreement and term of the Agreement, including suspension and termination, are dealt with in Sections 4, 6 and 7.

3.   The Model CAA is drafted as a bilateral reciprocal agreement based on the principle that automatic exchange is reciprocal and that the exchange will be done on a bilateral basis. To reduce the costs associated with signing multiple competent authority agreements the exchange of information could also be implemented on the basis of a multilateral competent authority agreement/arrangement. A multilateral version of the Model CAA is included as Annex 1. Although the agreement would be multilateral the exchange of information itself would be on a bilateral basis. Further there may be instances where jurisdictions wish to enter into a non-reciprocal bilateral agreement (e.g. where one jurisdiction does not have an income tax). A nonreciprocal version of the Model CAA is included as Annex 2. It has been

acknowledged, by the G20 and others, that developing countries may face particular capacity issues as regards automatic exchange of information and that this is an important issue which needs to be addressed and in July 2013 the G20 called on the Global Forum on Transparency and Exchange of Information for Tax Purposes to work with the OECD Task Force on Tax and Development, the World Bank and others to help developing countries identify their need for technical assistance and capacity building.

4.   Jurisdictions could also enter into a multilateral intergovernmental agreement or multiple intergovernmental agreements that would be international treaties in their own right or regional legislation covering both the reporting obligations and due diligence procedures coupled with a more limited competent authority agreement.

Commentary on the Preamble

1.   The preamble ("whereas clauses") provide relevant context and representations including a sentence referring to the underlying legal basis that permits the automatic exchange of information.

2.   The first clause serves as an introduction and may vary depending on the particular circumstances of the jurisdictions entering into the Agreement.

3.   The second clause sets out the representations by the Competent Authorities that the laws of their respective jurisdictions require, or are expected to require, financial institutions to report information regarding certain accounts, consistent with the scope of exchange contemplated by Section 2 of this Agreement.

4.   The alternative language used in this clause allows jurisdictions, that so wish, to sign the competent authority agreement even before one or both of the jurisdictions have the relevant rules on due diligence and reporting in place. See also paragraph 3 of Section 3 (paragraph 3 of the Commentary on Section 3) and Section 7 (paragraph 1 of the Commentary on Section 7).

5.   The third clause sets out the legal basis that authorises the automatic exchange of financial account information and allows the Competent Authorities to agree the scope and modalities of such automatic exchanges. The scope agreed to must be consistent with the scope of exchange contemplated by Section 2 of this Agreement. Other legal instruments (i.e. instruments other than income tax conventions or the Convention on Mutual Administrative Assistance in Tax Matters) that permit the automatic exchange of information for tax purposes include certain tax information exchange agreements, or regional tax co-operation agreements. On a regional basis the automatic exchange of information could also be implemented on the basis of e.g. EU law or Andean community legislation that covered the elements of the Model CAA and the CRS.

6.   The fourth clause sets out the representations by the Competent Authorities that they have in place *(i)* appropriate safeguards to ensure the confidentiality of the information received and *(ii)* an infrastructure that allows for an effective exchange relationship. The Commentary on Section 5 of the Model CAA provides more information.

Commentary on Section 1
concerning Definitions

Paragraph 1 – Definitions

1.   Paragraph 1 contains the definitions of the terms that are specific to the Agreement. The definitions of all the other terms used in the Agreement are contained in Section VIII of the Common Reporting Standard.

2.   Subparagraphs 1(a) and (b) are intended to include the description of the jurisdictions concluding the Agreement. Competent Authorities are free to agree on the definitions of the terms "[Jurisdiction A]" and "[Jurisdiction B]"; however, such definitions must be consistent with the definitions contained in the underlying legal instrument. Furthermore, Competent Authorities are free to include a geographic description (including a reference to continental shelves); however, only a political definition is necessary. An example of a political definition is "Mexico means the United Mexican States".

3.   The definition of the term "Competent Authority" contained in subparagraph 1(c) is intended to include a description of the competent authorities for purposes of the Agreement. This definition enables each jurisdiction to designate one or more authorities as being competent. However, such definition must be consistent with the definition contained in the underlying legal instrument.

4.   The terms contained in subparagraphs 1(d) through (k) align the scope of the exchange of information between the jurisdictions concluding the Agreement to the scope of the Common Reporting Standard. Such terms refer to:

- the financial institutions required to report: "[Jurisdiction A] Financial Institution", "[Jurisdiction B] Financial Institution", and "Reporting Financial Institution", which are consistent with the terms "Reporting Financial Institution" and "Participating Jurisdiction Financial Institution" contained in subparagraphs A(1) and (2) of Section VIII of the Common Reporting Standard (see paragraphs 2-6 of the Commentary on Section VIII);

- the financial accounts reported: "Reportable Account", "[Jurisdiction A] Reportable Account", and "[Jurisdiction B] Reportable Account", which are consistent with the term "Reportable Account" contained in subparagraph D(1) of Section VIII of the Common Reporting Standard (see paragraph 105 of the Commentary on Section VIII); and

- the account holders subject to reporting: "[Jurisdiction A] Person" and "[Jurisdiction B] Person", which are consistent with the terms "Reportable Person" and "Reportable Jurisdiction Person" contained in subparagraphs D(2) and (3) of Section VIII of the Common Reporting Standard (see paragraphs 106-116 of the Commentary on Section VIII).

5.   Subparagraph 1(l) contains the definition of the term "TIN", which is also a term defined in subparagraph E(5) of Section VIII of the Common Reporting Standard. Whilst the latter is intended to describe that a TIN is a Taxpayer Identification Number or a functional equivalent in the absence of a Taxpayer Identification Number (see paragraphs 146-149 of the Commentary on Section VIII), the purpose of the former is to identify the TINs of the jurisdictions concluding the Agreement. The terms "[Jurisdiction A] TIN" and "[Jurisdiction B] TIN" contained in subparagraphs 1(m) and (n) also serve this purpose.

6.   The term "Common Reporting Standard" is not defined in the Model Competent Authority Agreement, but it is defined in the multilateral version of the Model Competent Authority Agreement. It is possible that the Common Reporting Standard, including the IT modalities, will be updated from time to time as more jurisdictions implement, and obtain experience with, the Common Reporting Standard. In the context of a multilateral agreement competent authorities may sign on different dates and because of the differing dates of signature the Common Reporting Standard may have been updated in the interim. To address this situation, the multilateral version defines the Common Reporting Standard as "the standard for automatic exchange of financial account information developed by the OECD, with G20 countries, presented to the G20 in 2014 and published on the OECD website". In addition, to ensure that there is an understanding that all jurisdictions would be expected to implement the most recent version of the Standard, the third recital states that it is "expected that the laws of the Jurisdictions would be amended from time to time to reflect updates to the Common Reporting Standard and once such changes are enacted by a Jurisdiction the definition of "Common Reporting Standard" would be deemed to refer to the updated version in respect of that Jurisdiction". In a bilateral agreement, the same issue does not arise as competent authorities would generally sign on the same date. However, even in a bilateral agreement, competent authorities may wish to explicitly provide for updates to the Common Reporting Standard

in the same way as set out in the multilateral version (i.e. define the term "Common Reporting Standard" and add a recital setting out the expectation that jurisdictions would amend their laws to reflect updates to the Common Reporting Standard).

Paragraph 2 – General rule of interpretation

7.   Paragraph 2 sets out the general rule of interpretation. The first sentence of paragraph 2 makes clear that any capitalised terms used in the Model CAA but not defined therein are meant to be interpreted consistently with the meaning given to them in the Common Reporting Standard. This reflects the notion, also expressed in the preamble, that the jurisdictions have introduced reporting and due diligence procedures (including related definitions) consistent with the Common Reporting Standard.

8.   The second sentence of paragraph 2 provides that, unless the context otherwise requires or the Competent Authorities agree to a common meaning, any term not otherwise defined in this Agreement or in the Common Reporting Standard has the meaning that it has at that time under the law of the jurisdiction applying the Agreement. In this respect any meaning under the applicable tax laws of that jurisdiction will prevail over a meaning given to that term under other laws of that jurisdiction. Further, when looking at the context, the Competent Authorities should consider the Commentary on the Common Reporting Standard and any terms defined therein.

Commentary on Section 2
concerning Exchange of Information
with Respect to Reportable Accounts

1.   This Section provides that the information to be exchanged is the information required to be reported under the reporting and due diligence rules of the Common Reporting Standard. See Section I (General Reporting Requirements) of the CRS and the related Commentary.

2.   The first paragraph refers to the legal basis for the exchange and provides that the information will be exchanged on an annual basis. Information may also be exchanged more frequently than once a year; for example, when a Competent Authority receives corrected data from a Reporting Financial Institution, that information would generally be sent to the other Competent Authority as soon as possible after it has been received. The information to be exchanged is the information obtained pursuant to the CRS and is further specified in paragraph 2.

3.   Paragraph 1 makes clear that the exchange of information is subject to the applicable reporting and due diligence rules of the CRS. Thus, where those rules do not require the reporting of, for instance, a TIN with respect to a particular Reportable Account, there is also no obligation to exchange such information. See the exceptions contained in paragraphs C through F of Section I of the CRS and paragraphs 25-35 of the Commentary on Section I.

4.   Subparagraph 2(d) of Section 2 provides that a jurisdiction is required to exchange the account balance or value as of the end of the calendar year or other appropriate reporting period. However, paragraph 11 of the Commentary on Section I of the CRS provides that jurisdictions may, as an alternative, require financial institutions to report the average account balance or value during the relevant calendar year or other reporting period. Where a jurisdiction requires reporting of the average account balance or value rather than year-end balance, this should be set out in the Agreement, including the applicable rules to determine the average account balance or value, so that it is clear what is being exchanged.

Commentary on Section 3
concerning Time and Manner of
Exchange of Information

Paragraphs 1 and 2 – Amount, characterisation and currency of payments

1.   Paragraph 1 provides that for the purposes of the exchange of information in Section 2, the amount and characterisation of payments made with respect to a Reportable Account may be determined in accordance with the principles of the tax laws of the jurisdiction sending the information. Paragraph 2 provides that the information exchanged will identify the currency in which each amount is denominated.

Paragraphs 3 and 4 – Time of exchange of information

2.   Paragraph 3 provides that the information must be exchanged within nine months after the calendar year to which the information relates. The first year with respect to which the information is exchanged is left blank and is for jurisdictions to insert. The nine-month timeline in paragraph 3 is a minimum standard and jurisdictions are free to agree on shorter timelines. For example, Member States of the European Union are subject to a 6-month timeline under the Savings Directive.

3.   Paragraph 3 also provides that notwithstanding the year that the Competent Authorities have chosen as the year in respect of which the first exchange will take place, information is only required to be exchanged with respect to a calendar year if both jurisdictions have in effect legislation that requires reporting with respect to such calendar year that is consistent with the scope of exchange provided for in Section 2 and in the Common Reporting Standard. This sentence will not be operational if at the time the Agreement is signed both jurisdictions have in effect domestic legislation consistent with the Common Reporting Standard. If one or both of the jurisdictions do not have such legislation in place at the time of signature, the sentence will operate to ensure that once the Agreement has come into effect but the Common Reporting Standard has been in place for longer in

one of the jurisdictions, the only information that needs to be exchanged is years with respect to which both jurisdictions have the relevant reporting obligations in place. A Jurisdiction may however choose, subject to its domestic laws, to exchange with respect to the earlier years in which case this is also consistent with the CRS and the Model CAA.

4.   The following example illustrates the operation of paragraph 3 where one jurisdiction does not have legislation requiring reporting in effect for the calendar year that was agreed to in the first sentence of paragraph 3. Jurisdictions A and B sign the Model CAA on 30 April 2015 and agree that information will be exchanged with respect to 2016 and subsequent years. Jurisdiction A provides notice on 7 June 2015 that it has legislation in effect that requires reporting with respect to 2016. Jurisdiction B provides notice on 1 November 2015 that it has legislation in effect to provide reporting with respect to 2017. In this case the last sentence of paragraph 3 will operate such that Jurisdiction A does not have an obligation to exchange information in respect of 2016. Both jurisdictions A and B will have an obligation to exchange information with respect to 2017. However, Jurisdiction A may choose, subject to its domestic laws, to send information to Jurisdiction B in respect of 2016 even though Jurisdiction A will not receive information in respect of 2016.

5.   Paragraph 4 contains an exception with respect to the year gross proceeds are to be reported. It may be more difficult for Reporting Financial Institutions to implement procedures to obtain the total gross proceeds from the sale or redemption of property. Thus, when implementing the Common Reporting Standard, jurisdictions may choose to gradually introduce the reporting of such gross proceeds. If no transition is provided, paragraph 4 will be unnecessary. If a transition is provided for by one of the jurisdictions, paragraph 4 should be included which provides that notwithstanding paragraph 3, the information to be exchanged with respect to the year identified in paragraph 3 is the information described in paragraph 2 of Section 2, except for gross proceeds described in subparagraph 2(e)(2) of Section 2. In such a case, jurisdictions should specify the year for which gross proceeds are to be reported.

6.   Nothing in the Agreement prevents the application of the provisions of Sections 2 and 3 with respect to the information obtained prior to the effective date of the Agreement, as long as such information is provided after the Agreement is in effect and the provisions of Sections 2 and 3 have become effective. Competent Authorities may find it useful, however, to clarify the extent to which the provisions of Sections 2 and 3 are applicable to such information.

Paragraphs 5 and 6 – Information Technology modalities

CRS schema and user guide

7.   Paragraph 5 provides that the Competent Authorities will automatically exchange the information described in Section 2 in a common reporting standard schema in Extensible Markup Language. Guidance on the relevant schema and its use is contained in the CRS user guide, which is included in Annex 3.

Data transmission including encryption

8.   Paragraph 6 provides that the Competent Authorities will agree on one or more methods for data transmission, including encryption standards.

Appropriate minimum standards

9.   Any transmission method should meet appropriate minimum standards to ensure the confidentiality and integrity of data throughout the transmission. Confidentiality means that data or information is not made available or disclosed to unauthorised persons. Integrity means that data or information has not been modified or altered in an unauthorised manner. Such standards should be susceptible to changing technological capabilities over time. This includes the use of secure transmission channels and protocols that ensure confidentiality and integrity of the data through encryption or physical measures or a combination of both.

10.   The Model CAA does not mandate a single solution for data transmission or encryption, as this could limit the ability of Competent Authorities to agree systems and practices that are already successfully in use or may be appropriate in the particular circumstances. As the responsibility for the data remains with the sending jurisdiction until the data reaches the receiving jurisdiction, it is also possible that, depending on national requirements, different processes may be agreed for the two parts of a bilateral exchange (i.e. sending and receiving). For example, jurisdiction A may use browser based transmission and jurisdiction B a server routed through a secure network to exchange data. However, given that jurisdictions would enter into CRS based automatic exchange relationships with a number of jurisdictions, thought will need to be given to designing a sustainable international transmission architecture that mitigates the need for each jurisdiction having to potentially adopt and maintain multiple methods of transmission and/or encryption.

Encryption

11. Encryption is designed to protect both the confidentiality and the integrity of data. It ensures that data is transformed in order to render it unintelligible to anyone who does not possess the decryption key. All data files to be exchanged should therefore be encrypted to a minimum secure standard, and the transmission path should be encrypted or otherwise physically secured with audit controls in place to monitor access and file copies. One method of encryption in common use for exchange of information uses both a public and a private key. Public key cryptography has been in use for some decades and allows parties to exchange encrypted data without communicating a shared secret key in advance. The sending party encrypts the data file with a public key, and only the receiving party holds the secure private key that allows the data to be decrypted. There are standards for the length of encryption keys in use internationally that are recognised as providing the appropriate level of security for personal financial data, both now and for the foreseeable future, such as advanced encryption standard (AES) 256.

Electronic transmission methods

12. While it used to be common to send encrypted files of data on floppy discs, memory sticks and compact discs by physical handover or signed-for postal mail between Competent Authorities, additional administration and risk attach to transfer of portable media (even when integrity and confidentiality are assured by encryption). It is now technologically as straightforward to transfer data using an internet browser which can also inexpensively provide encryption, non-revocation and non-repudiation capabilities, so use of portable media would no longer be considered best practice. A transmission method that allows an integrated end-to-end transfer process for transmission of electronic files is the recommended best practice, whether server-to-server or browser based.[1] Secure email under minimum standards and specifications may alternatively be used, but may have higher installation costs or operating complexity in managing user accesses and data security, including file size

---

1. WEB SERVICES with ws-security is another affordable standard coming to be widely used in secure environments, formed by a set of services using HTTP protocol through standard methods such as GET and POST. Examples of transmission protocols that have been agreed internationally to meet requirement for secure transmission channels and protocols that ensure confidentiality and integrity of the data include transport layer security (TLS) v 1.1 for secure browser based exchanges and secure file transfer protocol (SFTP) for scheduled bulk transfer, but these are not the only protocols that may provide appropriate solutions.

limits and firewall issues. The importance of risk assessment and continuous reassessment of risk should be recognised.

Operational security implementation

13.   The confidentiality and security of data transmitted also depends on good managerial, organisational and operational procedures, as well as technical measures such as hardware and software tools. Although conformance with any particular standard is not mandated, ideally security should be managed in a manner that is consistent with best practice standards such as the ISO 27000 series Information Security standards as modified from time to time. More specifically, the data must be accessed only by authorised parties in the transmission process and access to any encryption keys, particularly the private key must be tightly controlled. Evidence of all authorised access to the data or keys should be maintained as an audit log. Further information on data safeguarding and confidentiality standards is contained in the Commentary on Section 5.

Commentary on Section 4
concerning Collaboration on
Compliance and Enforcement

1.   This Section deals with collaboration between the Competent Authorities on compliance and enforcement. It provides that if one Competent Authority has reason to believe that an error may have led to incorrect or incomplete information reporting or there is non-compliance by a Reporting Financial Institution that Competent Authority should notify the other Competent Authority. The notified Competent Authority will take all appropriate measures available under its domestic law to address the errors or non-compliance described in the notice. See the Commentary on Section IX of the Common Reporting Standard regarding the rules and administrative procedures that jurisdictions must have in place to ensure that the CRS is effectively implemented.

2.   The notice under this Section must be in writing and must clearly set out the error or non-compliance and the reasons for the belief that such error or non-compliance has occurred. The notified Competent Authority should provide a response or an update as soon as possible and no later than 90 calendar days of having received the notice from the other Competent Authority. If the issue has not been resolved, the Competent Authority should provide the other Competent Authority with updates every 90 days. If however, after reviewing and considering the notice in good faith, the notified Competent Authority does not agree that there is, or has been, an error or non-compliance as described in the notice it should, as soon as possible, advise the other Competent Authority in writing of such determination and explain the reasons for it.

3.   Section 4 does not contemplate direct contact between the Competent Authority from one jurisdiction with a Reporting Financial Institution in the other jurisdiction. As an alternative, two competent authorities may wish to allow for direct contact between a competent authority in one jurisdiction and a Reporting Financial Institution in the other jurisdiction in case of administrative or other minor errors. The decision to include such option will depend on the domestic law in the respective jurisdictions and may also be influenced by the volume of inquiries that a Competent Authority expects

to receive. If the Competent Authorities agree to such an approach, the following language would replace the current language of Section 4:

1. A Competent Authority may make an inquiry directly to a Reporting Financial Institution in the other jurisdiction where it has reason to believe that administrative errors or other minor errors may have led to incorrect or incomplete information reporting. A Competent Authority will notify the other Competent Authority when the first-mentioned Competent Authority makes such an inquiry of a Reporting Financial Institution in the other jurisdiction.

2. A Competent Authority will notify the other Competent Authority when the first-mentioned Competent Authority has reason to believe that there is non-compliance by a Reporting Financial Institution with the applicable reporting requirements and due diligence procedures consistent with the Common Reporting Standard. The notified Competent Authority will take all appropriate measures available under domestic law to address the non-compliance described in the notice.

4.   It is the domestic law of the jurisdiction of the Reporting Financial Institution, including protection of personal data that would be applicable to such direct contact.

Commentary on Section 5
concerning Confidentiality and Data Safeguards

1.   Confidentiality of taxpayer information has always been a fundamental cornerstone of tax systems. Both taxpayers and tax administrations have a legal right to expect that information exchanged remains confidential. In order to have confidence in their tax systems and comply with their obligations under the law, taxpayers need to know that the often sensitive financial information is not disclosed inappropriately, whether intentionally or by accident. Citizens and governments will only trust international exchange if the information exchanged is used and disclosed only in accordance with the instrument on the basis of which it was exchanged. This is a matter of both the legal framework but also of having systems and procedures in place to ensure that the legal framework is respected in practice and that there is no unauthorised disclosure of information. The ability to protect the confidentiality of tax information is also the result of a "culture of care" within a tax administration which includes the entire spectrum of systems, procedures and processes to ensure that the legal framework is respected in practice and information security and integrity is also maintained in the handling of information. As the sophistication of a tax administration increases, the confidentiality processes and practices must keep pace to ensure that information exchanged remains confidential.[2] Several jurisdictions have specific rules on the protection of personal data which also apply to taxpayer information.

2.   Section 5 together with Section 7 and the representations in the fourth clause of the preamble explicitly recognise the importance of confidentiality and data safeguards in connection with the automatic exchange of financial account information. The remainder of this Commentary briefly discusses paragraphs 1 and 2 followed by a comprehensive discussion of confidentiality and data safeguarding in connection with the Common Reporting Standard.

---

2.   OECD (2012), *Keeping it Safe: The OECD Guide on the Protection of Confidentiality of Information Exchanged for Tax Purposes*, OECD, Paris, available on www.oecd.org/ctp/exchange-of-tax-information/keeping-it-safe-report.pdf.

Paragraph 1 – Confidentiality including protection of personal data

3.　All information exchanged is subject to the confidentiality rules and other safeguards provided for in the underlying legal instrument. This includes the purposes for which the information may be used and limits to whom the information may be disclosed.

4.　Many jurisdictions have specific rules on the protection of personal data which apply to taxpayer information. For example, special data protection rules apply to information exchanges by EU Member States (whether the exchange is made to another EU Member State or a third jurisdiction). These rules include, inter alia, the data subject's right to information, access, correction, redress, and the existence of an oversight mechanism to protect the data subject's rights. Paragraph 1 of Section 5 provides that the supplying Competent Authority may, to the extent needed to ensure the necessary level of protection of personal data, specify in the Competent Authority Agreement the particular safeguards that must be respected, as required under its domestic law. The Competent Authority receiving the information must ensure the practical implementation and observance of any safeguarding specified. The Competent Authority receiving the information shall treat the information in compliance not only with its own domestic law, but also with additional safeguards that may be required to ensure data protection under the domestic law of the supplying Competent Authority. Such additional safeguards, as specified by the supplying Competent Authority, may for example relate to individual access to the data. The specification of the safeguards may not be necessary if the supplying Competent Authority is satisfied that the receiving Competent Authority ensures the necessary level of data protection with respect to the data being supplied. In any case, these safeguards should be limited to what is needed to ensure the protection of personal data without unduly preventing or delaying the effective exchange of information.

5.　Exchange of information instruments generally provide that information does not have to be supplied to another jurisdiction if the disclosure of the information would be contrary to the *ordre public* (public policy) of the jurisdiction supplying the information.[3] While it is rare for this to apply in the context of information exchange between Competent Authorities, certain jurisdictions may require their Competent Authorities to specify that information it supplies may not be used or disclosed in proceedings that could result in the imposition and execution of the death penalty or torture or other severe violations of human rights (such as for example when tax investigations are motivated by political, racial, or religious persecution) as that would contravene the public

---

3.　See for example subparagraph 3(c) of Article 26 of the OECD Model Tax Convention and subparagraph 2(d) of Article 21 of the Multilateral Convention on Mutual Administrative Assistance in Tax Matters.

policy of the supplying jurisdiction. In such a case, a provision to this effect could be included in the Competent Authority Agreement.

Paragraph 2 – Breach of confidentiality

6.   Ensuring the confidentiality of information received under the applicable legal instrument is critical. Paragraph 2 of Section 5 provides that in the event of any breach of confidentiality or failure of safeguards (including the additional safeguards (if any) specified by the supplying Competent Authority) the Competent Authority must immediately notify the other Competent Authority of such breach or failure including any sanctions or remedial actions consequently imposed. The content of any such notice must itself respect the confidentiality rules and must be in accordance with the domestic law of the jurisdiction where the breach or failure occurred. Further, Section 7 explicitly provides that non-compliance with the confidentiality and data safeguard provisions (including the additional safeguards (if any) specified by the supplying Competent Authority) would be considered significant non-compliance and a justification for immediate suspension of the Competent Authority Agreement.

Confidentiality and data safeguards under the Common Reporting Standard

7.   Three building blocks are essential in ensuring appropriate safeguards are in place to protect the information exchanged automatically: *(i)* the legal framework, *(ii)* information security management: practices and procedures, and *(iii)* monitoring compliance and sanctions to address a breach of confidentiality. Each one of these aspects is discussed further below. Annex 4 is a questionnaire[4] which translates the discussion into a series of questions and which jurisdictions may find a useful tool in assessing whether the required confidentiality and data safeguards are met. Jurisdictions may choose to design their own questionnaire to translate the principles of the confidentiality and data safeguard aspects of the CRS. Other jurisdictions may choose not to use a questionnaire as they already have an ongoing automatic exchange of information relationship with another jurisdiction and have previously satisfied themselves that the partner jurisdiction has appropriate safeguards in place to protect the information exchanged automatically.

---

4.   The example questionnaire in Annex 4 is the questionnaire used by the United States for the purposes of FATCA as of 20 March 2014 with the United States specificities removed.

1. Legal Framework

8.   The legal framework must ensure the confidentiality of exchanged tax information and limit its use to appropriate purposes in accordance with the terms of the exchange instrument. The two basic components of such a framework are the terms of the applicable instrument and a jurisdiction's domestic legislation.

9.   All bilateral and multilateral tax conventions and other legal instruments under which tax information is exchanged must contain provisions requiring that the confidentiality of exchanged information be maintained and that its use be limited to certain purposes. The OECD Model Tax Convention is illustrative. Paragraph 2 of Article 26 of the Model Tax Convention requires that taxpayer information received by a Competent Authority be treated as secret in the same manner as taxpayer information obtained under the jurisdiction's domestic laws. The disclosure of such information is restricted to "persons or authorities (including courts and administrative bodies)" involved in assessment, collection, administration, or enforcement of covered taxes, or in related prosecutions, appeals or oversight. It also allows use for another purpose if authorised by both competent authorities and if the laws of both states permit such use. Similarly Article 22 of the Multilateral Convention on Mutual Administrative Assistance in Tax Matters requires that information be treated as secret and protected in the same manner as information obtained under the domestic law of the party and imposes limitations on the use and disclosure of the information.

10.   Domestic legislation must include provisions sufficient to protect the confidentiality of taxpayer information and provide for specific and limited circumstances under which such information can be disclosed and used. Domestic law must also impose significant penalties or sanctions for improper disclosure or use of taxpayer information. Further, domestic law must provide that the jurisdiction's international exchange instruments are legally binding, such that confidentiality obligations in such instruments are also binding. Additionally, a jurisdiction's domestic law for safeguarding taxpayer data must apply to taxpayer information received from another government under an exchange instrument.

2. Information Security Management: Practices and Procedures

11.   In order for the legal protections afforded under the exchange instrument and domestic law to be meaningful, practices and procedures must be in place to ensure that exchanged taxpayer information can be used solely for tax purposes (or other specified purposes) and to prevent the disclosure of taxpayer information to persons or governmental authorities that

are not engaged in the assessment, collection, administration, or enforcement of covered taxes, or in related prosecutions, appeals or oversight.

12.   An information security management system is a set of policies, practices and procedures concerned with information security management including IT related risks. This is not just a technical issue but also a management, cultural and organisational issue. As discussed in more detail below the practices and procedures implemented by tax administrations should cover all aspects relevant to protecting confidentiality including a screening process for employees handling the information, limits on who can access the information and systems to detect and trace unauthorised disclosures. The information security management practices and procedures used by each jurisdiction's tax administration must adhere to internationally recognised standards or best practices that ensure the protection of confidential taxpayer data.[5] More specifically this would include the following baseline controls:

2.1. Employees (background checks, employment contracts, training)

13.   Tax administrations must ensure that individuals in positions of authority and access are trustworthy and meet security criteria, and their access privileges are appropriately managed and monitored. Employees, consultants and others with access to confidential information must be screened for potential security risks. Consultants with access to taxpayer information must be contractually bound by the same obligations as employees to keep taxpayer information confidential.

14.   Tax administrations must also ensure that employees with access to data are aware of the confidentiality requirements of their positions, the security risks associated with their activities, and applicable laws, policies, and procedures related to security/confidentiality. As long as employees continue to have access to data, annual or more frequent training must continue.

---

5.   The internationally accepted standards for information security are known as the "ISO/IEC 27000-series", which are published jointly by the International Organisation for Standardisation (ISO) and the International Electro-technical Commission (IEC). The series provides best practices on information security management, risks, and controls within the context of an overall information security management system. A tax administration should be able to document readily that it is compliant with the ISO/IEC 27000-series standards or that it has an equivalent information security framework and that taxpayer information obtained under a legal instrument is protected under that framework.

15.   In addition, there must be procedures in place to quickly end access to confidential information for terminated, transferred, or retired employees who no longer need such access. Further, confidentiality obligations must continue after access has ceased.

2.2. Access to premises and physical document storage

16.   Tax administrations must have security measures in place to restrict entry to their premises. Measures often include the presence of security guards, policies against unaccompanied visitors, security passes, or coded entry systems for employees and limits on employee access to areas where sensitive information is located.

17.   Tax administrations must also provide secure storage for confidential documents. Information can be secured in locked storage units or rooms, such as cabinets (whether locked with combinations or keys), safes and strong rooms. Access to combinations and keys must be limited. The security of physical storage cabinets must vary depending on the classification of their contents, and bulk tax data exchanged automatically must have an appropriate security classification. Tax administrations must also ensure this security continues when data is taken to alternate work sites.

2.3. Planning

18.   Tax administrations must have a plan to develop, document, update, and implement security for information systems.

2.4. Configuration Management

19.   Tax administrations must control and manage the configuration of information systems. To this end, they must develop, document, disseminate, and update relevant security controls.

2.5. Access Control

20.   Tax administrations must limit system access to authorised users and devices (including other information systems). Authorised users must be limited to accessing the transactions and functions they are permitted to undertake.

2.6. Identification and Authentication

21.   Information systems must have the means to store and authenticate the identities of users and devices that require access to information systems. Information systems must also be capable of identifying an unauthorised user and preventing him or her from accessing confidential information.

2.7. Audit and Accountability

22.   Unauthorised users can be held accountable only if their actions are traceable. Therefore, it is essential for tax administrations to create and retain information system audit records for monitoring, analysing, investigating, and reporting of unlawful, unauthorised, or inappropriate information system activity.

2.8. Maintenance

23.   Tax administrations must perform periodic and timely maintenance of systems, and provide effective controls over the tools, techniques, and mechanisms for system maintenance and the personnel that use them.

2.9. System and Communications Protection

24.   Tax administrations must monitor, control, and protect communications at external and internal boundaries of information systems. These controls must include procedures to remove residual data, provide transmission confidentiality, and validate cryptography.

2.10. System and Information Integrity

25.   Tax administrations must identify, report, and correct (or take remedial action for) information communication technology security incidents in a timely manner, providing protection from malicious code and monitoring system security alerts and advisories.

2.11. Security Assessments

26.   The tax administration must develop and regularly update a policy for reviewing the processes used to test, validate, and authorise the security controls for protecting data, correcting deficiencies and reducing vulnerabilities. The frequency of such updates will be risk-based but must be done at appropriate intervals in line with internationally recognised standards or best practices. It must also have a policy to review the manner in which

information system operations and connections are authorised, and the procedures for monitoring system security controls.

2.12. Contingency Planning

27.   Tax administrations must establish and implement plans for emergency response, backup operations, and post-disaster recovery of information systems.

2.13. Risk Assessment

28.   A tax administration must assess the potential risk of unauthorised access to taxpayer information, and the risk and magnitude of harm from unauthorised use, disclosure, disruption, modification, or destruction of such information or of the taxpayer information systems. It must update its risk assessment periodically or whenever there are significant changes to the information system, the facilities where the system resides, or other conditions that may impact the security or accreditation status of the system.

2.14. Systems and Services Acquisition

29.   Tax administrations must ensure that third-party providers of information systems that are engaged to process, store, and transmit information exchanged under the legal instrument use security controls consistent with the necessary computer security requirements.

2.15. Media Protection

30.   Tax administrations must protect information in printed form or on digital media, limit information access to authorised users, and sanitise or destroy digital media before disposal or reuse.

2.16. Data Identification

31.   Data exchanged under the legal instrument must always be protected against inadvertent disclosure. If the data is included in a file that includes other data and physical separation is impractical, procedures must be in place to ensure that the entire file is safeguarded and clearly labelled to indicate the inclusion of data exchanged under a legal instrument. The information itself also must be clearly labelled.

32.   Procedures must be in place to ensure that, before such a file is released to an individual or agency not authorised to access data exchanged under a legal instrument, all such data has been removed. In case the data is stored in a database procedures must be in place to ensure that, before access

to the database is provided to an individual or agency not authorised to access data exchanged under a legal instrument, all such data has been deleted from the database (or securely partitioned/protected in a way that prevents the unauthorised individual or agency from accessing that data).

2.17. Information Disposal Policies

33.   Tax administrations must have policies requiring data to be destroyed as soon as it is no longer needed and ensuring secure disposal of confidential information. Document shredding, burn boxes, or locked waste bin shredding is appropriate for paper documents, and electronic documents should be deleted when no longer necessary. Confidential information must be removed prior to the disposition of computers and information storage devices.

3. Monitoring compliance and sanctions to address a breach of confidentiality

34.   In addition to keeping information exchanged under a legal instrument confidential, tax administrations must be able to ensure that its use will be limited to the purposes defined by the applicable information exchange agreement. Thus, compliance with an acceptable information security framework alone is not sufficient to protect tax data that has been exchanged. In addition, domestic law must impose penalties or sanctions for improper disclosure or use of taxpayer information. To ensure implementation, such laws must be reinforced by adequate administrative resources and procedures.

3.1. Penalties and Sanctions

35.   Domestic law must impose penalties or sanctions for improper disclosure or use of taxpayer information, and tax administrations must in fact impose these penalties and sanctions against personnel who violate security policies and procedures to deter others from engaging in similar violations. To ensure implementation, such laws must be reinforced by adequate administrative resources and procedures. Tax administrations should implement a formal sanctions process for personnel and third-party providers who fail to comply with established information security policies and procedures. Policies should consider both civil and criminal sanctions for unauthorised inspection or disclosure.

3.2. Policing Unauthorised Access and Disclosure

36.   In addition to having policies that govern access to confidential information, tax administrations must also have processes in place to monitor compliance with these policies and detect any unauthorised access

and disclosure. If it occurs, there must be an investigation followed by the preparation of a report for management. The report must include:

- recommendations for minimising the repercussions of the incident;

- an analysis of how to avoid similar incidents in the future;

- recommendations for any penalties to be imposed on the person(s) responsible for the breach, noting that law enforcement authorities should be involved if intentional disclosure is suspected; and

- reasons for a high degree of confidence that, once implemented, recommended system changes and penalties will prevent similar future breaches.

37.   Additionally, tax administrations should have a process for review and approval of recommendations for policy and procedural changes to avoid future breaches. The tax administration's investigating authority or senior management must ensure that approved recommendations are implemented.

Commentary on Section 6
concerning Consultations and Amendments

1.   This Section deals with consultations between the Competent Authorities and amendments to the competent authority agreement.

Paragraph 1 – Consultations

2.   This paragraph provides that if any difficulties in the implementation or interpretation of this Agreement arise, either Competent Authority may request consultations to develop measures to ensure that this Agreement is fulfilled. Consultations may also be held to analyse the quality of the information received.

3.   The Competent Authorities may communicate with each other by letter, facsimile transmission, telephone, direct meetings, or any other convenient means for purposes of reaching an agreement on appropriate measures to ensure that this Agreement is fulfilled.

Paragraph 2 – Amendments

4.   This paragraph clarifies that the Agreement may be amended by written agreement of the Competent Authorities. Unless the Competent Authorities otherwise agree, such amendment is effective on the first day of the month next following a period of one month from the later of:

- the date of the signatures of such written agreement, or

- the date that notifications are exchanged for the purposes of such written agreement.

5.   As noted in the Introduction to the Commentaries on the Model Competent Authority Agreement jurisdictions could also enter into a multilateral intergovernmental agreement or multiple intergovernmental agreements that would be international treaties in their own right covering both the reporting obligations and due diligence procedures coupled with a more limited competent authority agreement. In such cases different rules regarding amendments may apply.

Commentary on Section 7
concerning Term of Agreement

Paragraph 1 – Entry into force

1.   Paragraph 1 provides for two alternatives regarding the effective date. First, where jurisdictions have entered into this agreement after both jurisdictions have the necessary laws in place to implement the Common Reporting Standard, they would decide on a date for the Agreement to come into effect. Second, if the Competent Authorities sign before one or both jurisdictions have the necessary laws in place, they would likely use this second alternative and the agreement would enter into effect on the date of the later of the notifications that the jurisdiction has the necessary rules in place to implement the agreement.

Paragraph 2 – Suspension

2.   Paragraph 2 provides details on the possibility for a Competent Authority to suspend the Agreement when it has determined that there is or has been significant non-compliance by the other Competent Authority with this Agreement. Where possible the Competent Authorities should try to resolve any issues of non-compliance, even those of significant non-compliance, before issuing a notice to suspend the operation of the Agreement.

3.   To suspend the Agreement a Competent Authority must give notice in writing to the other Competent Authority that it intends to suspend the Agreement. The notice should provide a detailed description of the significant non-compliance that has occurred, or is occurring, and where possible a description of the steps that should be taken to resolve the issue. The suspension will have immediate effect.

4.   The notified Competent Authority should, as soon as possible, undertake the necessary steps to address the significant non-compliance. As soon as the non-compliance is resolved, the notified Competent Authority should advise the other Competent Authority. Following successful resolution of the issue, the Competent Authority that sent the suspension notice should

confirm in writing to the notified Competent Authority that the Agreement is no longer suspended and exchanges of information should recommence as soon as possible.

5.   Paragraph 2 provides that significant non-compliance includes, but is not limited to:

- non-compliance with the confidentiality or data safeguard provisions of this Agreement (including the additional safeguards specified in the Competent Authority Agreement), for example information is used for purposes not authorised in the underlying legal instrument or domestic legislation is amended in such a way that the confidentiality of information is compromised;

- a failure by the Competent Authority to provide timely or adequate information as required under this Agreement;

- defining the status of Excluded Accounts or Non-Reporting Financial Institutions in a manner that frustrates the purposes of the Common Reporting Standard;

- a failure to have rules and administrative procedures in place to ensure the effective implementation of the reporting and due diligence procedures set out in the Common Reporting Standard.

6.   During the period of any suspension all information previously received under this Agreement will remain confidential and subject to the terms of Section 5 of the Agreement including any additional data safeguards specified by the supplying Competent Authority and the underlying legal instrument.

Paragraph 3 – Termination

7.   Paragraph 3 contains the termination clause. Either Competent Authority may terminate this Agreement by giving notice of termination in writing to the other Competent Authority. Such termination will become effective on the first day of the month following the expiration of a period of 12 months after the date of the notice of termination. For example, a Competent Authority may choose to terminate this Agreement when the Agreement has been suspended and the other Competent Authority has not resolved issues of significant non-compliance within a reasonable timeframe.

8.   The termination of the underlying legal instrument under which the Competent Authority Agreement is concluded would lead to the automatic termination of the Competent Authority Agreement. Accordingly in such circumstances the Competent Authority Agreement would not separately need to be terminated.

9.   Paragraph 3 clarifies that in the event of termination, all information previously received under this Agreement will remain confidential and subject to the terms of Section 5 of the Agreement including any additional data safeguards specified by the supplying Competent Authority and the underlying legal instrument.

B. Commentaries on the Common Reporting Standard

Introduction

[handwritten marginal notes:] Section I - who to be reported / II - VII Due diligence. / VIII Defn / IX Rule / admin procedure to ensure implementation / comp

The CRS contains the reporting and due diligence standards that underpin the automatic exchange of financial account information. An implementing jurisdiction must have rules in place that require financial institutions to report information consistent with the scope of reporting set out in Section I and to follow due diligence procedures consistent with the procedures contained in Sections II through VII of the CRS.

Capitalised terms used in the CRS are defined in Section VIII. An implementing jurisdiction may provide that the amount and characterisation of payments made with respect to a Reportable Account must be determined in accordance with the principles of its tax laws.

Section IX of the CRS describes the rules and administrative procedures a jurisdiction is expected to have in place to ensure effective implementation of, and compliance with, the CRS.

Commentary on Section I
concerning General Reporting Requirements

1.   Section I contains the general reporting requirements applicable to Reporting Financial Institutions. Paragraphs A and B specify the information to be reported as a general rule, while paragraphs C through F provide for a series of exceptions in connection with TIN, date of birth, place of birth and gross proceeds. Paragraph 1 of Section 2 of the Model Competent Authority Agreement makes clear that the information to be exchanged is the information required to be reported under the reporting and due diligence rules of the Common Reporting Standard, including the exceptions contained in paragraphs C through F of Section I.

2.   Reporting Financial Institutions would often inform Account Holders (e.g. through a change to terms and conditions) that information relating to their accounts, if their accounts are Reportable Accounts, will be reported and may be exchanged with other jurisdictions. In some jurisdictions, Reporting Financial Institutions may be required to do so under their jurisdiction's privacy and disclosure rules. Reporting Financial Institutions would need to comply with such rules in this regard (e.g. by providing Account Holders, upon request, with a copy of the information reported).

Paragraph A – Information to be reported

3.   Pursuant to paragraph A, each Reporting Financial Institution must report the following information with respect to each Reportable Account of such Reporting Financial Institution:

   a)   in the case of any individual that is an Account Holder and a Reportable Person: the name, address, jurisdiction(s) of residence, TIN(s) and date and place of birth;

   b)   in the case of any Entity that is an Account Holder and a Reportable Person: the name, address, jurisdiction(s) of residence and TIN(s);

   c)   in the case of any Entity that is an Account Holder and that is identified as having one or more Controlling Persons that is a Reportable Person:

(1) the name, address, jurisdiction(s) of residence and TIN(s) of the Entity; and

(2) the name, address, jurisdiction(s) of residence, TIN(s) and date and place of birth of each Controlling Person that is a Reportable Person;

d) the account number (or functional equivalent in the absence of an account number);

e) the name and identifying number (if any) of the Reporting Financial Institution; and

f) the account balance or value (including, in the case of a Cash Value Insurance Contract or Annuity Contract, the Cash Value or surrender value) as of the end of the relevant calendar year or other appropriate reporting period or, if the account was closed during such year or period, the closure of the account.

4.   In addition, the following information must also be reported:

a) in the case of any Custodial Account:

(1) the total gross amount of interest paid or credited to the account (or with respect to the account) during the calendar year or other appropriate reporting period;

(2) the total gross amount of dividends paid or credited to the account (or with respect to the account) during the calendar year or other appropriate reporting period;

(3) the total gross amount of other income generated with respect to the assets held in the account paid or credited to the account (or with respect to the account) during the calendar year or other appropriate reporting period; and

(4) the total gross proceeds from the sale or redemption of Financial Assets paid or credited to the account during the calendar year or other appropriate reporting period with respect to which the Reporting Financial Institution acted as a custodian, broker, nominee, or otherwise as an agent for the Account Holder.

b) in the case of any Depository Account: the total gross amount of interest paid or credited to the account during the calendar year or other appropriate reporting period.

c) in the case of any account other than a Custodial Account or a Depository Account: the total gross amount paid or credited to the Account Holder with respect to the account during the calendar year or other appropriate reporting period with respect to which the Reporting Financial Institution is the obligor or debtor, including the aggregate amount of any redemption payments made to the Account Holder during the calendar year or other appropriate reporting period.

Subparagraph A(1) – Address

5.   The address to be reported with respect to an account is the address recorded by the Reporting Financial Institution for the Account Holder, pursuant to the due diligence procedures in Sections II through VII. Consequently, in the case of an account held by an individual that is a Reportable Person, the address to be reported is the current residence address of the individual (see paragraphs 8 and 22 of the Commentary on Section III) unless the Reporting Financial Institution does not have such address in its records where it would report the mailing address it has on file. In the case of an account held by an Entity that is identified as having one or more Controlling Persons that is a Reportable Person, the address to be reported is the address of the Entity and the address of each Controlling Person of such Entity that is a Reportable Person.

Subparagraph A(1) – Jurisdiction(s) of residence

6.   The jurisdiction of residence to be reported with respect to an account is the jurisdiction of residence identified by the Reporting Financial Institution for the Reportable Person with respect to the relevant calendar year or other appropriate reporting period, pursuant to the due diligence procedures in Sections II through VII. In the case of a Reportable Person that is identified as having more than one jurisdiction of residence, the jurisdictions of residence to be reported are all the jurisdictions of residence identified by the Reporting Financial Institution for the Reportable Person with respect to the relevant calendar year or other appropriate reporting period. The jurisdiction(s) of residence that are identified as a result of the due diligence procedures in Sections II through VII are without prejudice to any residence determination made by the Reporting Financial Institution for any other tax purposes.

Subparagraph A(1) – TIN

7.   The TIN to be reported with respect to an account is the TIN assigned to the Account Holder by its jurisdiction of residence (i.e. not by a jurisdiction of source). In the case of a Reportable Person that is identified as having more than one jurisdiction of residence, the TIN to be reported is the Account Holder's TIN with respect to each Reportable Jurisdiction (subject

to the application of paragraphs C and D). As defined in subparagraph E(5) of Section VIII, the term "TIN" includes a functional equivalent in the absence of a Taxpayer Identification Number (see paragraph 148 of the Commentary on Section VIII).

Subparagraph A(2) – Account number

8.   The account number to be reported with respect to an account is the identifying number assigned by the Reporting Financial Institution for purposes other than to satisfy the reporting requirements of subparagraph A(1) or, if no such number is assigned to the account, a functional equivalent (i.e. a unique serial number or other number such Reporting Financial Institution assigns to the Financial Account that distinguishes the account from other accounts maintained by such institution). A contract or policy number would generally be considered functional equivalents of an account number.

Subparagraph A(3) – Identifying number

9.   The Reporting Financial Institution must report its name and identifying number (if any). Identifying information on the Reporting Financial Institution is intended to allow Participating Jurisdictions to easily identify the source of the information reported and subsequently exchanged in order to, e.g. follow-up on an error that may have led to incorrect or incomplete information reporting. The "identifying number" of a Reporting Financial Institution is the number assigned to a Reporting Financial Institution for identification purposes. Normally this number is assigned to the Reporting Financial Institution by its jurisdiction of residence or location, but it could also be assigned globally. Examples of identifying numbers include a TIN, business/company registration code/number, Global Legal Entity Identifier (LEI),[6] or Global Intermediary Identification Number (GIIN).[7] Participating Jurisdictions are expected to provide their Reporting Financial Institutions with guidance with respect to any identifying number to be reported. If no such number is assigned to the Reporting Financial Institution, then only the name and address of the Reporting Financial Institution are required to be reported.

---

6.   See the Regulatory Oversight Committee (ROC) of the Global Legal Entity Identifier System (GLEIS) webpage, available on www.leiroc.org/.
7.   The Global Intermediary Identification Number (GIIN) is an identification number that is assigned to certain financial institutions by the Internal Revenue Service (IRS) of the United States.

Subparagraph A(4) – Account balance or value

10.   The Reporting Financial Institution must report the balance or value of the account as of the end of the calendar year or other appropriate reporting period or, if the account was closed during such year or period, the closure of the account (see paragraph 14 below). An account with a balance or value that is negative must be reported as having an account balance or value equal to zero. In the case of an account that is a Cash Value Insurance or Annuity Contract, the Reporting Financial Institution must report the Cash Value or surrender value of the account.

11.   Some jurisdictions, however, already require financial institutions to report the average balance or value of the account during the calendar year or other appropriate reporting period. These jurisdictions are free to maintain reporting of that information instead of requiring reporting of the balance or value of the account as of the end of the calendar year or other appropriate reporting period, which can be done by replacing subparagraph A(4) by the following provision:

4. the [highest] average [monthly] account balance or value (including, in the case of a Cash Value Insurance Contract or Annuity Contract, the Cash Value or surrender value) during the relevant calendar year or other appropriate reporting period or, if the account was closed during such year or period, the closure of the account;

In such a case, subparagraph 2(d) of Section 2 of the Model Competent Authority Agreement should be modified accordingly (see paragraph 4 of the Commentary on Section 2 of the Model Competent Authority Agreement).

12.   In general, the balance or value of a Financial Account is the balance or value calculated by the Financial Institution for purposes of reporting to the Account Holder. In the case of an equity or debt interest in a Financial Institution, the balance or value of an Equity Interest is the value calculated by the Financial Institution for the purpose that requires the most frequent determination of value, and the balance or value of a debt interest is its principal amount. The balance or value of an Insurance or Annuity Contract is the balance or value as of the end of either the calendar year or other appropriate reporting period (see paragraph 15 below). The balance or value of the account is not to be reduced by any liabilities or obligations incurred by an account holder with respect to the account or any of the assets held in the account.

13.   Each holder of a jointly held account is attributed the entire balance or value of the joint account, as well as the entire amounts paid or credited to the joint account (or with respect to the joint account). The same is applicable with respect to:

- an account held by a Passive NFE with more than one Controlling Person that is a Reportable Person, where each Controlling Person is attributed the entire balance or value of the account held by the Passive NFE, as well as the entire amounts paid or credited to the account;

- an account held by an Account Holder that is a Reportable Person and is identified as having more than one jurisdiction of residence, where the entire balance or value of the account, as well as the entire amount paid or credited to the account, must be reported with respect to each jurisdiction of residence of the Account Holder;

- an account held by a Passive NFE with a Controlling Person that is a Reportable Person and is identified as having more than one jurisdiction of residence, where the entire balance or value of the account held by the Passive NFE, as well as the entire amount paid or credited to the account, must be reported with respect to each jurisdiction of residence of the Controlling Person; or

- an account held by a Passive NFE that is a Reportable Person with a Controlling Person that is a Reportable Person, where the entire balance or value of the account held by the Passive NFE, as well as the entire amount paid or credited to the account, must be reported with respect to both the Passive NFE and the Controlling Person.

14.   In the case of an account closure, the Reporting Financial Institution has no obligation to report the account balance or value before or at closure, but must report that the account was closed. In determining when an account is "closed", reference must be made to the applicable law in a particular jurisdiction. If the applicable law does not address closure of accounts, an account will be considered to be closed according to the normal operating procedures of the Reporting Financial Institution that are consistently applied for all accounts maintained by such institution. For example, an equity or debt interest in a Financial Institution would generally be considered to be closed upon termination, transfer, surrender, redemption, cancellation, or liquidation. An account with a balance or value equal to zero or that is negative will not be a closed account solely by reason of such balance or value.

Subparagraphs A(4) through (7) – Appropriate reporting period

15.   The information to be reported must be that as of the end of the relevant calendar year or other appropriate reporting period. In determining what is meant by "appropriate reporting period", reference must be made to the meaning that the term has at that time under each jurisdiction's reporting rules, which must be consistently applied for a reasonable number of years.

The period between the most recent contract anniversary date and the previous contract anniversary date (e.g. in the case of a Cash Value Insurance Contract), and a fiscal year other than the calendar year, would generally be considered appropriate reporting periods.

Subparagraph A(5)(a) – Other income

16.   The information to be reported, in the case of a Custodial Account, includes the total gross amount of other income generated with respect to the assets held in the account paid or credited to the account (or with respect to the account) during the calendar year or other appropriate reporting period. The term "other income" means any amount considered income under the laws of the jurisdiction where the account is maintained, other than any amount considered interest, dividends, or gross proceeds or capital gains from the sale or redemption of Financial Assets.

Subparagraph A(5)(b) – Gross proceeds

17.   In the case of a Custodial Account, information to be reported includes the total gross proceeds from the sale or redemption of Financial Assets paid or credited to the account during the calendar year or other appropriate reporting period with respect to which the Reporting Financial Institution acted as a custodian, broker, nominee, or otherwise as an agent for the Account Holder. The term "sale or redemption" means any sale or redemption of Financial Assets, determined without regard to whether the owner of such Financial Assets is subject to tax with respect to such sale or redemption.

18.   A clearing or settlement organisation that maintains Reportable Accounts and settles sales and purchases of securities between members of such organisation on a net basis may not know the gross proceeds from sales or dispositions. Where the clearing or settlement organisation does not know the gross proceeds, gross proceeds are limited to the net amount paid or credited to a member's account that is associated with sales or other dispositions of Financial Assets by such member as of the time that such transactions are settled under the settlement procedures of such organisation. The term "clearing or settlement organisation" means an entity that is in the business of clearing trades of securities for its member organisations and transferring, or instructing the transfer of, securities by credit or debit to the account of a member without the necessity of physical delivery of the securities.

19.   With respect to a sale that is effected by a broker that results in a payment of gross proceeds, the date the gross proceeds are considered paid

is the date that the proceeds of such sale are credited to the account of or otherwise made available to the person entitled to the payment.

20.   The total gross proceeds from a sale or redemption means the total amount realised as a result of a sale or redemption of Financial Assets. In the case of a sale effected by a broker, the total gross proceeds from a sale or redemption means the total amount paid or credited to the account of the person entitled to the payment increased by any amount not so paid by reason of the repayment of margin loans; the broker may (but is not required to) take commissions with respect to the sale into account in determining the total gross proceeds. In the case of a sale of an interest bearing debt obligation, gross proceeds includes any interest accrued between interest payment dates.

Subparagraph A(7) – Gross amounts

21.   The information to be reported, in the case of any account other than a Custodial Account or a Depository Account, includes the total gross amount paid or credited to the Account Holder with respect to the account during the calendar year or other appropriate reporting period with respect to which the Reporting Financial Institution is a creditor or debtor. Such "gross amount" includes, for example, the aggregate amount of:

- any redemption payments made (in whole or part) to the Account Holder during the calendar year or other appropriate reporting period; and

- any payments made to the Account Holder under a Cash Value Insurance Contract or an Annuity Contract during the calendar year or other appropriate reporting period, even if such payments are not considered Cash Value in accordance with subparagraph C(8) of Section VIII.

CRS schema and user guide

22.   As provided in the Model Competent Authority Agreement, Competent Authorities will use the Common Reporting Standard schema for purposes of exchanging the information to be reported. The schema may also be used by Reporting Financial Institutions for purposes of reporting the information (as permitted by domestic law). Both the diagrammatic representation of the schema and its user guide may be found in Annex 3. The user guide may be particularly useful for Reporting Financial Institutions as it contains more detailed information on each data element and any attributes that apply to such data element. For example, the user guide describes the three data elements that apply specifically to the place of birth (i.e. CountryInfo, City and CitySubentity) and clarifies that, where the place

of birth is required to be reported, the data elements CountryInfo (identified by country code or name) and City must both be reported and the data element CitySubentity is optional.

Paragraph B – Currency

23.   The information must be reported in the currency in which the account is denominated and the information reported must identify the currency in which each amount is denominated. In the case of an account denominated in more than one currency, the Reporting Financial Institution may elect to report the information in a currency in which the account is denominated and is required to identify the currency in which the account is reported.

24.   If the balance or value of a financial account or other amount is denominated in a currency other than the currency used by a Participating Jurisdiction when implementing the Common Reporting Standard (for purposes of thresholds or limits), a Reporting Financial Institution must calculate the balance or value by applying a spot rate to translate such balance or value into the currency equivalent. For the purpose of a Reporting Financial Institution reporting an account, the spot rate must be determined as of the last day of the calendar year or other appropriate reporting period for which the account is being reported.

Paragraphs C through F – Exceptions

TIN and date of birth

25.   Paragraph C contains an exception applicable to Preexisting Accounts: the TIN or date of birth is not required to be reported if (i) such TIN or date of birth is not in the records of the Reporting Financial Institution, and (ii) there is not otherwise a requirement for such TIN or date of birth to be collected by such Reporting Financial Institution under domestic law. Thus, the TIN or date of birth is required to be reported if either:

  • the TIN or date of birth is in the records of the Reporting Financial Institution (whether or not there is an obligation to have it in the records); or

  • the TIN or date of birth is not in the records of the Reporting Financial Institution, but it is otherwise required to be collected by such Reporting Financial Institution under domestic law (e.g. AML/KYC Procedures).

26.   The "records" of a Reporting Financial Institution include the customer master file and electronically searchable information (see paragraph 34 below). A "customer master file" includes the primary files of a Reporting Financial Institution for maintaining account holder information, such as information used for contacting account holders and for satisfying AML/KYC Procedures. Reporting Financial Institutions would generally have a two-year period to complete the review procedures for identifying Reportable Accounts among Lower Value Accounts (see paragraph 51 of the Commentary on Section III) and, thus, could first review their electronic records (or obtain TIN or date of birth from the Account Holder) and then review their paper records.

27.   In addition, even where a Reporting Financial Institution does not have the TIN or date of birth for a Preexisting Account in its records and is not otherwise required to collect such information under domestic law, the Reporting Financial Institution is required to use reasonable efforts to obtain the TIN and date of birth with respect to Preexisting Accounts by the end of the second calendar year following the year in which such Accounts were identified as Reportable Accounts, unless one of the exceptions in paragraph D applies with respect to the TIN and it is not required to be reported.

28.   "Reasonable efforts" means genuine attempts to acquire the TIN and date of birth of the Account Holder of a Reportable Account. Such efforts must be made, at least once a year, during the period between the identification of the Preexisting Account as a Reportable Account and the end of the second calendar year following the year of that identification. Examples of reasonable efforts include contacting the Account Holder (e.g. by mail, in-person or by phone), including a request made as part of other documentation or electronically (e.g. by facsimile or by e-mail); and reviewing electronically searchable information maintained by a Related Entity of the Reporting Financial Institution, in accordance with the aggregation principles set forth in paragraph C of Section VII. However, reasonable efforts do not necessarily require closing, blocking, or transferring the account, nor conditioning or otherwise limiting its use. Notwithstanding the foregoing, reasonable efforts may continue to be made after the abovementioned period.

29.   Paragraph D contains an exception applicable to both Preexisting and New Accounts. A TIN is not required to be reported if either:

a)   a TIN is not issued by the relevant Reportable Jurisdiction; or

b)   the domestic law of the relevant Reportable Jurisdiction does not require the collection of the TIN issued by such Reportable Jurisdiction.

30.   A TIN is considered not to be issued by a Reportable Jurisdiction *(i)* where the jurisdiction does not issue a Taxpayer Identification Number nor

a functional equivalent in the absence of a Taxpayer Identification Number (see paragraph 148 of the Commentary on Section VIII), or *(ii)* where the jurisdiction has not issued a TIN to a particular individual or Entity. As a consequence, a TIN is not required to be reported with respect to a Reportable Account held by a Reportable Person that is resident in such a Reportable Jurisdiction, or with respect to whom a TIN has not been issued. However, if and when a Reportable Jurisdiction starts issuing TINs and issues a TIN to a particular Reportable Person, the exception contained in paragraph D no longer applies and the Reportable Person's TIN would be required to be reported if the Reporting Financial Institution obtains a self-certification that contains such TIN, or otherwise obtains such TIN.

31.   The exception described in clause *(ii)* of paragraph D focuses on the domestic law of the Account Holder's jurisdiction. Where a Reportable Jurisdiction has issued a TIN to a Reportable Person that holds a Reportable Account and the collection of such TIN cannot be required under such jurisdiction's domestic law (e.g. because under such law the provision of the TIN by a taxpayer is on a voluntary basis), the Reporting Financial Institution that maintains such account is not required to obtain and report the TIN. However, the Reporting Financial Institution is not prevented from asking for, and collecting the Account Holder's TIN for reporting purposes if the Account Holder choses to provide it. In this case, the Reporting Financial Institution must report the TIN. In practice, there may be only a few jurisdictions where this is the case (e.g. Australia).

32.   Participating Jurisdictions are expected to provide Reporting Financial Institutions with information with respect to the issuance, collection and, to the extent possible and practical, structure and other specifications of taxpayer identification numbers. The OECD will endeavour to facilitate its dissemination.

Place of birth

33.   Paragraph E contains an exception for both Preexisting and New Accounts: the place of birth is not required to be reported unless the Reporting Financial Institution is otherwise required to obtain and report it under domestic law and it is available in the electronically searchable data maintained by the Reporting Financial Institution. Thus, the place of birth is required to be reported if, with respect to the relevant Account Holder, both:

- the Reporting Financial Institution is otherwise required to obtain the place of birth and report it under domestic law; and

- the place of birth is available in the electronically searchable information maintained by the Reporting Financial Institution.

34. The term "electronically searchable information/data" means information that a Reporting Financial Institution maintains in its tax reporting files, customer master files, or similar files, and that is stored in the form of an electronic database against which standard queries in programming languages, such as Structured Query Language, may be used. Information, data, or files are not electronically searchable merely because they are stored in an image retrieval system (such as portable document format (.pdf) or scanned documents). "Reporting" for this purpose does not include information that is provided only upon request.

Gross proceeds

35. Paragraph F contains an exception with respect to the year the information is to be reported. It may be more difficult for Reporting Financial Institutions to implement procedures to obtain the total gross proceeds from the sale or redemption of Financial Assets. Thus, when implementing the Common Reporting Standard, jurisdictions may consider (if necessary) gradually introducing the reporting of such gross proceeds. In that case, the transitory provision would be drafted as paragraph F.

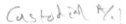

Commentary on Section II
concerning General Due Diligence Requirements

1.   This Section contains the general due diligence requirements. It also deals with reliance on service providers and alternative due diligence procedures for Preexisting Accounts.

Paragraphs A through C – General Due Diligence Requirements

2.   An account is treated as a Reportable Account, according to paragraph A, beginning as of the date it is identified as such pursuant to the due diligence procedures in Sections II through VII. Once an account is a Reportable Account, it maintains such status until the date it ceases to be a Reportable Account (e.g. because the Account Holder ceases to be a Reportable Person or the account becomes an Excluded Account, is closed, or is transferred in its entirety), even if the account balance or value is equal to zero or is negative, or there was not any amount paid or credited to the account (or with respect to the account). Where an account is identified as a Reportable Account based on its status at the end of the calendar year or reporting period, information with respect to that account must be reported as if it were a Reportable Account through the full calendar year or reporting period in which it was identified as such. Where a Reportable Account is closed, information with respect to that account must be reported until the date of closure. Unless otherwise provided, information with respect to a Reportable Account must be reported annually in the calendar year following the year to which the information relates.

3.   The following examples illustrate, in general, the application of paragraph A:

- • Example 1 (Account that becomes a Reportable Account): An account is opened on 28 May 00 and is identified as a Reportable Account on 3 December 01. Because the account was identified as a Reportable Account in calendar year 01, information with respect to that Reportable Account must be reported in calendar year 02 with respect to the full calendar year 01 and on an annual basis thereafter.

- Example 2 (Account that ceases to be a Reportable Account): The facts are the same as in Example 1. However, on 24 March 02, the Account Holder ceases to be a Reportable Person and, as a consequence, the account ceases to be a Reportable Account. Because the account ceased to be a Reportable Account on 24 March 02, information with respect to that account is not required to be reported in calendar year 03 nor afterwards, unless the account once again becomes a Reportable Account in calendar year 03 or any subsequent calendar year.

- Example 3 (Account that is closed): An account is opened on 9 September 04 and becomes a Reportable Account on 8 February 05. However, on 27 September 05, the Account Holder closes the account. Because the account was a Reportable Account between 8 February and 27 September 05 and was closed in calendar year 05, information with respect to that account (including the closure of the account) must be reported in calendar year 06 with respect to the part of calendar year 05 between 1 January and 27 September.

- Example 4 (Account that ceases to be a Reportable Account and is closed): The facts are the same as in Example 2, except that on 4 July 02 the Account Holder closes the account. Because the account ceased to be a Reportable Account on 24 March 02, information with respect to that account is not required to be reported in calendar year 03.

4.   Whilst the balance or value of an account is part of the information to be reported, it is also relevant for other purposes, such as the due diligence procedures for Preexisting Entity Accounts (see paragraphs A and B, and subparagraph E(1) and (2) of Section V) and the account balance aggregation rules (see subparagraphs C(1) and (2) of Section VII). According to paragraph B, the balance or value of an account is to be determined as of the last day of the calendar year or other appropriate reporting period.

5.   Where a balance or value threshold is to be determined as of the last day of a calendar year (see, e.g. subparagraph C(6) of Section III, and paragraphs A and B of Section V), according to paragraph C, the relevant balance or value must be determined as of the last day of the reporting period that ends with or within that calendar year. Thus, if the reporting period ends with the calendar year, then the relevant balance or value must be determined as of 31 December of the calendar year. However, if the reporting period ends within the calendar year, then the relevant balance or value must be determined as of the last day of the reporting period, but within the calendar year.

Paragraph D – Reliance on Service Providers

6.   According to paragraph D, each Jurisdiction may allow Reporting Financial Institutions to use service providers to fulfil the reporting and due diligence obligations imposed on such Reporting Financial Institutions (e.g. a jurisdiction may permit Reporting Financial Institutions to rely on due diligence procedures performed by service providers). In such cases, Reporting Financial Institutions must satisfy the requirements contained in domestic law and remain responsible for their reporting and due diligence obligations (i.e. the service provider's actions are imputed to the Reporting Financial Institution), including their obligations under domestic law on confidentiality and data protection. This alternative allows a Reporting Financial Institution to use a service provider that is resident in the same or in a different jurisdiction as the Reporting Financial Institution. Also, it does not modify the time and manner of the reporting and due diligence obligations, which remain the same as if they were still being fulfilled by the Reporting Financial Institution. For example, the service provider must report the information as the Reporting Financial Institution would have (e.g. to the same jurisdiction) and identify the Reporting Financial Institution with respect to which it fulfils the reporting and due diligence obligations.

7.   The following example illustrates the application of paragraph D: Investment Entity P is a mutual fund managed by Fund manager M that is resident in Participating Jurisdiction B and does not qualify as an Exempt Collective Investment Vehicle. Participating Jurisdiction B allows Reporting Financial Institutions to use service providers to fulfil all their CRS related obligations. Because Investment Entity P is a Reporting Financial Institution in Participating Jurisdiction B, Investment Entity P may use Fund manager M to perform the due diligence procedures and comply with its reporting and other CRS obligations.

Paragraph E – Alternative due diligence procedures for Preexisting Accounts

8.   According to paragraph E, each Jurisdiction may allow Reporting Financial Institutions to apply (i) the due diligence procedures for New Accounts to Preexisting Accounts, and (ii) the due diligence procedures for High Value Accounts to Lower Value Accounts. It may also permit Reporting Financial Institutions to make such election either with respect to all relevant Preexisting Accounts or, separately, with respect to any clearly identified group of such accounts (such as by line of business or the location where the account is maintained).

9.   Where a Jurisdiction allows New Account due diligence procedures to be used for Preexisting Accounts, the rules otherwise applicable to

Preexisting Accounts continue to apply. Thus, a Reporting Financial Institution can apply the due diligence procedures for New Accounts without forgoing access to relieving provisions that apply to Preexisting Accounts, such as paragraphs C of Section I, A of Section III, and A of Section V, which continue to apply in such circumstances. Also, consistent with subparagraph B(1) of Section III, the reporting of a single residence for a Preexisting Individual Account is sufficient to satisfy the reporting requirements of Section I.

Commentary on Section III concerning Due Diligence for Preexisting Individual Accounts

1.   This Section contains the due diligence procedures for purposes of identifying Reportable Accounts among Preexisting Individual Accounts. It distinguishes between Lower Value Accounts and High Value Accounts.

Paragraph A – Accounts not required to be reviewed, identified or reported

2.   Paragraph A exempts from review all Preexisting Individual Accounts that are Cash Value Insurance Contracts and Annuity Contracts, provided that the Reporting Financial Institution is effectively prevented by law from selling such contracts to residents of a Reportable Jurisdiction. A Reporting Financial Institution is "effectively prevented by law" from selling Cash Value Insurance Contracts or Annuity Contracts to residents of a Reportable Jurisdiction if:

   a)   the law of the Reporting Financial Institution's jurisdiction prohibits or otherwise effectively prevents the sale of such contracts to residents in another jurisdiction; or

   b)   the law of a Reportable Jurisdiction prohibit or otherwise effectively prevents the Reporting Financial Institution from selling such contracts to residents of such Reportable Jurisdiction.

3.   Where the applicable law does not prohibit Reporting Financial Institutions from selling insurance or annuity contracts outright, but requires them to fulfil certain conditions prior to being able to sell such contracts to residents of the Reportable Jurisdiction (such as obtaining a license and registering the contracts), a Reporting Financial Institution that has not fulfilled the required conditions under the applicable law will be considered to be "effectively prevented by law" from selling such contracts to residents of such Reportable Jurisdiction.

Paragraph B – Due diligence for Lower Value Accounts

4.   Paragraph B contains the procedures that apply with respect to Lower Value Accounts. Such procedures are the residence address test and the electronic record search.

5.   When implementing the Common Reporting Standard, jurisdictions may allow Reporting Financial Institutions to apply *(i)* either the residence address test or the electronic record search set forth in subparagraphs B(2) through (6), or *(ii)* only the electronic record search. In the first case, jurisdictions may also allow Reporting Financial Institutions to make an election to apply the residence address test either with respect to all Lower Value Accounts or, separately, with respect to any clearly identified group of such accounts (such as by line of business or the location where the account is maintained).

6.   Where domestic law allows Reporting Financial Institutions to apply the residence address test and a Reporting Financial Institution elects to apply it, the Reporting Financial Institution must apply such a test with respect to each Lower Value Account or clearly identified group of such accounts (as permitted by domestic law). If the Reporting Financial Institution decides not to apply the test or one or more of the requirements of the test are not satisfied, then it must perform the electronic record search with respect to the Lower Value Account.

Subparagraph B(1) – Residence address test

7.   Subparagraph B(1) contains the "residence address" test. Under this test, a Reporting Financial Institution must have policies and procedures in place to verify the residence address based on Documentary Evidence. For purposes of determining whether an individual Account Holder is a Reportable Person, the Reporting Financial Institution may treat such individual as being a resident for tax purposes of the jurisdiction in which an address is located if:

   a)   the Reporting Financial Institution has in its records a residence address for the individual Account Holder;

   b)   such residence address is current; and

   c)   such residence address is based on Documentary Evidence.

8.   The first requirement is that the Reporting Financial Institution has in its records a residence address for the individual Account Holder (see paragraph 26 of the Commentary on Section I). In general, an "in-care-of" address or a post office box is not a residence address. However, a post office box would generally be considered a residence address where it forms part of an address together with, e.g. a street, an apartment or suite number, or a

rural route, and thus clearly identifies the actual residence of the Account Holder. Similarly, in special circumstances such as that of military personnel, an "in-care-of" address may constitute a residence address. Jurisdictions implementing the Common Reporting Standard may determine other special circumstances where an "in-care-of" address or a post office box is used that clearly identify a residence address, provided that such determination does not frustrate the purposes of the Common Reporting Standard.

9.   The second requirement is that the residence address in the Reporting Financial Institution's records is current. A residence address is considered to be "current" where it is the most recent residence address that was recorded by the Reporting Financial Institution with respect to the individual Account Holder. However, a residence address is not considered to be "current" if it has been used for mailing purposes and mail has been returned undeliverable-as-addressed (other than due to an error). Notwithstanding the foregoing, a residence address associated with an account that is a dormant account would be considered to be "current" during the dormancy period. An account (other than an Annuity Contract) is a "dormant account" if *(i)* the Account Holder has not initiated a transaction with regard to the account or any other account held by the Account Holder with the Reporting Financial Institution in the past three years; *(ii)* the Account Holder has not communicated with the Reporting Financial Institution that maintains such account regarding the account or any other account held by the Account Holder with the Reporting Financial Institution in the past six years; and *(iii)* in the case of a Cash Value Insurance Contract, the Reporting Financial Institution has not communicated with the Account Holder that holds such account regarding the account or any other account held by the Account Holder with the Reporting Financial Institution in the past six years. Alternatively, an account (other than an Annuity Contract) may also be considered as a "dormant account" under applicable laws or regulations or the normal operating procedures of the Reporting Financial Institution that are consistently applied for all accounts maintained by such institution in a particular jurisdiction, provided that such laws or regulations or such procedures contain substantially similar requirements to those in the previous sentence. An account ceases to be a dormant account when *(i)* the Account Holder initiates a transaction with regard to the account or any other account held by the Account Holder with the Reporting Financial Institution; *(ii)* the Account Holder communicates with the Reporting Financial Institution that maintains such account regarding the account or any other account held by the Account Holder with the Reporting Financial Institution; or *(iii)* the account ceases to be a dormant account under applicable laws or regulations or the Reporting Financial Institution's normal operating procedures.

10.   The third requirement is that the current residence address in the Reporting Financial Institution's records is based on Documentary Evidence (see paragraphs 150-162 of the Commentary on Section VIII). This

requirement is satisfied if the Reporting Financial Institution's policies and procedures ensure that the current residence address in its records is the same address, or in the same jurisdiction, as that on the Documentary Evidence (e.g. identity card, driving license, voting card, or certificate of residence). The third requirement is also met if the Reporting Financial Institution's policies and procedures ensure that where it has government-issued Documentary Evidence but such Documentary Evidence does not contain a recent residence address or does not contain an address at all (e.g. certain passports), the current residence address in the Reporting Financial Institution's records is the same address, or in the same jurisdiction, as that on recent documentation issued by an authorised government body or a utility company, or on a declaration of the individual Account Holder under penalty of perjury. Acceptable documentation issued by an authorised government body includes, for example, formal notifications or assessments by a tax administration. Acceptable documentation issued by utility companies relates to supplies linked to a particular property and includes a bill for water, electricity, telephone (landline only), gas, or oil. A declaration of the individual Account Holder under penalty of perjury is acceptable only if *(i)* the Reporting Financial Institution has been required to collect it under domestic law for a number of years; *(ii)* it contains the Account Holder's residence address; and *(iii)* it is dated and signed by the individual Account Holder under penalty of perjury. In such circumstances, the standards of knowledge applicable to Documentary Evidence would also apply to the documentation relied upon by the Reporting Financial Institution (see paragraphs 2-3 of the Commentary on Section VII). Alternatively, a Reporting Financial Institution can meet the third requirement if its policies and procedures ensure that the jurisdiction in the residence address corresponds to the jurisdiction of issuance of government-issued Documentary Evidence.

11.   There may also be accounts opened at a time when there were no AML/KYC requirements and the Reporting Financial Institution therefore did not review any Documentary Evidence in the initial on-boarding process. The FATF Recommendations, which set out the international standards on combating money laundering and include the requirement to verify the identity of the customers on the basis of reliable independent sources, were first issued in 1990 and subsequently revised in 1996, 2003 and 2012.[8] Even for accounts opened before the introduction of such requirements and "grandfathered" under the rules, there is a requirement to apply customer due diligence measures to existing customers on the basis of materiality and

---

8.   FATF/OECD (2013), *International Standards on Combating Money Laundering and the Financing of Terrorism and Proliferation*, The FATF Recommendations February 2012, FATF/OECD, Paris, available on www.fatf-gafi.org/media/fatf/documents/recommendations/pdfs/FATF_Recommendations.pdf.

risk. In addition, with respect to Reportable Accounts that are Preexisting Accounts, Reporting Financial Institutions are already required to use reasonable efforts and contact their customers to obtain their TIN and date of birth (subject to the application of paragraphs C and D of Section I). It would be expected that such a contact would also be used to request Documentary Evidence. As a result, such instances of accounts without Documentary Evidence should be exceptional, relate to low-risk accounts, and affect accounts opened prior to 2004. In such instances, the third requirement contained in subparagraph B(1) may also be satisfied if the Reporting Financial Institution's policies and procedures ensure that current residence address in its records is in the same jurisdiction *(i)* as that of the address on the most recent documentation collected by such Reporting Financial Institution (e.g. a utility bill, real property lease, or declaration by the individual Account Holder under penalty of perjury); and *(ii)* as that reported by the Reporting Financial Institution with respect to the individual Account Holder under any other applicable tax reporting requirements (if any). Alternatively to meet the third requirement in the abovementioned circumstances, in the case of a Cash Value Insurance Contract, a Reporting Financial Institution may rely on the current residence address in its records until *(i)* there is a change in circumstances that causes the Reporting Financial Institution to know or have reason to know that such residence address is incorrect or unreliable, or *(ii)* the time of pay-out (full or partial) or maturity of the Cash Value Insurance Contract. The pay-out or maturity of such contract will constitute a change in circumstances and will trigger the relevant procedures (see paragraph 13 below).

12.   The following examples illustrate the application of Reporting Financial Institutions' policies and procedures with respect to subparagraph B(1):

- •   Example 1 (Identity card): M, a bank that is a Reporting Financial Institution, has policies and procedures in place, pursuant to which it has collected a copy of the identity card of all its Preexisting Individual Accounts and pursuant to which it ensures that the current residence address in its records for those accounts is in the same jurisdiction as the address on their identity card. M may treat such Account Holders as being resident for tax purposes of the jurisdiction in which such address is located.

- •   Example 2 (Passport and utility bill): M has account opening procedures in place pursuant to which it relies on the Account Holder's passport to confirm the identity of the Account Holder and on recent utility bills to verify their residence address, as recorded in M's systems. M may treat its Preexisting Individual Account Holders as being resident for tax purposes of the jurisdiction recorded in its systems.

- Example 3 (Utility bill with reporting obligations): H, a bank that is a Reporting Financial Institution, has a number of accounts opened prior to 1990 that has been grandfathered from the application of AML/KYC Procedures and the related rules on materiality and risk have not required re-documenting the accounts. H has in its records a current residence address for these accounts that is supported by utility bills collected upon account opening. Such address is also the same address as that periodically reported by H with respect to those accounts under its non-CRS tax reporting obligations. Because H's records do not contain any Documentary Evidence associated with these accounts and H is not required to collect it under AML/KYC Procedures, and the current residence address in H's records is the same as that on the most recent documentation collected by H and as that reported by H under its non-CRS tax reporting obligations, H may treat its Account Holders as being resident for tax purposes of the jurisdiction in which such address is situated.

13.   If a Reporting Financial Institution has relied on the residence address test described in subparagraph B(1) and there is a change in circumstances (see paragraph 17 below) that causes the Reporting Financial Institution to know or have reason to know that the original Documentary Evidence (or other documentation as described in paragraph 10 above) is incorrect or unreliable, the Reporting Financial Institution must, by the later of the last day of the relevant calendar year or other appropriate reporting period, or 90 calendar days following the notice or discovery of such change in circumstances, obtain a self-certification and new Documentary Evidence to establish the residence(s) for tax purposes of the Account Holder. If the Reporting Financial Institution cannot obtain the self-certification and new Documentary Evidence by such date, the Reporting Financial Institution must apply the electronic record search procedure described in subparagraphs B(2) through (6). The following examples illustrate the procedures to be followed in case of a change in circumstances:

- Example 1: I, a bank that is a Reporting Financial Institution, has relied on the residence address test to treat an individual Account Holder, P, as a resident of Reportable Jurisdiction X. Five years later, P communicates to I that he has moved to jurisdiction Y, which is also a Reportable Jurisdiction, and provides his new address. I obtains from P a self-certification and new Documentary Evidence confirming that he is resident for tax purposes in jurisdiction Y. I must treat P as a resident of Reportable Jurisdiction Y.

- Example 2: The facts are the same as in Example 1, except that I does not obtain a self-certification from P. I must apply the electronic record search procedure described in subparagraphs B(2) through (6) and, as a result, treat P as a resident of, at least, jurisdiction Y (based on the new address provided by the Account Holder).

Subparagraphs B(2) through (6) – Electronic record search

14. Subparagraphs B(2) through (6) describe the "electronic record search" procedure. Under this procedure, the Reporting Financial Institution must review electronically searchable data maintained by the Reporting Financial Institution for any of the indicia described in subparagraph B(2).

15. Subparagraph B(3) makes clear that if none of the indicia listed in subparagraph B(2) are discovered in the electronic search, no further action is required until there is a change in circumstances that results in one or more indicia being associated with the account, or the account becomes a High Value Account.

16. If any of the indicia listed in subparagraph B(2)(a) through (e) are discovered in the electronic search, or if there is a change in circumstances that results in one or more indicia being associated with the account, then, according to subparagraph B(4), the Reporting Financial Institution must treat the Account Holder as a resident for tax purposes of each Reportable Jurisdiction for which an indicium is identified, unless it elects to apply the curing procedure described in subparagraph B(6) and one of the exceptions in such subparagraph applies with respect to that account. However, in case of a change in circumstances, a Reporting Financial Institution may choose to treat a person as having the same status that it had prior to the change in circumstances until the later of the last day of the relevant calendar year or other appropriate reporting period or 90 calendar days following the date that the indicium was identified due to the change in circumstances.

17. A "change in circumstances" includes any change that results in the addition of information relevant to a person's status or otherwise conflicts with such person's status. In addition, a change in circumstances includes any change or addition of information to the account holder's account (including the addition, substitution, or other change of an account holder) or any change or addition of information to any account associated with such account (applying the account aggregation rules described in subparagraphs C(1) through (3) of Section VII) if such change or addition of information affects the status of the account holder.

18. Despite the fact that the indicia described in subparagraph B(2) should limit the number of instances in which the electronic record search results in indicia for different Reportable Jurisdictions, these instances may still occur in practice. Some of these cases may be "false" indications of residence in a Reportable Jurisdiction. Some others may be genuine cases of Account Holders that are resident in multiple jurisdictions. Reporting

Financial Institutions would often contact their customers to resolve such cases (by applying the curing procedure described in subparagraph B(6)) and advise them that if the conflicting indicia cannot be cured, information may be exchanged with two or more jurisdictions. Such course of action would often already result from customer relationship considerations and the need to handle customer information with care. The same would apply in the context of the due diligence procedures for Preexisting Individual Accounts that are High Value Accounts. To the extent an Account Holder would nevertheless be reported as resident of more than one jurisdiction, it is expected that the Competent Authorities would exchange all jurisdictions of residence to each respective jurisdiction. This would allow the relevant Competent Authorities to resolve any residence questions.

19.   Subparagraph B(5) contains a special procedure in case a "hold mail" instruction or "in-care-of" address is discovered in the electronic search, and none of the other indicia listed in subparagraph B(2)(a) through (e) and no other address (within such indicia) are identified for the Account Holder in such electronic search.

Subparagraph B(2) – Indicia

20.   Subparagraph B(2) contains the actual "electronic record search". Under this procedure, the Reporting Financial Institution must review electronically searchable data maintained by the Reporting Financial Institution for any of the following indicia (see paragraph 34 of the Commentary on Section I) and apply subparagraphs B(3) through (6):

a) identification of the Account Holder as a resident of a Reportable Jurisdiction;

b) current mailing or residence address (including a post office box) in a Reportable Jurisdiction;

c) one or more telephone numbers in a Reportable Jurisdiction and no telephone number in the jurisdiction of the Reporting Financial Institution;

d) standing instructions (other than with respect to a Depository Account) to transfer funds to an account maintained in a Reportable Jurisdiction;

e) currently effective power of attorney or signatory authority granted to a person with an address in a Reportable Jurisdiction; or

f) a "hold mail" instruction or "in-care-of" address in a Reportable Jurisdiction if the Reporting Financial Institution does not have any other address on file for the Account Holder.

21.   The indicium contained in subparagraph B(2)(a) is an identification of the Account Holder as a resident of a Reportable Jurisdiction. This indicium is met if the Reporting Financial Institution's electronically searchable information contains a designation of the Account Holder as a Reportable Jurisdiction's resident for tax purposes.

22.   The indicium contained in subparagraph B(2)(b) is a current mailing or residence address (including a post office box) in a Reportable Jurisdiction. A mailing or residence address is considered to be "current" where it is the most recent mailing or residence address that was recorded by the Reporting Financial Institution with respect to the individual Account Holder. A mailing or residence address associated with an account that is a dormant account (see paragraph 9 above) would be considered to be "current" during the dormancy period. Where the Reporting Financial Institution has recorded two or more mailing or residence addresses with respect to the Account Holder and one of such addresses is that of a service provider of the Account Holder (e.g. external asset manager, investment advisor, or attorney), the Reporting Financial Institution is not required to treat the service provider's address as an indicium of residence of the Account Holder.

23.   The indicium contained in subparagraph B(2)(c) is one or more telephone numbers in a Reportable Jurisdiction and no telephone number in the jurisdiction of the Reporting Financial Institution. The telephone number(s) in a Reportable Jurisdiction is only required to be treated as an indicium of residence of the Account Holder where it is a "current" telephone number(s) in a Reportable Jurisdiction. For these purposes, a telephone number(s) is considered to be "current" where it is the most recent telephone number(s) that was recorded by the Reporting Financial Institution with respect to the individual Account Holder. Where the Reporting Financial Institution has recorded two or more telephone numbers with respect to the Account Holder and one of such telephone numbers is that of a service provider of the Account Holder (e.g. external asset manager, investment advisor, or attorney), the Reporting Financial Institution is not required to treat the service provider's telephone number as an indicium of residence of the Account Holder.

24.   The indicium contained in subparagraph B(2)(d) is standing instructions (other than with respect to a Depository Account) to transfer funds to an account maintained in a Reportable Jurisdiction. The term "standing instructions to transfer funds" means current payment instructions provided by the account holder, or an agent of the account holder, that will repeat without further instructions being provided by the account holder. Therefore, for example, a transfer instruction to make an isolated payment is not a standing instruction to transfer funds, even if the instructions are given one year in advance. However, an instruction to make payments indefinitely is a standing

instruction to transfer funds for the period during which such instructions are in effect, even if such instructions are amended after a single payment.

25.   The following example illustrates the application of subparagraph B(2)(d): An individual, K, holds a Custodial Account with E, a custodial bank resident in Reportable Jurisdiction R. K also holds a Depository Account with F, a commercial bank resident in Reportable Jurisdiction S. K has provided E with standing instructions to transfer to the Depository Account, all the income generated with respect to the securities held in the Custodial Account. Because the standing instructions are with respect to a Custodial Account and the funds are to be transferred to an account maintained in a Reportable Jurisdiction, then such standing instructions are an indicium of residence in Reportable Jurisdiction S.

26.   The indicia contained in subparagraph B(2)(f) cover a "hold mail" instruction and a "in-care-of" address in a Reportable Jurisdiction if the Reporting Financial Institution does not have any other address on file for the Account Holder. A "hold mail" instruction is a current instruction by the Account Holder, or an agent of the Account Holder, to keep the Account Holder's mail until such instruction is amended. Where such an instruction is in place and the Reporting Financial Institution does not have any address on file for the Account Holder, the indicium is met. An instruction to send all correspondence electronically is not a "hold mail" instruction. Where the Reporting Financial Institution holds an "in-care-of" address in a Reportable Jurisdiction and does not have any other address on file for the Account Holder, the indicium is also met.

Subparagraph B(5) – Special procedure

27.   Subparagraph B(5) contains a special procedure in case a "hold mail" instruction or "in-care-of" address is discovered in the electronic search, and none of the other indicia listed in subparagraph B(2)(a) through (e) and no other address (within such indicia) are identified for the Account Holder in such electronic search.

28.   Where the special procedure is applicable, the Reporting Financial Institution must, in the order most appropriate to the circumstances, apply the paper record search described in subparagraph C(2), or seek to obtain from the Account Holder a self-certification or Documentary Evidence to establish the residence(s) for tax purposes of such Account Holder. If the paper search fails to establish an indicium and the attempt to obtain the self-certification or Documentary Evidence is not successful, the Reporting Financial Institution must report the account as an undocumented account.

29.   Once a Reporting Financial Institution determines that a Lower Value Account is an undocumented account, the Reporting Financial Institution is

not required to re-apply the procedure set forth in subparagraph B(5) to the same Lower Value Account in any subsequent year until there is a change in circumstances that results in one or more indicia being associated with the account, or the account becomes a High Value Account. However, the Reporting Financial Institution must report the Lower Value Account as an undocumented account until such account ceases to be undocumented.

Subparagraph B(6) – Curing procedure

30.   Subparagraph B(6) contains a procedure for curing a finding of indicia under subparagraph B(2). A Reporting Financial Institution is not required to treat an Account Holder as a resident of a Reportable Jurisdiction if:

   a)   the Account Holder information contains a current mailing or residence address in the Reportable Jurisdiction, one or more telephone numbers in the Reportable Jurisdiction (and no telephone number in the jurisdiction of the Reporting Financial Institution) or standing instructions (with respect to Financial Accounts other than Depository Accounts) to transfer funds to an account maintained in a Reportable Jurisdiction, the Reporting Financial Institution obtains, or has previously reviewed and maintains a record of:

   i)   a self-certification from the Account Holder of the jurisdiction(s) of residence of such Account Holder that does not include such Reportable Jurisdiction; and

   ii) Documentary Evidence establishing the Account Holder's non-reportable status.

   b)   the Account Holder information contains a currently effective power of attorney or signatory authority granted to a person with an address in the Reportable Jurisdiction, the Reporting Financial Institution obtains, or has previously reviewed and maintains a record of:

   i)   a self-certification from the Account Holder of the jurisdiction(s) of residence of such Account Holder that does not include such Reportable Jurisdiction; or

   ii) Documentary Evidence establishing the Account Holder's non-reportable status.

31.   A self-certification or Documentary Evidence that has been previously reviewed may be relied upon for purposes of the curing procedure unless the Reporting Financial Institution knows or has reasons to know that the self-certification or Documentary Evidence is incorrect or unreliable (see paragraphs 2-3 of the Commentary on Section VII).

32.   The self-certification that is part of the curing procedure does not need to contain an express confirmation that an Account Holder is not resident in a given Reportable Jurisdiction provided the Account Holder confirms that it contains all its jurisdictions of residence (i.e. the information with respect to the Account Holder's jurisdiction(s) of residence is correct and complete). Documentary Evidence is sufficient to establish an Account Holder's non-reportable status if the Documentary Evidence *(i)* confirms that the Account Holder is resident in a jurisdiction other than the relevant Reportable Jurisdiction; *(ii)* contains a current residence address outside the relevant Reportable Jurisdiction; or *(iii)* is issued by an authorised government body of a jurisdiction other than the relevant Reportable Jurisdiction (see paragraph 150-162 of the Commentary on Section VIII).

Paragraph C – Due diligence for Higher Value Accounts

33.   Paragraph C contains the enhanced review procedures that apply with respect to High Value Accounts. Such procedures are the electronic record search, the paper record search and the relationship manager inquiry.

Subparagraph C(1) – Electronic record search

34.   The "electronic record search" is required with respect to all High Value Accounts. As provided in subparagraph C(1), the Reporting Financial Institution must review electronically searchable data maintained by the Reporting Financial Institution for any of the indicia described in subparagraph B(2) (see paragraph 34 of the Commentary on Section I).

Subparagraph C(2) and (3) – Paper record search

35.   If the Reporting Financial Institution's electronically searchable databases include fields for, and capture all of the information described in, subparagraph C(3), then a further paper record search is not required. This means that the Reporting Financial Institution's electronically searchable database has fields for the information described in subparagraph C(3) from which, via an electronic search, it can determine whether information is contained in such fields. Thus, the exception for the paper record search would not be available where a field was simply left blank unless, pursuant to the Reporting Financial Institution's policies and procedures, the fact that such field is left blank means that the information described in subparagraph C(3) is not in the Reporting Financial Institution's records (e.g. because a telephone number has not been provided, or a power of attorney has not been granted).

36.   A Reporting Financial Institution is not required to perform the paper record search described in subparagraph C(2) to the extent the Reporting

Financial Institution's electronically searchable information includes the information described in subparagraph C(3). Thus, if the Reporting Financial Institution's electronically searchable information does not include all the information described in subparagraph C(3), then the Reporting Financial Institution is only required to perform the paper record search with respect to the information described in subparagraph C(3) that is not included in its electronically searchable information. For example, a Reporting Financial Institution's electronically searchable database that includes all the information described in subparagraph C(3) apart from the one contained in subparagraph C(3)(d) (i.e. standing instructions to transfer funds), only causes the Reporting Financial Institution to perform the paper record search with respect to the information described in subparagraph C(3)(d). Similarly, a Reporting Financial Institution's electronically searchable database that does not include all the information described in subparagraph C(3) with respect to a clearly identified group of High Value Accounts, only causes the Reporting Financial Institution to perform the paper record search with respect to such group of accounts and limited to the information described in subparagraph C(3) that is not included in its electronically searchable information.

37.   When the Reporting Financial Institution is required to perform the "paper record search" with respect to a High Value Account, it must also review the current customer master file and, to the extent not contained in the current customer master file, the documents listed in subparagraph C(2) associated with the account and obtained by the Reporting Financial Institution within the last five years for any of the indicia described in subparagraph B(2).

Subparagraph C(4) – Relationship manager inquiry

38.   The "relationship manager inquiry" is required in addition to the electronic and paper record searches. As provided in subparagraph C(4), the Reporting Financial Institution must treat as a Reportable Account any High Value Account assigned to a relationship manager (including any Financial Accounts aggregated with that High Value Account) if the relationship manager has actual knowledge that the Account Holder is a Reportable Person.

39.   A "relationship manager" is an officer or other employee of a Reporting Financial Institution who is assigned responsibility for specific account holders on an on-going basis (including as an officer or employee that is a member of a Reporting Financial Institution's private banking department), advises account holders regarding their banking, investment, trust, fiduciary, estate planning, or philanthropic needs, and recommends, makes referrals to, or arranges for the provision of financial products, services, or other assistance by internal or external providers to meet those needs.

40.   Relationship management must be more than ancillary or incidental to the job function of a person for the person to be considered a relationship manager. As such, a person whose functions do not involve direct client contact or which are of a back office, administrative or clerical nature is not considered a relationship manager. It is recognised that regular contact can exist between an Account Holder and an employee of a Reporting Financial Institution without causing the employee to be a relationship manager. For example, a person at a Reporting Financial Institution who is largely responsible for processing transactions/orders or ad hoc requests may end up knowing an Account Holder well. However, the person is not considered a relationship manager unless that person is ultimately charged with managing the Account Holder's affairs at the Reporting Financial Institution.

41.   Notwithstanding paragraphs 39-40 above, a person is only a relationship manager for purposes of subparagraph C(4) with respect to an account that has an aggregate balance or value of more than USD 1 000 000, taking into account the account aggregation and currency translation rules described in paragraph C of Section VII. Thus, in determining whether an officer or employee of a Reporting Financial Institution is a relationship manager, *(i)* the employee must satisfy the definition of relationship manager and *(ii)* the aggregate balance or value the Account Holder's accounts must exceed USD 1 000 000.

42.   The following examples illustrate how to determine whether an employee of a Reporting Financial Institution is a relationship manager:

- Example 1: An individual, P, holds a custodial account with R, a bank that is a Reporting Financial Institution. The value in P's account at the end of year is USD 1 200 000. An employee of R's private banking department, O, oversees the account of P on an on-going basis. Because O satisfies the definition of "relationship manager" and the value in P's account is more than USD 1 000 000, O is a relationship manager with respect to P's account.

- Example 2: Same facts as Example 1, except that the value in P's custodial account at the end of year is USD 800 000. In addition, P also holds a depository account with R, the balance of which at the end of year is USD 400 000. Both accounts are associated with P and with one another by reference to R's internal identification number. Because O satisfies the definition of "relationship manager" and, once the account aggregation rules have been applied, the aggregated balance or value in P's accounts is more than USD 1 000 000, O is a relationship manager with respect to P's accounts.

- Example 3: Same facts as Example 2, except that O's functions do not involve direct contact with P. Because O does not satisfy the definition of "relationship manager", O is not a relationship manager with respect to P's accounts.

Subparagraph C(5) – Effect of finding indicia

43.   If none of the indicia listed in subparagraph B(2) are discovered in the enhanced review of High Value Accounts, and the account is not identified as held by a Reportable Person in subparagraph C(4), then, according to subparagraph C(5)(a), further action is not required until there is a change in circumstances that results in one or more indicia being associated with the account.

44.   If any of the indicia listed in subparagraph B(2)(a) through (e) are discovered in the enhanced review of High Value Accounts, or if there is a subsequent change in circumstances that results in one or more indicia being associated with the account, then, pursuant to subparagraph C(5)(b), the Reporting Financial Institution must treat the account as a Reportable Account with respect to each Reportable Jurisdiction for which an indicium is identified unless it elects to apply the curing procedure contained in subparagraph B(6) and one of the exceptions in such subparagraph applies with respect to that account. An indicium discovered in one review procedure such as the paper record search or the relationship manager inquiry, cannot be used to cure an indicium identified in another review procedure such as the electronic record search. For example, a current residence address in a Reportable Jurisdiction within the knowledge of the relationship manager cannot be used to cure a different residence address currently on file with the Reporting Financial Institution discovered in the paper record search

45.   If a "hold mail" instruction or "in-care-of" address is discovered in the enhanced review of High Value Accounts, and no other address and none of the other indicia listed in subparagraph B(2)(a) through (e) are identified for the Account Holder, then, according to subparagraph C(5)(c), the Reporting Financial Institution must obtain from such Account Holder a self-certification or Documentary Evidence to establish the residence(s) for tax purposes of the Account Holder. If the Reporting Financial Institution cannot obtain such self-certification or Documentary Evidence, it must report the account as an undocumented account until such account ceases to be undocumented.

Subparagraphs C(6) through (9) – Additional procedures

46.   According to subparagraph C(6), if a Preexisting Individual Account is not a High Value Account as of 31 December [xxxx] (i.e. it is a Lower Value Account), but becomes a High Value Account as of the last day of a subsequent calendar year, the Reporting Financial Institution must complete the enhanced review for High Value Accounts with respect to such account within the calendar year following the year in which the account becomes a High Value Account. If based on such review such account is identified as

a Reportable Account, the Reporting Financial Institution must report the required information about such account with respect to the year in which it is identified as a Reportable Account and subsequent years on an annual basis, unless the Account Holder ceases to be a Reportable Person.

47.   While the selection of the year referred to in subparagraph C(6) is a decision of the jurisdiction implementing the Common Reporting Standard, it is expected that the year selected for that purpose is the same year as the year selected for the term "Preexisting Account".

48.   According to subparagraph C(7), once a Reporting Financial Institution applies the enhanced review procedures of High Value Accounts, the Reporting Financial Institution is not required to re-apply such procedures, other than the relationship manager inquiry, to the same High Value Account in any subsequent year unless the account is undocumented. In such a case, the Reporting Financial Institution should re-apply them annually until such account ceases to be undocumented. Similarly, with respect to the relationship manager inquiry, annual verifications would suffice without there being a requirement for a relationship manager to confirm on an account-by-account basis that it does not have actual knowledge that each Account Holder assigned to him is a Reportable Person.

49.   According to subparagraph C(8), if there is a change of circumstances with respect to a High Value Account that results in one or more indicia described in subparagraph B(2) being associated with the account, then the Reporting Financial Institution must treat the account as a Reportable Account with respect to each Reportable Jurisdiction for which an indicium is identified unless it elects to apply subparagraph B(6) and one of the exceptions in such subparagraph applies with respect to that account. However, a Reporting Financial Institution may choose to treat a person as having the same status that it had prior to the change in circumstances during the 90 calendar days following the date that the indicium was identified due to the change in circumstances (see also paragraph 17 above).

50.   A Reporting Financial Institution must have appropriate communication channels and procedures in place to ensure that a relationship manager identifies any change in circumstances of an account, as provided in subparagraph C(9). For example, if a relationship manager is notified that the Account Holder has a new mailing address in a Reportable Jurisdiction, the Reporting Financial Institution is required to treat the new address as a change in circumstances and, if it elects to apply subparagraph B(6), is required to obtain the appropriate documentation from the Account Holder.

Paragraphs D and E – Timing of review and additional procedures

51.   Paragraph D contains the rule governing the timing of the review procedures for identifying Reportable Accounts among Preexisting Individual Accounts. Such rule requires that the review must be completed by [xx/xx/xxxx]. While the selection of this date is a decision of the jurisdiction implementing the Common Reporting Standard, it is expected that the date selected for that purpose is the year following the year selected for the term "Preexisting Account" with respect to High Value Accounts, and the second year following the year selected for such term with respect to Lower Value Accounts.

52.   Paragraph E contain an additional procedure applicable to Preexisting Individual Accounts: any Preexisting Individual Account that has been identified as a Reportable Account under Section III must be treated as a Reportable Account in all subsequent years, unless the Account Holder ceases to be a Reportable Person.

Commentary on Section IV
concerning Due Diligence for New Individual Accounts

1.   This Section contains the due diligence procedures for New Individual Accounts and provides for the collection of a self-certification (and confirmation of its reasonableness).

2.   According to paragraph A, upon account opening, the Reporting Financial Institution must:

- obtain a self-certification, which may be part of the account opening documentation, that allows the Reporting Financial Institution to determine the Account Holder's residence(s) for tax purposes; and

- confirm the reasonableness of such self-certification based on the information obtained by the Reporting Financial Institution in connection with the opening of the account, including any documentation collected pursuant to AML/KYC Procedures.

3.   If the self-certification establishes that the Account Holder is resident for tax purposes in a Reportable Jurisdiction, then, as provided in paragraph B, the Reporting Financial Institution must treat the account as a Reportable Account.

4.   The self-certification must allow determining the Account Holder's residence(s) for tax purposes. Generally, an individual will only have one jurisdiction of residence. However, an individual may be resident for tax purposes in two or more jurisdictions. The domestic laws of the various jurisdictions lay down the conditions under which an individual is to be treated as fiscally "resident". They cover various forms of attachment to a jurisdiction which, in the domestic taxation laws, form the basis of a comprehensive taxation (full liability to tax). They also cover cases where an individual is deemed, according to the taxation laws of a jurisdiction, to be resident of that jurisdiction (e.g. diplomats or other persons in government service). To solve cases of double residence, tax conventions contain special rules which give the attachment to one jurisdiction a preference over the attachment of the other jurisdiction for purposes of those conventions. Generally, an individual will be resident for tax purposes in a jurisdiction if, under the laws of that jurisdiction (including tax conventions), he pays or

should be paying tax therein by reason of his domicile, residence or any other criterion of a similar nature, and not only from sources in that jurisdiction. Dual resident individuals may rely on the tiebreaker rules contained in tax conventions (if applicable) to solve cases of double residence for determining their residence for tax purposes (see paragraph 23 below).

5.   The following examples illustrate how an individual's residence for tax purposes may be determined:

- Example 1: An individual has his permanent home in Jurisdiction A and is taxed as being a resident of Jurisdiction A. He has had a stay of more than six months in Jurisdiction B and according to the legislation of the latter Jurisdiction he is, in consequence of the length of the stay, taxed as being a resident of that Jurisdiction. Thus, he is resident of both Jurisdictions.

- Example 2: Same facts as Example 1, except that the individual only had a stay of eight weeks in Jurisdiction B and according to the legislation of that Jurisdiction he is not, by reason of the length of the stay, taxed as being a resident of Jurisdiction B. Thus, he is only resident of Jurisdiction A.

6.   Participating Jurisdictions are expected to help taxpayers determine, and provide them with information with respect to, their residence(s) for tax purposes. That may be done, for example, through the various service channels used for providing information or guidance to taxpayers on the application of tax laws (e.g. phone, walk-in offices, internet). The OECD will endeavour to facilitate the dissemination of such information.

Requirements for validity of self-certifications

7.   A "self-certification" is a certification by the Account Holder that provides the Account Holder's status and any other information that may be reasonably requested by the Reporting Financial Institution to fulfil its reporting and due diligence obligations, such as whether the Account Holder is resident for tax purposes in a Reportable Jurisdiction. With respect to New Individual Accounts, a self-certification is valid only if it is signed (or otherwise positively affirmed) by the Account Holder, it is dated at the latest at the date of receipt, and it contains the Account Holder's:

a)   name;

b)   residence address;

c)   jurisdiction(s) of residence for tax purposes;

d)   TIN with respect to each Reportable Jurisdiction (see paragraph 8 below); and *e)* date of birth (see paragraph 8 below).

The self-certification may be pre-populated by the Reporting Financial Institution to include the Account Holder's information, except for the jurisdiction(s) of residence for tax purposes, to the extent already available in its records.

8.   If the Account Holder is resident for tax purposes in a Reportable Jurisdiction, the self-certification must include *(i)* the Account Holder's TIN with respect to each Reportable Jurisdiction, subject to paragraph D of Section I (see paragraphs 29-32 of the Commentary on Section I); and *(ii)* the Account Holder's date of birth. The self-certification would not need to include the place of birth of the Account Holder as, according to paragraph E of Section I, the place of birth is not required to be reported unless the Reporting Financial Institution is otherwise required to obtain and report it under domestic law and it is available in the electronically searchable data maintained by the Reporting Financial Institution.

9.   The self-certification may be provided in any manner and in any form (e.g. electronically, such as portable document format (.pdf) or scanned documents). If the self-certification is provided electronically, the electronic system must ensure that the information received is the information sent, and must document all occasions of user access that result in the submission, renewal, or modification of a self-certification. In addition, the design and operation of the electronic system, including access procedures, must ensure that the person accessing the system and furnishing the self-certification is the person named in the self-certification, and must be capable of providing upon request a hard copy of all self-certifications provided electronically. Where the information is provided as part of the account opening documentation, it does not need to be on any one specific page of the documentation or any specific form, provided that it is complete.

10.   The following examples illustrate how a self-certification may be provided:

- Example 1: Individual A completes an online application to open an account with Reporting Financial Institution K. All the information required for self-certification is entered by A on an electronic application (including a confirmation of A's jurisdiction of residence for tax purposes). A's information, as provided in the electronic self-certification, is confirmed by K's service provider to be reasonable based on the information it has collected pursuant to AML/KYC Procedures. A's self-certification is valid.

- Example 2: Individual B makes an application in person to open an account with bank L. B produces his identity card as proof of identification and provides all the information required for self-certification to an employee of L who enters the information into the L's systems. The application is subsequently signed by B. B's self-certification is valid.

11.   A self-certification may be signed (or otherwise positively affirmed) by any person authorised to sign on behalf of the Account Holder under domestic law. A person authorised to sign a self-certification generally includes an executor of an estate, any equivalent of the former title, and any other person that has been provided written authorisation by the Account Holder to sign documentation on such person's behalf.

12.   A self-certification remains valid until there is a change of circumstances that causes the Reporting Financial Institution to know, or have reason to know, that the original self-certification is incorrect or unreliable (see paragraphs 17 of the Commentary on Section III and 2-3 of the Commentary on Section VII). When that is case, according to paragraph C, the Reporting Financial Institution cannot rely on the original self-certification and must obtain either *(i)* a valid self-certification that establishes the residence(s) for tax purposes of the Account Holder, or *(ii)* a reasonable explanation and documentation (as appropriate) supporting the validity of the original self-certification (and retain a copy or a notation of such explanation and documentation). Therefore, a Reporting Financial Institution is expected to institute procedures to ensure that any change that constitutes a change in circumstances is identified by the Reporting Financial Institution. In addition, a Reporting Financial Institution is expected to notify any person providing a self-certification of the person's obligation to notify the Reporting Financial Institution of a change in circumstances.

13.   A change in circumstances affecting the self-certification provided to the Reporting Financial Institution will terminate the validity of the self-certification with respect to the information that is no longer reliable, until the information is updated (see paragraph 17 of the Commentary on Section III).

14.   A self-certification becomes invalid on the date that the Reporting Financial Institution holding the self-certification knows or has reason to know that circumstances affecting the correctness of the self-certification have changed. However, a Reporting Financial Institution may choose to treat a person as having the same status that it had prior to the change in circumstances until the earlier of 90 calendar days from the date that the self-certification became invalid due to the change in circumstances, the date that the validity of the self-certification is confirmed, or the date that a new self-certification is obtained. A Reporting Financial Institution may rely on a self-certification without having to inquire into possible changes of circumstances that may affect the validity of the statement, unless it knows or has reason to know that circumstances have changed.

15.   If the Reporting Financial Institution cannot obtain a confirmation of the validity of the original self-certification or a valid self-certification during such 90-day period, the Reporting Financial Institution must treat the Account Holder as resident of the jurisdiction in which the Account Holder claimed to be resident in the original self-certification and the jurisdiction in which the Account Holder may be resident as a result of the change in circumstances.

16.   A Reporting Financial Institution may retain an original, certified copy, or photocopy (including a microfiche, electronic scan, or similar means of electronic storage) of the self-certification. Any documentation that is stored electronically must be made available in hard copy form upon request.

Curing self-certification errors

17.   A Reporting Financial Institution may treat a self-certification as valid, notwithstanding that the self-certification contains an inconsequential error, if the Reporting Financial Institution has sufficient documentation on file to supplement the information missing from the self-certification due to the error. In such case, the documentation relied upon to cure the inconsequential error must be conclusive. For example, a self-certification in which the individual submitting the form abbreviated the jurisdiction of residence may be treated as valid, notwithstanding the abbreviation, if the Reporting Financial Institution has government issued identification for the person from a jurisdiction that reasonably matches the abbreviation. On the other hand, an abbreviation for the jurisdiction of residence that does not reasonably match the jurisdiction of residence shown on the person's passport is not an inconsequential error. A failure to provide a jurisdiction of residence is not an inconsequential error. In addition, information on a self-certification that contradicts other information contained on the self-certification or in the customer master file is not an inconsequential error.

Self-certifications furnished on account-by-account basis

18.   In general, a Reporting Financial Institution with which a customer may open an account must obtain a self-certification on an account-by-account basis. However, a Reporting Financial Institution may rely upon the self-certification furnished by a customer for another account if both accounts are treated as a single account for purposes of satisfying the standards of knowledge requirements set forth in paragraph A of Section VII.

Documentation collected by other persons

19.   As provided in paragraph D of Section II, a Participating Jurisdiction may allow Reporting Financial Institutions to use service providers to fulfil their reporting and due diligence obligations. In such cases, a Reporting Financial Institution may use the documentation (including a self-certification) collected by service providers (e.g. data providers, financial advisors, insurance agents), subject to the conditions described in domestic law. The reporting and due diligence obligations remain, however, the responsibility of the Reporting Financial Institution.

20.   A Reporting Financial Institution may rely on documentation (including a self-certification) collected by an agent (including a fund advisor for mutual funds, hedge funds, or a private equity group) of the Reporting Financial Institution. The agent may retain the documentation as part of an information system maintained for a single Reporting Financial Institution or multiple Reporting Financial Institutions provided that under the system, any Reporting Financial Institution on behalf of which the agent retains documentation may easily access data regarding the nature of the documentation, the information contained in the documentation (including a copy of the documentation itself) and its validity, and must allow such Reporting Financial Institution to easily transmit data, either directly into an electronic system or by providing such information to the agent, regarding any facts of which it becomes aware that may affect the reliability of the documentation. The Reporting Financial Institution must be able to establish, to the extent applicable, how and when it has transmitted data regarding any facts of which it became aware that may affect the reliability of the documentation and must be able to establish that any data it has transmitted has been processed and appropriate due diligence has been exercised regarding the validity of the documentation. The agent must have a system in effect to ensure that any information it receives regarding facts that affect the reliability of the documentation or the status assigned to the customer are provided to all Reporting Financial Institutions for which the agent retains the documentation.

21.   A Reporting Financial Institution that acquires an account from a predecessor or transferor in a merger or bulk acquisition of accounts for value would generally be permitted to rely upon valid documentation (including a valid self-certification) or copies of valid documentation collected by the predecessor or transferor. In addition, a Reporting Financial Institution that acquires an account in a merger or bulk acquisition of accounts for value from another Reporting Financial Institution that has completed all the due diligence required under Sections II through VII with respect to the accounts transferred, would generally be permitted to also rely upon the predecessor's or transferor's determination of status of an Account Holder until the acquirer

knows, or has reason to know, that the status is inaccurate or a change in circumstances occurs (see paragraph 17 of the Commentary on Section III).

Reasonableness of self-certifications

22.   As mentioned in paragraph 2 above, upon account opening, once the Reporting Financial Institution has obtained a self-certification that allows it to determine the Account Holder's residence(s) for tax purposes, the Reporting Financial Institution must confirm the reasonableness of such self-certification based on the information obtained in connection with the opening of the account, including any documentation collected pursuant to AML/KYC Procedures (i.e. the "reasonableness" test).

23.   A Reporting Financial Institution is considered to have confirmed the "reasonableness" of a self-certification if, in the course of account opening procedures and upon review of the information obtained in connection with the opening of the account (including any documentation collected pursuant to AML/KYC Procedures), it does not know or have reason to know that the self-certification is incorrect or unreliable (see paragraphs 2-3 of the Commentary on Section VII). Reporting Financial Institutions are not expected to carry out an independent legal analysis of relevant tax laws to confirm the reasonableness of a self-certification.

24.   The following examples illustrate the application of the "reasonableness" test:

- • Example 1: A Reporting Financial Institution obtains a self-certification from the Account Holder upon account opening. The jurisdiction of the residence address contained in the self-certification conflicts with that contained in the documentation collected pursuant to AML/KYC Procedures. Because of the conflicting information, the self-certification is incorrect or unreliable and, as a consequence, it fails the reasonableness test.

- • Example 2: A Reporting Financial Institution obtains a self-certification from the Account Holder upon account opening. The residence address contained in the self-certification is not in the jurisdiction in which the Account Holder claims to be resident for tax purposes. Because of the conflicting information, the self-certification fails the reasonableness test.

25.   In the case of a self-certification that would otherwise fail the reasonableness test, it is expected that in the course of the account opening procedures the Reporting Financial Institution would obtain either *(i)* a valid self-certification, or *(ii)* a reasonable explanation and documentation (as appropriate) supporting the reasonableness of the self-certification (and retain

a copy or a notation of such explanation and documentation). Examples of such "reasonable explanation" include a statement by the individual that he or she *(1)* is a student at an educational institution in the relevant jurisdiction and holds the appropriate visa (if applicable); *(2)* is a teacher, trainee, or intern at an educational institution in the relevant jurisdiction or a participant in an educational or cultural exchange visitor program, and holds the appropriate visa (if applicable); *(3)* is a foreign individual assigned to a diplomatic post or a position in a consulate or embassy in the relevant jurisdiction; or *(4)* is a frontier worker or employee working on a truck or train travelling between jurisdictions. The following example illustrates the application of this paragraph: A Reporting Financial Institution obtains a self-certification for the Account Holder upon account opening. The jurisdiction of residence for tax purposes contained in the self-certification conflicts with the residence address contained in the documentation collected pursuant to AML/KYC Procedures. The Account Holder explains that she is a diplomat from a particular jurisdiction and that, as a consequence, she is resident in such jurisdiction; she also presents her diplomatic passport. Because the Reporting Financial Institution obtained a reasonable explanation and documentation supporting the reasonableness of the self-certification, the self-certification passes the reasonableness test.

Commentary on Section V concerning Due Diligence for Preexisting Entity Accounts

1.   This Section describes the due diligence procedures for Preexisting Entity Accounts.

Paragraph A – Accounts not required to be reviewed, identified or reported

2.   Paragraph A exempts from review all Preexisting Entity Accounts with an account balance or value that does not exceed USD 250 000 as of 31 December [xxxx], until such balance or value exceeds USD 250 000 as of the last day of any subsequent calendar year. This threshold is provided to reduce the compliance burden for financial institutions, recognising that the due diligence procedures for accounts held by Entities are more complex than those for accounts held by individuals.

3.   However, the application of paragraph A is subject to *(i)* the implementing jurisdiction allowing Reporting Financial Institutions to apply the exception, and *(ii)* the Reporting Financial Institution electing to apply it, either with respect to all Preexisting Entity Accounts or, separately, with respect to any clearly identified group of such accounts. Thus, if the implementing rules in a jurisdiction do not provide for such an election or the Reporting Financial Institution does not make such an election, all Preexisting Entity Accounts are required to be reviewed in accordance with the procedures set forth in paragraph D.

4.   While the selection of the years referred to in paragraphs A and B is a decision of the jurisdiction implementing the Common Reporting Standard, it is expected that the year selected for that purpose is the same year as the year selected for the term "Preexisting Account".

Paragraphs B and C – Accounts subject to be reviewed and reporting

5.   According to paragraph B, any Preexisting Entity Account not described in paragraph A (i.e. with an account balance or value that exceeds USD 250 000 as of 31 December of any calendar year) must be reviewed in accordance with the procedures set forth in paragraph D. Thus, a Preexisting Entity Account is required to be reviewed where:

   a)   it has an account balance or value that exceeds USD 250 000 as of 31 December [xxxx]; or

   b)   it does not exceed USD 250 000 as of 31 December [xxxx] but the account balance or value of which exceeds USD 250 000 as of the last day of any subsequent calendar year.

6.   However, a Preexisting Entity Account not described in paragraph A must only be treated as a Reportable Account, according to paragraph C, if it is held by one or more Entities that are either:

   a)   Reportable Persons, or

   b)   Passive NFEs with one or more Controlling Persons who are Reportable Persons.

7.   A Preexisting Entity Account held by a Passive NFE with one or more Controlling Persons who are Reportable Persons does not fail to qualify as a Reportable Account under paragraph C, solely because the Entity itself is not a Reportable Person or any of the Controlling Persons of the Passive NFE is resident in the same jurisdiction as the Passive NFE.

Paragraph D – Review procedures

8.   Paragraph D contains the review procedures to identify Reportable Accounts among Preexisting Entity Accounts. Such procedures require Reporting Financial Institutions to determine:

   a)   whether a Preexisting Entity Account is held by one or more Entities that are Reportable Persons; and

   b)   whether the Preexisting Entity Account is held by one or more Entities that are Passive NFEs with one or more of the Controlling Persons who are Reportable Persons.

Subparagraph D(1) – Review procedure for Account Holders

9.   Subparagraph D(1) contains the review procedure to determine whether a Preexisting Entity Account is held by one or more Entities that are

Reportable Persons. If any of the Entities is a Reportable Person, then the account must be treated as a Reportable Account.

10.   A Reporting Financial Institution must review information maintained for regulatory or customer relationship purposes (including information collected pursuant to AML/KYC Procedures) to determine whether the information indicates that the Account Holder is resident in a Reportable Jurisdiction. For this purpose, information indicating that the Account Holder is resident in a Reportable Jurisdiction includes:

- a place of incorporation or organisation in a Reportable Jurisdiction;

- an address in a Reportable Jurisdiction (for example, this would be likely to apply for Entities treated as fiscally transparent and could reflect the registered address, principal office, or place of effective management); or

- an address of one or more of the trustees of a trust in a Reportable Jurisdiction.

However, the existence of a permanent establishment (including a branch) in a Reportable Jurisdiction (including an address of a permanent establishment) is not by itself an indication of residence for this purpose.

11.   If the information indicates that the Account Holder is resident in a Reportable Jurisdiction, then, as provided in subparagraph D(1)(b), the Reporting Financial Institution must treat the account as a Reportable Account unless it obtains a self-certification from the Account Holder, or reasonably determines based on information in its possession or that is publicly available, that the Account Holder is not a Reportable Person with respect to such Reportable Jurisdiction.

12.   "Publicly available" information includes information published by an authorised government body (for example, a government or an agency thereof, or a municipality) of a jurisdiction, such as information in a list published by a tax administration that contains the names and identifying numbers of financial institutions (e.g. the IRS FFI list); information in a publicly accessible register maintained or authorised by an authorised government body of a jurisdiction; information disclosed on an established securities market (see paragraph 112 of the Commentary on Section VIII); and any publicly accessible classification with respect to the Account Holder that was determined based on a standardised industry coding system and that was assigned e.g. by a trade organisation or a chamber of commerce, consistent with normal business practices (see paragraph 154 of the Commentary on Section VIII). In this respect, the Reporting Financial Institution is expected to retain a notation of the type of information reviewed, and the date the information was reviewed.

13.   In determining whether a Preexisting Entity Account is held by one or more Entities that are Reportable Persons, the Reporting Financial Institution may follow the guidance in subparagraphs D(1)(a) and (b) in the order most appropriate under the circumstances. That would allow a Reporting Financial Institution, for example, to determine under subparagraph D(1)(b) that a Preexisting Entity Account is held by an Entity that is not a Reportable Person (e.g. a corporation that is publicly traded) and, thus, the account is not a Reportable Account.

14.   As mentioned in paragraph 7 of the Commentary on Section IV, a "self-certification" is a certification by the Account Holder that provides the Account Holder's status and any other information that may be reasonably requested by the Reporting Financial Institution to fulfil its reporting and due diligence obligations, such as whether the Account Holder is resident for tax purposes in a Reportable Jurisdiction or whether the Account Holder is a Passive NFE. With respect to Preexisting Entity Accounts, a self-certification is valid only if it is signed (or otherwise positively affirmed) by the person with authority to sign for the Account Holder, it is dated at the latest at the date of receipt, and it contains the Account Holder's:

a) name;

b) address;

c) jurisdiction(s) of residence for tax purposes; and

d) TIN with respect to each Reportable Jurisdiction.

The self-certification may be pre-populated by the Reporting Financial Institution to include the Account Holder's information, except for the jurisdiction(s) of residence for tax purposes, to the extent already available in its records.

15.   A person with authority to sign a self-certification generally includes an officer or director of a corporation, a partner of a partnership, a trustee of a trust, any equivalent of the former titles, and any other person that has been provided written authorisation by the Account Holder to sign documentation on such person's behalf.

16.   A self-certification with respect to Preexisting Entity Accounts may also contain the Account Holder's status. When that is the case, the Account Holder's status may be any of the following:

a) Financial Institution:

(1) Investment Entity described in subparagraph A(6)(b) of Section VIII.

(2) Financial Institution (other).

b) NFE:

   (1) corporation that is publicly traded or an affiliate of a publicly traded corporation.

   (2) Governmental Entity.

   (3) International Organisation.

   (4) Active NFE (other than 1 through 3).

   (5) Passive NFE (not including an Investment Entity described in subparagraph A(6)(b) of Section VIII).

When requesting a self-certification, Reporting Financial Institutions are expected to provide Account Holders with the information that is relevant for the latter to determine their status (e.g. the definition of the term "Active NFE" contained in subparagraph D(9) of Section VIII).

17.   The requirements for the validity of self-certifications with respect to New Individual Accounts are applicable for the validity of self-certifications with respect to Preexisting Entity Accounts (see paragraphs 7-16 of the Commentary on Section IV). The same is applicable with respect to curing self-certification errors, the requirement to obtain self-certifications on an account-by-account basis, and documentation collected by other persons (see paragraphs 17-21 of the Commentary on Section IV).

Subparagraph D(2) – Review procedure for Controlling Persons

18.   Subparagraph D(2) contains a review procedure to determine whether a Preexisting Entity Account is held by one or more Entities that are Passive NFEs with one or more Controlling Persons that are Reportable Persons. If any of the Controlling Persons of a Passive NFE is a Reportable Person, then the account must be treated as a Reportable Account (even if the Controlling Person is resident in the same jurisdiction as the Passive NFE).

19.   In making these determinations, the Reporting Financial Institution must follow the guidance in subparagraphs D(2)(a) through (c) in the order most appropriate under the circumstances. Those subparagraphs are aimed at determining:

   a) whether the Account Holder is a Passive NFE;

   b) the Controlling Persons of such Passive NFE; and

   c) whether any of such Controlling Persons is a Reportable Person.

20.   For purposes of determining whether the Account Holder is a Passive NFE, according to subparagraph D(2)(a), the Reporting Financial Institution must obtain a self-certification from the Account Holder to establish its

status, unless it has information in its possession or that is publicly available (see paragraph 12 above), based on which it can reasonably determine that the Account Holder is an Active NFE or a Financial Institution other than a non-participating professionally managed investment entity (i.e. an Investment Entity described in subparagraph A(6)(b) of Section VIII that is not a Participating Jurisdiction Financial Institution). For example, a Reporting Financial Institution could reasonably determine that the Account Holder is an Active NFE where the Account Holder is legally prohibited from conducting activities or operations, or holding assets, for the production of passive income (see paragraph 126 of the Commentary on Section VIII). The self-certification to establish the Account Holder's status must comply with the requirements for the validity of self-certification with respect to Preexisting Entity Accounts (see paragraphs 13-17 above). A Reporting Financial Institution that cannot determine the status of the Account Holder as an Active NFE or a Financial Institution other than non-participating professionally managed investment entity must presume that it is a Passive NFE.

21.   For the purposes of determining the Controlling Persons of an Account Holder, according to subparagraph D(2)(b), a Reporting Financial Institution may rely on information collected and maintained pursuant to AML/KYC Procedures.

22.   For the purposes of determining whether a Controlling Person of a Passive NFE is a Reportable Person, a Reporting Financial Institution may also rely on information collected and maintained pursuant to AML/KYC Procedures. However, in the case of a Preexisting Entity Account with an account balance or value that exceeds USD 1 000 000, subparagraph D(2)(c)(ii) prescribes the collection of a self-certification from either the Account Holder or the Controlling Person, which may be provided in the same self-certification as the one provided by the Account Holder to certify its own status. The self-certification with respect to the Controlling Person is valid only if it is signed (or otherwise positively affirmed) by the Controlling Person or a person with authority to sign for the Account Holder or the Controlling Person, it is dated at the latest at the date of receipt, and it contains each Controlling Person's:

  a) name;

  b) address;

  c) jurisdiction(s) of residence for tax purposes;

  d) TIN with respect to each Reportable Jurisdiction (see paragraph 8 of the Commentary on Section IV); and

  e) date of birth (see paragraph 8 of the Commentary on Section IV).

The self-certification may be pre-populated by the Reporting Financial Institution to include the Controlling Person's information, except for the jurisdiction(s) of residence for tax purposes, to the extent already available in its records.

23.   The requirements for the validity of self-certifications with respect to New Individual Accounts are applicable for the validity of self-certifications for determining whether a Controlling Person of a Passive NFE is a Reportable Person (see paragraphs 7-16 of the Commentary on Section IV). The same is applicable with respect to curing self-certification errors, the requirement to obtain self-certifications on an account-by-account basis, and documentation collected by other persons (see paragraphs 17-21 of the Commentary on Section IV).

24.   If a self-certification is required to be collected and is not obtained with respect to a Controlling Person of a Passive NFE, the Reporting Financial Institution must rely on the indicia described in subparagraph B(2) of Section III that it has in its records for such Controlling Person in order to determine whether it is a Reportable Person. If the Reporting Financial Institution has none of such indicia in its records, then no further action would be required until there is a change in circumstances that results in one or more indicia with respect to the Controlling Person being associated with the account.

Paragraph E – Timing of review and additional procedures

25.   Subparagraphs E(1) and (2) contain the rules governing the timing of the review procedures for identifying Reportable Accounts among Preexisting Entity Accounts. Such rules require that the review must be completed:

a)   for accounts with an account balance or value that exceeds USD 250 000 as of 31 December [xxxx], by 31 December [xxxx]; and

b)   for accounts with an account balance or value that does not exceed USD 250 000 as of 31 December [xxxx], but exceeds USD 250 000 as of 31 December of a subsequent year, within the calendar year following the year in which the account balance or value exceeds USD 250 000.

26.   While the selection of the years referred to in subparagraphs E(1) and (2) is a decision of the jurisdiction implementing the Common Reporting Standard, it is expected that the years elected for that purpose are the same year as the year selected for the term "Preexisting Account". In the case of the second year referred to in subparagraph E(1), however, it is expected that the year selected for that purpose is, at the earliest, the second calendar year following the year selected for the term "Preexisting Account".

27.   Subparagraph E(3) contains an additional procedure applicable to Preexisting Entity Accounts: if there is a change of circumstances with respect to a Preexisting Entity Account that causes the Reporting Financial Institution to know, or have reason to know, that the self-certification or other documentation associated with an account is incorrect or unreliable, the Reporting Financial Institution must re-determine the status of the account in accordance with the procedures set forth in paragraph D. The standards of knowledge applicable to Documentary Evidence also apply to any other documentation relied upon pursuant to the procedures set forth in paragraph D (see paragraphs 14 of the Commentary on Section IV and 2-3 of the Commentary on Section VII). In such case, a Reporting Financial Institution must apply the following procedures by the later of the last day of the relevant calendar year or other appropriate reporting period, or 90 calendar days following the notice or discovery of the change in circumstances:

- with respect to the determination whether the Account Holder is a Reportable Person: a Reporting Financial Institution must obtain either *(i)* a self-certification, or *(ii)* a reasonable explanation and documentation (as appropriate) supporting the reasonableness of the original self-certification or documentation (and retain a copy or a notation of such explanation and documentation). If the Reporting Financial Institution fails to either obtain a self-certification or confirm the reasonableness of the original self-certification or documentation, it must treat the Account Holder as a Reportable Person with respect to both jurisdictions.

- with respect to the determination whether the Account Holder is a Financial Institution, Active NFE or Passive NFE: a Reporting Financial Institution must obtain additional documentation or a self-certification (as appropriate) to establish the status of the Account Holder as an Active NFE or Financial Institution. If the Reporting Financial Institution fails to do so, it must treat the Account Holder as a Passive NFE.

- with respect to the determination whether the Controlling Person of a Passive NFE is a Reportable Person: a Reporting Financial Institution must obtain either *(i)* a self-certification, or *(ii)* a reasonable explanation and documentation (as appropriate) supporting the reasonableness of a previously collected self-certification or documentation (and retain a copy or a notation of such explanation and documentation). If the Reporting Financial Institution fails to either obtain a self-certification or confirm the reasonableness of the previously collected self-certification or documentation, it must rely on the indicia described in subparagraph B(2) of Section III it has in its records for such Controlling Person to determine whether it is a Reportable Person.

Commentary on Section VI
concerning Due Diligence for New Entity Accounts

1.   This Section describes the due diligence procedures for New Entity Accounts. The procedures are broadly the same as those for Preexisting Entity Accounts. However, the USD 250 000 threshold does not apply as it should be easier to collect self-certifications for New Entity Accounts.

2.   Paragraph A contains the review procedures to identify Reportable Accounts among New Entity Accounts. Such procedures require Reporting Financial Institutions to determine:

a)   whether a New Entity Account is held by one or more Entities that are Reportable Persons; and

b)   whether a New Entity Account is held by one or more Entities that are Passive NFEs with one or more Controlling Persons who are Reportable Persons.

Subparagraph A(1) – Review procedure for Account Holders

3.   Subparagraph A(1) contains the review procedure to determine whether a New Entity Account is held by one or more Entities that are Reportable Persons. If any of the Entities is a Reportable Person, then the account must be treated as a Reportable Account.

4.   In order to determine whether an Entity is a Reportable Person, subparagraph A(1)(a) requires that, upon account opening, the Reporting Financial Institution:

*   obtains a self-certification that allows the Reporting Financial Institution to determine the Account Holder's residence(s) for tax purposes; and

*   confirms the reasonableness of such self-certification based on the information obtained by the Reporting Financial Institution in connection with the opening of the account, including any documentation collected pursuant to AML/KYC Procedures.

5.   If the self-certification indicates that the Account Holder is resident in a Reportable Jurisdiction, then, as provided in subparagraph A(1)(b), the Reporting Financial Institution must treat the account as a Reportable Account unless it reasonably determines based on information in its possession or that is publicly available (see paragraph 12 of the Commentary on Section V), that the Account Holder is not a Reportable Person with respect to such Reportable Jurisdiction (e.g. a corporation that is publicly traded or a Governmental Entity).

6.   In determining whether a New Entity Account is held by one or more Entities that are Reportable Persons, the Reporting Financial Institution may follow the guidance on subparagraphs A(1)(a) and (b) in the order most appropriate under the circumstances. That would allow a Reporting Financial Institution, for example, to determine under subparagraph A(1)(b) that a New Entity Account is held by an Entity that is not a Reportable Person (e.g. a corporation that is publicly traded) and, thus, the account is not a Reportable Account.

7.   The self-certification must allow determining the Account Holder's residence(s) for tax purposes. It may be rare in practice for an Entity to be subject to tax as a resident in more than one jurisdiction, but it is, of course, possible. The domestic laws of the various jurisdictions lay down the conditions under which an Entity is to be treated as fiscally "resident". They cover various forms of attachment to a jurisdiction which, in the domestic taxation laws, form the basis of a comprehensive taxation (full tax liability). To solve cases of double residence, tax conventions contain special rules which give the attachment to one jurisdiction a preference over the attachment of the other jurisdiction for purposes of those conventions. Generally, an Entity will be resident for tax purposes in a jurisdiction if, under the laws of that jurisdiction (including tax conventions), it pays or should be paying tax therein by reason of his domicile, residence, place of management or incorporation, or any other criterion of a similar nature, and not only from sources in that jurisdiction. Dual resident Entities may rely on the tiebreaker rules contained in tax conventions (if applicable) to solve cases of double residence for determining their residence for tax purposes (see paragraph 13 below).

8.   The following examples illustrate how an Entity's residence for tax purposes may be determined:

- Example 1: A company is incorporated in Jurisdiction A and has its place of effective management in Jurisdiction B. Under the laws of Jurisdiction A, residence for tax purposes is determined by reference to place of incorporation. The same applies under the laws of Jurisdiction B. Thus, the company is resident only in Jurisdiction A.

- Example 2: Same facts as Example 1, except that, under the laws of Jurisdiction B, residence for tax purposes is determined by reference to place of effective management. Thus, the company is resident in both Jurisdictions A and B.

- Example 3: Same facts as Example 1, except that, under the laws of Jurisdictions A and B, residence for tax purposes is determined by reference to place of effective management. Thus, the company is resident only in Jurisdiction B.

- Example 4: Same facts as Example 1, except that, under the laws of Jurisdiction A, residence for tax purposes is determined by reference to place of effective management and, under the laws of Jurisdiction B, residence for tax purposes is determined by reference to place of incorporation. Thus, the company is not resident in either Jurisdiction A or B.

9.   Participating Jurisdictions are expected to help taxpayers determine, and provide them with information with respect to, their residence(s) for tax purposes. That may be done, for example, through the various service channels used for providing information or guidance to taxpayers on the application of tax laws (e.g. phone, walk-in offices, internet). The OECD will endeavour to facilitate the dissemination of such information.

10.   As the definition of the term "Reportable Jurisdiction Person" makes clear, an Entity such as a partnership, limited liability partnership or similar legal arrangement that has no residence for tax purposes shall be treated as resident in the jurisdiction in which its place of effective management is situated (see paragraph 109 of the Commentary on Section VIII). When that is the case and such an Entity certifies that it has no residence for tax purposes, subparagraph A(1)(b) allows Reporting Financial Institutions to rely on the address of its principal office as a proxy for determining its residence (see paragraph 153 of the Commentary on Section VIII). Examples of Entities that have no residence for tax purposes include those treated as fiscally transparent, and those with the same fact pattern as Example 4 of paragraph 8 above.

Validity of self-certifications

11.   As mentioned in paragraph 7 of the Commentary on Section IV, a "self-certification" is a certification by the Account Holder that provides the Account Holder's status and any other information that may be reasonably requested by the Reporting Financial Institution to fulfil its reporting and due diligence obligations, such as whether the Account Holder is resident for tax purposes in a Reportable Jurisdiction or whether the Account Holder is a Passive NFE. With respect to New Entity Accounts, a self-certification

is valid only if it complies with the requirements for the validity of self-certifications for Preexisting Entity Accounts (see paragraphs 14-18 of the Commentary on Section V). The same is applicable with respect to curing self-certification errors, the requirement to obtain self-certifications on an account-by-account basis, and documentation collected by other persons.

Reasonableness of self-certifications

12.   As mentioned in paragraph 4 above, upon account opening, once the Reporting Financial Institution has obtained a self-certification that allows it to determine the Account Holder's residence(s) for tax purposes, the Reporting Financial Institution must confirm the reasonableness of such self-certification based on the information obtained in connection with the opening of the account, including any documentation collected pursuant to AML/KYC Procedures (i.e. the "reasonableness" test).

13.   A Reporting Financial Institution is considered to have confirmed the "reasonableness" of a self-certification if, in the course of account opening procedures and upon review of the information obtained in connection with the opening of the account (including any documentation collected pursuant to AML/KYC Procedures), it does not know or have reason to know that the self-certification is incorrect or unreliable (see paragraphs 2-3 of the Commentary on Section VII). Reporting Financial Institutions are not expected to carry out an independent legal analysis of relevant tax laws to confirm the reasonableness of a self-certification.

14.   The following examples illustrate the application of the "reasonableness" test:

- Example 1: A Reporting Financial Institution obtains a self-certification from the Account Holder upon account opening. The address contained in the self-certification conflicts with that contained in the documentation collected pursuant to AML/ KYC Procedures. Because of the conflicting information, the self-certification is incorrect or unreliable and, as a consequence, it fails the reasonableness test.

- Example 2: A Reporting Financial Institution obtains a self-certification from the Account Holder upon account opening. The documentation collected pursuant to AML/KYC Procedures only indicates the Account Holder's place of incorporation. In the self-certification, the Account Holder claims to be resident for tax purposes in a jurisdiction that is different from its jurisdiction of incorporation. The Account Holder explains to the Reporting Financial Institution that under relevant tax laws its residence for tax purposes is determined by reference to place of effective management, and that the jurisdiction where its effective management is situated differs from the jurisdiction in which it was incorporated. Thus, because there is a reasonable explanation of the conflicting information, the self-certification is not incorrect or unreliable and, as a consequence, passes the reasonableness test.

15.   In the case a self-certification that fails the reasonableness test, it is expected that the Reporting Financial Institution would obtain a valid self-certification in the course of the account opening procedures.

Subparagraph A(2) – Review procedure for Controlling Persons

16.   Subparagraph A(2) contains a review procedure to determine whether a New Entity Account is held by one or more Entities that are Passive NFEs with one or more Controlling Persons that are Reportable Persons. If any of the Controlling Persons of a Passive NFE is a Reportable Person, then the account must be treated as a Reportable Account (even if the Controlling Person is resident in the same jurisdiction as the Passive NFE).

17.   In making these determinations, the Reporting Financial Institution must follow the guidance in subparagraphs A(2)(a) through (c) in the order most appropriate under the circumstances. Those subparagraphs are aimed at determining:

a)   whether the Account Holder is a Passive NFE;

b)   the Controlling Persons of such Passive NFE; and

c)   whether any of such Controlling Persons is a Reportable Person.

18.   For purposes of determining whether the Account Holder is a Passive NFE, according to subparagraph A(2)(a), the Reporting Financial Institution must rely on a self-certification from the Account Holder to establish its status, unless it has information in its possession or that is publicly available (see paragraph 12 of the Commentary on Section V), based on which it can reasonably determine that the Account Holder is an Active NFE or a Financial Institution other than non-participating professionally managed investment entity (i.e. an Investment Entity described in subparagraph A(6)(b) of Section VIII that is not a Participating Jurisdiction Financial Institution). Such self-certification must comply with the requirements for the validity of self-certification with respect to Preexisting Entity Accounts (see paragraph 11 above). As mentioned in paragraph 18 of the Commentary on Section IV, a Reporting Financial Institution may rely upon the self-certification furnished by a customer for another account if both accounts are treated as a single account for purposes of satisfying the standards of knowledge requirements set forth in paragraph A of Section VII. A Reporting Financial Institution that cannot determine the status of the Account Holder as an Active NFE or

a Financial Institution other than non-participating professionally managed investment entity must presume that it is a Passive NFE.

19.   For the purposes of determining the Controlling Persons of an Account Holder, according to subparagraph A(2)(b), a Reporting Financial Institution may rely on information collected and maintained pursuant to AML/KYC Procedures.

20.   For the purposes of determining whether a Controlling Person of a Passive NFE is a Reportable Person, a Reporting Financial Institution may only rely on a self-certification from either the Account Holder or the Controlling Person (see paragraphs 22-23 of the Commentary on Section V).

21.   If there is a change in circumstances (see paragraph 17 of the Commentary on Section III) with respect to a New Entity Account that causes the Reporting Financial Institution to know, or have reason to know, that the self-certification or other documentation associated with an account is incorrect or unreliable, the Reporting Financial Institution must re-determine the status of the account in accordance with the procedures set forth in paragraph 27 of the Commentary on Section V.

Commentary on Section VII
concerning Special Due Diligence Requirements

1.   This Section contains special due diligence rules that Reporting Financial Institutions are required to apply in addition to the general due diligence requirements set forth in Section II and to any specific due diligence procedures applicable to the accounts maintained by them. Such rules are the standards of knowledge applicable to a self-certification and Documentary Evidence, an alternative due diligence procedure for Cash Value Insurance Contracts and Annuity Contracts held by individual beneficiaries, and the account aggregation and currency translation rules.

Paragraph A – Reliance on Self-Certification and Documentary Evidence

2.   Paragraph A contains the standards of knowledge applicable to a self-certification or Documentary Evidence. It provides that a Reporting Financial Institution may not rely on a self-certification or Documentary Evidence if the Reporting Financial Institution knows (i.e. has actual knowledge) or has reason to know that the self-certification or Documentary Evidence is incorrect or unreliable.

3.   A Reporting Financial Institution has reason to know that a self-certification or Documentary Evidence is unreliable or incorrect if its knowledge of relevant facts or statements contained in the self-certification or other documentation, including the knowledge of the relevant relationship managers, if any (see paragraphs 38-42 and 50 of the Commentary on Section III), is such that a reasonably prudent person in the position of the Reporting Financial Institution would question the claim being made. A Reporting Financial Institution also has reason to know that a self-certification or Documentary Evidence is unreliable or incorrect if there is information in the documentation or in the Reporting Financial Institution's account files that conflicts with the person's claim regarding its status.

Standards of knowledge applicable to self-certifications

4.   A Reporting Financial Institution has reason to know that a self-certification provided by a person is unreliable or incorrect if the self-certification is incomplete with respect to any item on the self-certification that is relevant to the claims made by the person, the self-certification contains any information that is inconsistent with the person's claim, or the Reporting Financial Institution has other account information that is inconsistent with the person's claim. A Reporting Financial Institution that relies on a service provider to review and maintain a self-certification is considered to know or have reason to know the facts within the knowledge of the service provider.

Standards of knowledge applicable to Documentary Evidence

5.   A Reporting Financial Institution may not rely on Documentary Evidence provided by a person if the Documentary Evidence does not reasonably establish the identity of the person presenting the Documentary Evidence. For example, Documentary Evidence is not reliable if it is provided in person by an individual and the photograph or signature on the Documentary Evidence does not match the appearance or signature of the person presenting the document. A Reporting Financial Institution may not rely on Documentary Evidence if the Documentary Evidence contains information that is inconsistent with the person's claim as to its status, the Reporting Financial Institution has other account information that is inconsistent with the person's status, or the Documentary Evidence lacks information necessary to establish the person's status.

6.   A Reporting Financial Institution is not obliged to rely upon an audited financial statement to establish that an account holder meets a certain asset threshold. However, if a Reporting Financial Institution elects to do so, it has reason to know that the status claimed is unreliable or incorrect only if the total assets shown on the audited financial statement for the account holder are not within the permissible thresholds, or the notes or footnotes to the financial statement indicate that the account holder is not eligible for the status claimed. If a Reporting Financial Institution elects to rely upon an audited financial statement to establish that the account holder is an Active NFE, it will be required to review the balance sheet and income statement to determine whether the account holder meets the income and asset thresholds set forth in subparagraph D(9)(a) of Section VIII and the notes or footnotes of the financial statement for an indication that the account holder is a financial institution. If a Reporting Financial Institution elects to rely upon an audited financial statement to establish a status for an account holder that does not require the account holder to meet an asset or income threshold, it will be required to review only the notes or footnotes to the financial statement

to determine whether the financial statement supports the claim of status. If a Reporting Financial Institution does not elect to rely upon an audited financial statement to establish the status of the account holder (for example, because it has other documentation that establishes the account holder's status), the Reporting Financial Institution is not required to independently evaluate the financial statement solely because it also has collected the audited financial statement in the course of its account opening or other procedures.

7. A Reporting Financial Institution is not obliged to rely upon organisational documents to establish that an Entity has a particular status. However, if a Reporting Financial Institution elects to do so, it will only be required to review the document to the extent needed to establish that the requirements applicable to the particular status are met, and that the document was executed, but will not be required to review the remainder of the document.

Limits on reason to know

8. For purposes of determining whether a Reporting Financial Institution that maintains a Preexisting Entity Account has reason to know that the status applied to the Entity is unreliable or incorrect, the Reporting Financial Institution is only required to review information contradicting the status claimed if such information is contained in the current customer master file, the most recent self-certification and Documentary Evidence for the person, the most recent account opening contract, and the most recent documentation obtained by the Reporting Financial Institution for purposes of AML/KYC Procedures or for other regulatory purposes.

9. A Reporting Financial Institution that maintains multiple accounts for a single person will have reason to know that a status for the person is inaccurate based on account information for another account held by the person only to the extent that the accounts are either required to be aggregated under the rules set forth in paragraph C of Section VII for account aggregation or otherwise treated as a single account for purposes of satisfying the standards of knowledge requirements set forth in paragraph A of Section VII.

10. A Reporting Financial Institution does not know or have reason to know that a self-certification or Documentary Evidence is unreliable or incorrect solely because of a change of address in the same jurisdiction as that of the previous address. In addition, a Reporting Financial Institution does not know or have reason to know that a self-certification or Documentary Evidence is unreliable or incorrect solely because it discovers any of the indicia listed in subparagraph B(2)(c) through (e) of Section III and such

indicia conflicts with the self-certification or Documentary Evidence. The following examples illustrate the application of the limits on the standards of knowledge:

- Example 1: A, a bank that is a Reporting Financial Institution, maintains a Depository Account for P, an individual Account Holder. The Depository Account is a Preexisting Account and A has relied on the address in its records for P, as supported by his passport and a utility bill collected upon opening of the account, to determine that P is resident for tax purposes in jurisdiction X (application of the residence address test). Five years later, P provides a power of attorney to his sister, who lives in jurisdiction Y, to operate his account. The fact that P has provided such power of attorney is not sufficient to give A reason to know that the Documentary Evidence relied upon to treat P as a resident of jurisdiction X is unreliable or incorrect.

- Example 2: B, an insurance company that is a Reporting Financial Institution, has entered into a Cash Value Insurance Contract with Q. Since the contract is a New Individual Account, B has obtained a self-certification from Q and confirmed its reasonableness on the basis of the AML/KYC documentation collected from Q. The self-certification confirms that Q is resident for tax purposes in jurisdiction V. Two years after B entered into the contract with Q, Q provides a telephone number in jurisdiction W to B. Although B did not previously have any telephone number in its records for Q, the sole receipt of a telephone number in jurisdiction W, does not constitute a reason to know that the original self-certification is unreliable or incorrect.

Paragraph B – Alternative Procedures for Cash Value Insurance and Annuity Contracts

11.   Paragraph B contains an alternative procedure for Cash Value Insurance Contracts and Annuity Contracts held by individual beneficiaries that simplifies the due diligence procedures otherwise applicable. A Reporting Financial Institution may presume that an individual beneficiary (other than the owner) of a Cash Value Insurance Contract or an Annuity Contract receiving a death benefit is not a Reportable Person and may treat such Financial Account as other than a Reportable Account unless the Reporting Financial Institution has actual knowledge, or reason to know, that the beneficiary is a Reportable Person.

12.   A Reporting Financial Institution has reason to know that a beneficiary of a Cash Value Insurance Contract or an Annuity Contract is a Reportable Person if the information collected by the Reporting Financial Institution and

associated with the beneficiary contains indicia as described in paragraph B of Section III. If a Reporting Financial Institution has actual knowledge, or reason to know, that the beneficiary is a Reportable Person, the Reporting Financial Institution must follow the procedures in paragraph B of Section III.

13.   An alternative procedure similar to that discussed may be necessary for certain employer-sponsored group insurance contracts or annuity contracts. When a group insurance contract or group annuity contract is issued to an employer and individual employees are the insured/beneficiaries, the insurance company does not have a direct relationship with the employee/certificate holders at inception of the contract. Jurisdictions wishing to provide such a procedure may include the following provision:

A Reporting Financial Institution may treat a Financial Account that is a member's interest in a Group Cash Value Insurance Contract or Group Annuity Contract as a Financial Account that is not a Reportable Account until the date on which an amount is payable to the employee/certificate holder or beneficiary, if the Financial Account that is a member's interest in a Group Cash Value Insurance Contract or Group Annuity Contract meets the following requirements:

a) the Group Cash Value Insurance Contract or Group Annuity Contract is issued to an employer and covers twenty-five or more employee/certificate holders;

b) the employee/certificate holders are entitled to receive any contract value related to their interests and to name beneficiaries for the benefit payable upon the employee's death; and

c) the aggregate amount payable to any employee/certificate holder or beneficiary does not exceed USD 1 000 000.

The term "Group Cash Value Insurance Contract" means a Cash Value Insurance Contract that (i) *provides coverage on individuals who are affiliated through an employer, trade association, labour union, or other association or group; and* (ii) *charges a premium for each member of the group (or member of a class within the group) that is determined without regard to the individual health characteristics other than age, gender, and smoking habits of the member (or class of members) of the group. The term "Group Annuity Contract" means an Annuity Contract under which the obligees are individuals who are affiliated through an employer, trade association, labour union, or other association or group.*

Paragraph C – Account Aggregation and Currency Translation Rules

Subparagraphs C(1) through (3) – Account aggregation rules

14.   Subparagraphs C(1) through (3) contain the account aggregation rules that Reporting Financial Institutions must follow for purposes of determining the aggregate balance or value of Financial Accounts.

15.   The first and second account aggregation rules are identical, except that the first rule is applicable to Financial Accounts held by an individual and the second rule to those held by an Entity. The rules provide that:

- a Reporting Financial Institution is required to aggregate (or take into account) all Financial Accounts maintained by the Reporting Financial Institution, or by a Related Entity, but only to the extent that the Reporting Financial Institution's computerised systems link the Financial Accounts by reference to a data element such as client number or TIN, and allow account balances or values to be aggregated.

- each holder of a jointly held Financial Account shall be attributed the entire balance or value of the jointly held Financial Account for purposes of applying the aggregation requirements.

16.   The third account aggregation rule is a special rule applicable to determine whether a Financial Account is a High Value Account. By virtue of this rule, a Reporting Financial Institution is required, in addition to the other account aggregation rules, to aggregate all Financial Accounts that a relationship manager knows, or has reason to know, are directly or indirectly owned, controlled, or established (other than in a fiduciary capacity) by the same person (see paragraphs 3 above and 38-42 of the Commentary on Section III). This requirement includes aggregating all accounts that the relationship manager has associated with one another through a name, relationship code, customer identification number, TIN, or similar indicator, or that the relationship manager would typically associate with each other under the procedures of the financial institution (or the department, division, or unit with which the relationship manager is associated).

17.   In some jurisdictions, domestic law does not allow the application of the account aggregation rules as envisaged under subparagraphs C(1) through (3). For example, a Reporting Financial Institution's computerised systems may be able to link all the Financial Accounts that are maintained by the Reporting Financial Institution and its Related Entities, but domestic law may limit one or more of such Related Entities from sharing the account holder's personal data with the Reporting Financial Institution. When that is the case, the Reporting Financial Institution is required to apply the account aggregation rules as set forth in subparagraphs C(1) through (3), but only to the extent permitted by domestic law.

18.   The following examples illustrate the application of the account aggregation rules:

- Example 1 (Reporting Financial Institution not required to aggregate accounts): An Entity, U, holds a depository account with AP, a commercial bank that is a Reporting Financial Institution. The balance in U's account at the end of Year 1 is USD 160 000. U also holds another depository account with AP, with a USD 165 000 balance at the end of Year 1. AP's retail banking businesses share computerised information management systems, but U's accounts are not associated with one another in the shared computerised information system. Because the accounts are not associated in AP's system, AP is not required to aggregate the accounts under subparagraphs C(2) and (3) and both accounts are eligible for the exception described in paragraph A of Section V as neither account exceeds the USD 250 000 threshold.

- Example 2 (Reporting Financial Institution required to aggregate accounts): Same facts as Example 1, except that both of U's depository accounts are associated with U and with one another by reference to AP's internal identification number. The system shows the account balances for both accounts, and such balances may be electronically aggregated, though the system does not show a combined balance for the accounts. In determining whether such accounts meet the exception described in paragraph A of Section V for accounts with an aggregate balance or value of USD 250 000 or less, AP is required to aggregate the account balances of all depository accounts under the account aggregation rules. Under those rules, U is treated as holding depository accounts with AP with an aggregate balance of USD 325 000. Accordingly, neither account is eligible for the exception, because the accounts, when aggregated, exceed the USD 250 000 threshold.

- Example 3 (Aggregation rules for joint accounts maintained by a Reporting Financial Institution): In Year 1, an individual, U, holds a custodial account that is a preexisting account at custodial institution SH, a Reporting Financial Institution. The balance in U's SH custodial account at the end of Year 1 is USD 700 000. U also holds a joint custodial account that is a preexisting account with her sister, A, with another custodial institution, SH2. The balance in the joint account at the end of Year 1 is also USD 700 000. SH and SH2 are Related Entities and share computerised information management systems. Both U's custodial account at SH and U and A's custodial account at SH2 are associated with U and with one another by reference to SH's internal identification number and the system allows the balances to be aggregated. In determining whether such accounts meet the definition of "High Value Account", SH is required to aggregate the account balances of accounts held in whole or in part by the same account holder under the account aggregation rules. Under those rules, U is treated as having financial accounts with SH and SH2, each with an aggregate balance of USD 1 400 000. Accordingly, both of U's accounts are High Value Accounts. A is only treated as having a financial account with SH2 with a balance of USD 700 000 since she is not an Account Holder of U's custodial account at SH. Accordingly, A's account is a Lower Value Account.

19. The following additional examples illustrate the application of the special aggregation rule applicable to relationship managers:

- Example 1 (Accounts held by a Passive NFE and by one of its Controlling Person): A Passive NFE, T, holds a depository account with A, a commercial bank that is a Reporting Financial Institution. One of T's Controlling Persons, N, also holds a depository account with A. Both accounts are associated with N and with one another by reference to A's internal identification number. In addition, A has assigned a relationship manager to N. Because the accounts are associated in A's system and by a relationship manager, A is required to aggregate the accounts under subparagraphs C(1) through (3).

- Example 2 (Accounts held by different Passive NFEs with a common Controlling Person): Same facts as Example 1. In addition, another Passive NFE, I, holds a depository account with A. N is also one of I's Controlling Persons. I's account is not associated with N nor with T's and N's accounts by reference to A's internal identification number. Because the accounts are associated by a relationship manager, A is required to aggregate the accounts under subparagraphs C(1) through (3).

Subparagraph C(4) – Currency translation rule

20. Subparagraph C(4) contains the currency translation rule, according to which all dollar amounts are in US dollars and shall be read to include equivalent amounts in other currencies, as determined by domestic law. When implementing the Common Reporting Standard, jurisdictions are expected to use the amounts that are equivalent in their currency to the US dollar threshold amounts described in the Standard. However, they are not required to use the exact equivalent amounts to the US dollar threshold amounts; approximate equivalent amounts are sufficient.

21. When implementing the Common Reporting Standard, jurisdictions may permit Reporting Financial Institutions to apply the US dollar threshold

amounts described in the Standard along with the equivalent amounts in other currencies. This would allow financial institutions that operate in several jurisdictions to apply the threshold amounts in the same currency in all the jurisdictions in which they operate.

Commentary on Section VIII concerning Defined Terms

1.   Section VIII contains the defined terms, grouped around 5 themes: A) Reporting Financial Institution; B) Non-Reporting Financial Institution, C) Financial Account, D) Reportable Account and E) Miscellaneous.

Paragraph A – Reporting Financial Institution

Subparagraphs A(1) and (2) – Reporting Financial Institution

Reporting Financial Institution

2.   Subparagraph A(1) defines the term "Reporting Financial Institution" as any Participating Jurisdiction Financial Institution that is not a Non-Reporting Financial Institution. Therefore, for a Financial Institution to be a Reporting Financial Institution, it needs, first, to be a Participating Jurisdiction Financial Institution and, then, not to be a Non-Reporting Financial Institution. Paragraph B sets forth the meaning of the term "Non-Reporting Financial Institution" through several definitions.

Participating Jurisdiction Financial Institution

3.   The term "Participating Jurisdiction Financial Institution" is defined in subparagraph A(2) to mean:

- any Financial Institution that is resident in a Participating Jurisdiction, but excluding any branch of that Financial Institution that is located outside such Participating Jurisdiction; and

- any branch located in a Participating Jurisdiction of a Financial Institution that itself is not resident in such Participating Jurisdiction.

4.   For this purpose, a Financial Institution is "resident" in a Participating Jurisdiction if it is subject to the jurisdiction of such Participating Jurisdiction (i.e. the Participating Jurisdiction is able to enforce reporting by the Financial Institution). In general, where a Financial Institution is resident for tax purposes in a Participating Jurisdiction, it is subject to the jurisdiction of such

Participating Jurisdiction and it is, thus, a Participating Jurisdiction Financial Institution. In the case of a trust that is a Financial Institution (irrespective of whether it is resident for tax purposes in a Participating Jurisdiction), the trust is considered to be subject to the jurisdiction of a Participating Jurisdiction if one or more of its trustees are resident in such Participating Jurisdiction except if the trust reports all the information required to be reported pursuant to the CRS with respect to Reportable Accounts maintained by the trust to another Participating Jurisdiction because it is resident for tax purposes in such other Participating Jurisdiction. However, where a Financial Institution (other than a trust) does not have a residence for tax purposes (e.g. because it is treated as fiscally transparent, or it is located in a jurisdiction that does not have an income tax), it is considered to be subject to the jurisdiction of a Participating Jurisdiction and it is, thus, a Participating Jurisdiction Financial Institution if:

a) it is incorporated under the laws of the Participating Jurisdiction;

b) it has its place of management (including effective management) in the Participating Jurisdiction; or

c) it is subject to financial supervision in the Participating Jurisdiction.

In this context, the term "Participating Jurisdiction" refers to a jurisdiction that has implemented the Common Reporting Standard.

5. Where a Financial Institution (other than a trust) is resident in two or more Participating Jurisdictions, such Financial Institution will be subject to the reporting and due diligence obligations of the Participating Jurisdiction in which it maintains the Financial Account(s).

6. A "branch" is a unit, business, or office of a Financial Institution that is treated as a branch under the regulatory regime of a jurisdiction or that is otherwise regulated under the laws of a jurisdiction as separate from other offices, units, or branches of the Financial Institution. A branch includes a unit, business, or office of a Financial Institution located in a jurisdiction in which the Financial Institution is resident, and a unit, business, or office of a Financial Institution located in the jurisdiction in which the Financial Institution is created or organised. All units, businesses, or offices of a Reporting Financial Institution in a single jurisdiction shall be treated as a single branch.

Subparagraphs A(3) through (8) – Financial Institution

7. The term "Financial Institution" means a Custodial Institution, a Depository Institution, an Investment Entity, or a Specified Insurance Company, as defined in subparagraph A(3).

8.   Whether an Entity is subject to the financial laws and regulations of a Participating Jurisdiction, or is subject to supervision and examination by agencies having regulatory oversight of financial institutions, is relevant to, but not necessarily determinative of, whether that Entity qualifies as a Financial Institution under subparagraph A(3).

Custodial Institution

9.   Subparagraph A(4) defines the term "Custodial Institution" as any Entity that holds, as a substantial portion of its business, Financial Assets for the account of others.

10.   It further establishes the "substantial portion" test. An Entity holds Financial Assets for the account of others as a substantial portion of its business if the Entity's gross income attributable to the holding of Financial Assets and related financial services equals or exceeds 20% of the Entity's gross income during the shorter of:

- the three-year period that ends on 31 December (or the final day of a non-calendar year accounting period) prior to the year in which the determination is being made; or

- the period during which the Entity has been in existence.

"Income attributable to holding Financial Assets and related financial services" means custody, account maintenance, and transfer fees; commissions and fees earned from executing and pricing securities transactions with respect to Financial Assets held in custody; income earned from extending credit to customers with respect to Financial Assets held in custody (or acquired through such extension of credit); income earned on the bid-ask spread of Financial Assets held in custody; and fees for providing financial advice with respect to Financial Assets held in (or potentially to be held in) custody by the entity; and for clearance and settlement services.

11.   Entities that safe keep Financial Assets for the account of others, such as custodian banks, brokers and central securities depositories, would generally be considered Custodial Institutions. Entities that do not hold Financial Assets for the account of others, such as insurance brokers, will not be Custodial Institutions.

Depository Institution

12.   Subparagraph A(5) defines the term "Depository Institution" as any Entity that accepts deposits in the ordinary course of a banking or similar business.

13.   An Entity is considered to be engaged in a "banking or similar business" if, in the ordinary course of its business with customers, the Entity accepts deposits or other similar investments of funds and regularly engages in one or more of the following activities:

  a)   makes personal, mortgage, industrial, or other loans or provides other extensions of credit;

  b)   purchases, sells, discounts, or negotiates accounts receivable, instalment obligations, notes, drafts, checks, bills of exchange, acceptances, or other evidences of indebtedness;

  c)   issues letters of credit and negotiates drafts drawn thereunder;

  d)   provides trust or fiduciary services;

  e)   finances foreign exchange transactions; or

  f)   enters into, purchases, or disposes of finance leases or leased assets.

An Entity is not considered to be engaged in a banking or similar business if the Entity solely accepts deposits from persons as a collateral or security pursuant to a sale or lease of property or pursuant to a similar financing arrangement between such Entity and the person holding the deposit with the Entity.

14.   Savings banks, commercial banks, savings and loan associations, and credit unions would generally be considered Depository Institutions. However, whether an Entity conducts a banking or similar business is determined based upon the character of the actual activities of such Entity.

Investment Entity

15.   The term "Investment Entity" includes two types of Entities: Entities that primarily conduct as a business investment activities or operations on behalf of other persons, and Entities that are managed by those Entities or other Financial Institutions.

16.   Subparagraph A(6)(a) defines the first type of "Investment Entity" as any Entity that primarily conducts as a business one or more of the following activities or operations for or on behalf of a customer:

  a)   trading in money market instruments (cheques, bills, certificates of deposit, derivatives, etc.); foreign exchange; exchange, interest rate and index instruments; transferable securities; or commodity futures trading;

  b)   individual and collective portfolio management; or

  c)   otherwise investing, administering, or managing Financial Assets or money on behalf of other persons.

Such activities or operations do not include rendering non-binding investment advice to a customer.

17.   Subparagraph A(6)(b) defines the second type of "Investment Entity" as any Entity the gross income of which is primarily attributable to investing, reinvesting, or trading in Financial Assets, if the Entity is managed by another Entity that is a Depository Institution, a Custodial Institution, a Specified Insurance Company, or an Investment Entity described in subparagraph A(6)(a). An Entity is "managed by" another Entity if the managing Entity performs, either directly or through another service provider, any of the activities or operations described in subparagraph A(6)(a) on behalf of the managed Entity. However, an Entity does not manage another Entity if it does not have discretionary authority to manage the Entity's assets (in whole or part). Where an Entity is managed by a mix of Financial Institutions, NFEs or individuals, the Entity is considered to be managed by another Entity that is a Depository Institution, a Custodial Institution, a Specified Insurance Company, or an Investment Entity described in subparagraph A(6)(a), if any of the managing Entities is such another Entity.

18.   An Entity is treated as primarily conducting as a business one or more of the activities described in subparagraph A(6)(a), or an Entity's gross income is primarily attributable to investing, reinvesting, or trading in Financial Assets for purposes of subparagraph A(6)(b), if the Entity's gross income attributable to the relevant activities equals or exceeds 50% of the Entity's gross income during the shorter of:

- the three-year period ending on 31 December of the year preceding the year in which the determination is made; or

- the period during which the Entity has been in existence.

19.   The term "Investment Entity", as defined in subparagraph A(6), does not include an Entity that is an Active NFE because it meets any of the criteria in subparagraphs D(9)(d) through (g) (i.e. holding NFEs and treasury centres that are members of a nonfinancial group; start-up NFEs; and NFEs that are liquidating or emerging from bankruptcy).

20.   An Entity would generally be considered an Investment Entity if it functions or holds itself out as a collective investment vehicle, mutual fund, exchange traded fund, private equity fund, hedge fund, venture capital fund, leveraged buy-out fund or any similar investment vehicle established with an investment strategy of investing, reinvesting, or trading in Financial Assets. An Entity that primarily conducts as a business investing, administering, or managing non-debt, direct interests in real property on behalf of other persons, such as a type of real estate investment trust, will not be an Investment Entity.

21. Subparagraph A(6) also states that the definition of the term "Investment Entity" shall be interpreted in a manner consistent with similar language set forth in the definition of "financial institution" in the Financial Action Task Force Recommendations.[9]

22. The following examples illustrate the application of subparagraph A(6):

- Example 1 (Investment advisor): Fund manager is an Investment Entity within the meaning of subparagraph A(6)(a). Fund manager, among its various business operations, organises and manages a variety of funds, including Fund A, a fund that invests primarily in equities. Fund manager hires Investment advisor, an Entity, to provide advice and discretionary management of a portion of the Financial Assets held by Fund A. Investment advisor earned more than 50% of its gross income for the last three years from providing similar services. Because Investment advisor primarily conducts a business of managing Financial Assets on behalf of clients, Investment advisor is an Investment Entity under subparagraph A(6)(a). It is recognised, however, that only the Investment Entity maintaining the Financial Accounts will be responsible for the reporting and due diligence obligations with respect to such Financial Accounts (see paragraphs 57-65 of the Commentary on Section VIII).

- Example 2 (Entity that is managed by a Financial Institution): The facts are the same as in Example 1. In addition, in every year since it was organised, Fund A has earned more than 50% of its gross income from investing in Financial Assets. Accordingly, Fund A is an Investment Entity under subparagraph A(6)(b) because it is managed by Fund manager and Investment advisor and its gross income is primarily attributable to investing, reinvesting, or trading in Financial Assets.

- Example 3 (Investment manager): Investment manager, a Jurisdiction B Entity, is an Investment Entity within the meaning of subparagraph A(6)(a). Investment manager organises and registers Fund A in Jurisdiction A. Investment manager is authorised to facilitate purchases and sales of Financial Assets held by Fund A in accordance with Fund A's investment strategy. In every year since it was organised, Fund A has earned more than 50% of its gross income from investing, reinvesting, or trading in Financial Assets. Accordingly, Fund A is an Investment Entity under subparagraph A(6)(b).

---

9. FATF/OECD (2013), *International Standards on Combating Money Laundering and the Financing of Terrorism and Proliferation*, The FATF Recommendations February 2012, FATF/OECD, Paris, available on www.fatf-gafi.org/media/fatf/documents/recommendations/pdfs/FATF_Recommendations.pdf.

- Example 4 (Real estate investment fund that is managed by a Financial Institution): The facts are the same as in Example 3, except that Fund A's assets consist solely of non-debt, direct interests in real property located within and outside of Jurisdiction B. Fund A is not an Investment Entity under subparagraph A(6)(b), even though it is managed by Investment manager, because less than 50% of its gross income is attributable to investing, reinvesting, or trading in Financial Assets.

- Example 5 (Trust managed by an individual): X, an individual, establishes Trust A, an irrevocable trust for the benefit of X's children, Y and Z. X appoints Trustee A, an individual, to act as the trustee of Trust A. Trust A's assets consist solely of Financial Assets, and its income consists solely of income from those Financial Assets. Pursuant to the terms of the trust instrument, Trustee A manages and administers the assets of the trust. Trustee A does not hire any Entity as a service provider to perform any of the activities described in subparagraph A(6)(a). Trust A is not an Investment Entity under subparagraph A(6)(b) because it is managed solely by Trustee A, an individual.

- Example 6 (Individual broker): B, an individual broker, primarily conducts a business of providing advice to clients, has discretionary authority to manage clients' assets, and uses the services of an entity to conduct and execute trades on behalf of clients. B provides services as an investment advisor and manager to E, a corporation. E has earned 50% or more of its gross income for the past three years from investing, reinvesting, or trading in Financial Assets. Because B is an individual, notwithstanding that B primarily conducts certain investment-related activities, B is not an Investment Entity under subparagraph A(6)(a). Further, E is not an Investment Entity under subparagraph A(6)(b) because E is managed by B, an individual.

Financial Asset

23.   The term "Financial Asset" is used in the definition of the terms "Custodial Institution", "Investment Entity", "Custodial Account" and "Excluded Account". While it does not refer to assets of every kind, it intends to encompass any assets that may be held in an account maintained by a Financial Institution with the exception of a non-debt, direct interest in real property.

24.   Within that context, subparagraph A(7) provides that the term "Financial Asset" includes a security (for example, a share of stock in a corporation; partnership or beneficial ownership interest in a widely held

or publicly traded partnership or trust; note, bond, debenture, or other evidence of indebtedness), partnership interest, commodity, swap (for example, interest rate swaps, currency swaps, basis swaps, interest rate caps, interest rate floors, commodity swaps, equity swaps, equity index swaps, and similar agreements), Insurance Contract or Annuity Contract, or any interest (including a futures or forward contract or option) in a security, partnership interest, commodity, swap, Insurance Contract, or Annuity Contract. However, the term "Financial Asset" does not include a non-debt, direct interest in real property; or a commodity that is a physical good, such as wheat.

25.   Negotiable debt instruments that are traded on a regulated market or over-the-counter market and distributed and held through Financial Institutions, and shares or units in a real estate investment trust, would generally be considered Financial Assets.

Specified Insurance Company

26.   Subparagraph A(8) defines the term "Specified Insurance Company" as any Entity that is an insurance company (or the holding company of an insurance company) that issues, or is obligated to make payments with respect to, a Cash Value Insurance Contract or an Annuity Contract.

27.   An "insurance company" is an Entity *(i)* that is regulated as an insurance business under the laws, regulations, or practices of any jurisdiction in which the Entity does business; *(ii)* the gross income of which (for example, gross premiums and gross investment income) arising from insurance, reinsurance, and Annuity Contracts for the immediately preceding calendar year exceeds 50% of total gross income for such year; or *(iii)* the aggregate value of the assets of which associated with insurance, reinsurance, and Annuity Contracts at any time during the immediately preceding calendar year exceeds 50% of total assets at any time during such year.

28.   Most life insurance companies would generally be considered Specified Insurance Companies. Entities that do not issue Cash Value Insurance Contracts or Annuity Contracts nor are obligated to make payments with respect to them, such as most non-life insurance companies, most holding companies of insurance companies, and insurance brokers, will not be Specified Insurance Companies.

29.   The reserving activities of an insurance company will not cause the company to be a Custodial Institution, a Depository Institution, or an Investment Entity.

Paragraph B – Non-Reporting Financial Institution

Subparagraph B(1) – In general

30.   Subparagraph B(1) sets out the various categories of Non-Reporting Financial Institutions (i.e. Financial Institutions that are excluded from reporting). "Non-Reporting Financial Institution" means any Financial Institution that is:

a)   a Governmental Entity, International Organisation or Central Bank, other than with respect to a payment that is derived from an obligation held in connection with a commercial financial activity of a type engaged in by a Specified Insurance Company, Custodial Institution, or Depository Institution;

b)   a Broad Participation Retirement Fund; a Narrow Participation Retirement Fund; a Pension Fund of a Governmental Entity, International Organisation or Central Bank; or a Qualified Credit Card Issuer;

c)   any other Entity that presents a low risk of being used to evade tax, has substantially similar characteristics to any of the Entities described in subparagraphs B(1)(a) and (b), and is defined in domestic law as a Non-Reporting Financial Institution, provided that the status of such Entity as a Non-Reporting Financial Institution does not frustrate the purposes of the Common Reporting Standard;

d)   an Exempt Collective Investment Vehicle; or

e)   a trust to the extent that the trustee of the trust is a Reporting Financial Institution and reports all information required to be reported pursuant to Section I with respect to all Reportable Accounts of the trust.

Subparagraphs B(2) through (4) – Governmental Entity, International Organisation and Central Bank

31.   A Financial Institution that is a Governmental Entity, International Organisation or Central Bank is a Non-Reporting Financial Institution, according to subparagraph B(1)(a), other than with respect to a payment that is derived from an obligation held in connection with a commercial financial activity of a type engaged in by a Specified Insurance Company, Custodial Institution, or Depository Institution. Thus, for example, a Central Bank that conducts a commercial financial activity, such as acting as an intermediary on behalf of persons other than in the bank's capacity as a Central Bank, is not a Non-Reporting Financial Institution under subparagraph B(1)(a) with respect to payments received in connection with an account held in connection with such activity.

Governmental Entity

32.   Subparagraph B(2) defines the term "Governmental Entity" as the government of a jurisdiction, any political subdivision of a jurisdiction (which, for the avoidance of doubt, includes a state, province, county, municipality, or local authority), or any wholly owned agency or instrumentality of a jurisdiction or of any one or more of the foregoing. It also includes the integral parts, controlled entities, and political subdivisions of a jurisdiction. An "integral part" and a "controlled entity" are defined in subparagraphs B(2)(a) and (b), which require that no portion of their income inure to the benefit of private persons. While subparagraph B(2)(c) clarifies when that is the case, income may also be considered to inure to the benefit of private persons if such income benefits private persons through the use of a Governmental Entity as a conduit for personal investment, or private persons who divert such income from its intended use by exerting influence or control through means explicitly or implicitly approved of by the jurisdiction.

33.   In order to promote international trade and development, many jurisdictions have established export or development financing programmes or agencies which may either provide loans directly or insure or guarantee loans granted by commercial lenders. Those agencies would generally be considered Governmental Entities and, thus, Non-Reporting Financial Institutions (see paragraph 31 above).

International Organisation

34.   The term "International Organisation", as defined in subparagraph B(3), means any international organisation or wholly owned agency or instrumentality thereof. It includes any intergovernmental organisation (including a supranational organisation) *(1)* that is comprised primarily of governments; *(2)* that has in effect a headquarters or substantially similar agreement with the jurisdiction; and *(3)* the income of which does not inure to the benefit of private persons (under the principles of subparagraph B(2)(c)). Arrangements substantially similar to headquarters arrangements include, for example, arrangements that entitle the organisation's offices or establishments in the jurisdiction (e.g. a subdivision, or a local or regional office) to privileges and immunities.

Central Bank

35.   According to subparagraph B(4), the term "Central Bank" means an institution that is by law or government sanction the principal authority, other than the government of the jurisdiction itself, issuing instruments intended to circulate as currency. Such an institution is generally the custodian of the banking reserves of the jurisdiction under whose law it is organised. This

term may include an instrumentality that is separate from the government of the jurisdiction, whether or not owned in whole or in part by the jurisdiction.

Subparagraphs B(5) through (7) – Funds

Broad Participation Retirement Fund

36.   Subparagraph B(5) defines the term "Broad Participation Retirement Fund" as a fund established to provide retirement, disability, or death benefits, or any combination thereof, to beneficiaries that are current or former employees (or persons designated by such employees) of one or more employers in consideration for services rendered, provided that the fund:

   a)   does not have a single beneficiary with a right to more than five per cent of the fund's assets;

   b)   is subject to regulation and provides information reporting to the tax authorities; and

   c)   satisfies at least one of the four requirements listed in subparagraph B(5)(c) (i.e. the fund is tax-favoured; most contributions are received from sponsoring employers; distributions or withdrawals are only allowed upon the occurrence of specified events; and contributions by employees are limited by amount).

37.   Information reporting required in subparagraph B(5)(b) may vary among jurisdictions. While one jurisdiction could require that the fund provides annual information about its beneficiaries, another jurisdiction could require that the fund provides monthly information about contributions and associated tax relief, and annual information about its beneficiaries and total contributions from sponsoring employers. However, whether a fund provides information reporting to the relevant tax authorities in the jurisdiction in which the fund is established or operates is determinative of whether a fund satisfies the requirement under that subparagraph.

Narrow Participation Retirement Fund

38.   The term "Narrow Participation Retirement Fund", as defined in subparagraph B(6), means a fund established to provide retirement, disability, or death benefits to beneficiaries that are current or former employees (or persons designated by such employees) of one or more employers in consideration for services rendered, provided that all requirements listed in that subparagraph are satisfied.

39.   Subparagraph B(6)(c) requires that the employee and employer contributions to the fund are limited by reference to earned income and

compensation of the employee, respectively. While that subparagraph excludes certain transfers of assets from the threshold (i.e. those from retirement and pension accounts described in subparagraph C(17)(a)), other transfers of assets could also be excluded, such as those from other plans described in subparagraphs B(5) through (7).

40.   Information reporting required in subparagraph B(6)(e) may vary among jurisdictions. As mentioned in paragraph 37 above, whether a fund provides information reporting to the relevant tax authorities in the jurisdiction in which the fund is established or operates is determinative of whether a fund satisfies the requirement under that subparagraph.

Pension Fund of a Governmental Entity, International Organisation or Central Bank

41.   According to subparagraph B(7), the term "Pension Fund of a Governmental Entity, International Organisation or Central Bank" means a fund established by a Governmental Entity, International Organisation or Central Bank to provide retirement, disability, or death benefits to beneficiaries or participants that are current or former employees (or persons designated by such employees), or that are not current or former employees, if the benefits provided to such beneficiaries or participants are in consideration of personal services performed for the Governmental Entity, International Organisation or Central Bank.

Subparagraph B(8) – Qualified Credit Card Issuer

42.   Subparagraph B(8) defines the term "Qualified Credit Card Issuer" as a Financial Institution satisfying the following requirements:

a)   the Financial Institution is a Financial Institution solely because it is an issuer of credit cards that accepts deposits only when a customer makes a payment in excess of a balance due with respect to the card and the overpayment is not immediately returned to the customer; and

b)   beginning on or before [xx/xx/xxxx], the Financial Institution implements policies and procedures either to prevent a customer from making an overpayment in excess of USD 50 000, or to ensure that any customer overpayment in excess of USD 50 000 (and of the balance due with respect to the card) is refunded to the customer within 60 calendar days, in each case applying the rules set forth in paragraph C of Section VII for account aggregation and currency translation. For this purpose, a customer overpayment does not refer to credit balances to the extent of disputed charges but does include credit balances resulting from merchandise returns.

43.   While the selection of the date referred to in subparagraph B(8)(b) is a decision of the jurisdiction implementing the Common Reporting Standard, it is expected that the date selected for that purpose is the same date as the one selected for the term "New Account". For this purpose, a Financial Institution that is formed or organised after the selected date must satisfy the requirement described in subparagraph B(8)(b) within six months after the date such Financial Institution was formed or organised.

44.   A Reporting Financial Institution that does not satisfy the requirements to be a Qualified Credit Card Issuer, but accepts deposits when a customer makes a payment in excess of a balance due with respect to a credit card or other revolving credit facility, may still not report a Depository Account if it qualifies as an Excluded Account under subparagraph C(17)(f).

Subparagraph B(1)(c) – Low-risk Non-Reporting Financial Institutions

45.   A Financial Institution can also be a Non-Reporting Financial Institution, according to subparagraph B(1)(c), provided that:

a)   the Financial Institution presents a low risk of being used to evade tax;

b)   the Financial Institution has substantially similar characteristics to any of the Financial Institutions described in subparagraphs B(1)(a) and (b);

c)   the Financial Institution is defined in domestic law as a Non-Reporting Financial Institution; and

d)   the status of the Financial Institution as a Non-Reporting Financial Institution does not frustrate the purposes of the Common Reporting Standard.

46.   This "open" category of Non-Reporting Financial Institution is intended to accommodate jurisdiction-specific types of financial institutions that satisfy the requirements listed in subparagraph B(1)(c), and avoids the need to negotiate classes of Non-Reporting Financial Institutions when concluding an agreement on the automatic exchange of financial account information.

47.   The first requirement described in subparagraph B(1)(c) is that the Financial Institution presents a low risk of being used to evade tax. Factors that may be considered to determine such a risk include:

a)   low-risk factors:

   (1) the Financial Institution is subject to regulation.

   (2) information reporting by the Financial Institution to the tax authorities is required.

b) high-risk factors:

(1) the type of Financial Institution is not subject to AML/KYC Procedures.

(2) the type of Financial Institution is allowed to issue shares in bearer form and is not subject to effective measures implementing the FATF Recommendations with respect to transparency and beneficial ownership of legal persons.[10]

(3) the type of Financial Institution is promoted as a tax minimisation vehicle.

48. The second requirement described in subparagraph B(1)(c) is that the Financial Institution has substantially similar characteristics to any of the Financial Institutions described in subparagraphs B(1)(a) and (b). This requirement cannot be used solely to eliminate a specific element of a description. Each jurisdiction may evaluate the application of this requirement to a type of Financial Institution that does not satisfy all the requirements of a particular description listed in subparagraphs B(1)(a) or (b). As part of such evaluation, a jurisdiction must identify which requirements are satisfied and which are not satisfied, and with respect to the requirements that are not satisfied, must identify the existence of a substitute requirement that provides equivalent assurance that the relevant type of Financial Institution presents a low-risk of tax evasion.

49. The third requirement described in subparagraph B(1)(c) is that the Financial Institution is defined in domestic law as a Non-Reporting Financial Institution. This requirement is satisfied where a jurisdiction defines a specific type of Financial Institution as a Non-Reporting Financial Institution, and that definition is contained in domestic law. For such purpose, a jurisdiction would typically be consistent with the types of Financial Institutions treated as "exempt beneficial owners" or "deemed-compliant FFIs" in the intergovernmental agreement concluded between such jurisdiction and the United States to improve international tax compliance including with respect to FATCA, provided that such types of Financial Institution satisfy all the requirements listed in subparagraph B(1)(c). It is expected that each jurisdiction would have only one single list of domestically-defined Non-Reporting Financial Institutions (as opposed to different lists for different Participating Jurisdictions) and that it would make such a list publicly available.

---

10. FATF/OECD (2013), *International Standards on Combating Money Laundering and the Financing of Terrorism and Proliferation*, The FATF Recommendations February 2012, FATF/OECD, Paris, available on www.fatf-gafi.org/media/fatf/documents/recommendations/pdfs/FATF_Recommendations.pdf.

50.   The fourth requirement described in subparagraph B(1)(c) is that the status of the Financial Institution as a Non-Reporting Financial Institution does not frustrate the purposes of the Common Reporting Standard. It is expected that this requirement will be monitored, inter alia, through the following:

  a)   the administrative procedures that a jurisdiction must have in place to ensure that the Financial Institutions defined in domestic law as Non-Reporting Financial Institutions continue to have a low risk of being used to evade tax (see subparagraph A(4) of Section IX);

  b)   the potential suspension of a Competent Authority Agreement where the other Competent Authority has defined the status of Financial Institutions as Non-Reporting Financial Institutions in a manner that frustrates the purposes of the Common Reporting Standard (see paragraph 2 of Section 7 of the Model Competent Authority Agreement); and

  c)   the mechanism to review the implementation of the Common Reporting Standard mandated to the Global Forum on Transparency and Exchange of Information for Tax Purposes by the G20 (see paragraph 51 of the G20 Leaders' Declaration, Saint Petersburg Summit, 5-6 September 2013).[11]

51.   The following examples illustrate the application of subparagraph B(1)(c):

  •   Example 1 (Non-profit organisation): A type of non-profit organisation that is a Financial Institution does not satisfy all the requirements of any particular description listed in subparagraphs B(1)(a) or (b). This type of Non-Reporting Financial Institution cannot be defined in domestic law as a Non-Reporting Financial Institution solely because it is a non-profit organisation.

  •   Example 2 (Retirement fund also for self-employed individuals): A type of retirement fund that is a Financial Institution satisfies all the requirements listed in subparagraph B(5). However, under the laws of the jurisdiction in which the fund is established or operates, it is required to also provide benefits to beneficiaries that are self-employed individuals. Because there is an overall, substitute requirement that provides equivalent assurance that the fund presents a low-risk of tax evasion, this type of Financial Institution could be defined in domestic law as a Non-Reporting Financial Institution.

  •   Example 3 (Unlimited retirement fund): A type of retirement fund that is a Financial Institution satisfies all the requirements listed in

---

11.   Available on https://www.g20.org/.

subparagraph B(6), apart from the one contained in subparagraph B(6)(c) (i.e. employee and employer contributions are not limited). However, the tax relief associated to the employee and employer contributions is limited by reference to earned income and compensation of the employee, respectively. Because there is a substitute requirement that provides equivalent assurance that the fund presents a low-risk of tax evasion, this type of Financial Institution could be defined in domestic law as a Non-Reporting Financial Institution.

• Example 4 (Investment vehicle exclusively for retirement funds): A type of investment vehicle that is Financial Institution is established exclusively to earn income for the benefit of one or more retirement or pension funds described in subparagraphs B(5) through (7), or retirement or pension accounts described in subparagraphs C(17)(a). Because all the income of the vehicle inures to the benefit of Non-Reporting Financial Institutions or Excluded Accounts, and there is an overall, substitute requirement that provides equivalent assurance that the vehicle presents a low-risk of tax evasion, this type of Financial Institution could be defined in domestic law as a Non-Reporting Financial Institution.

Subparagraph B(9) – Exempt Collective Investment Vehicle

52.   The term "Exempt Collective Investment Vehicle", as defined in subparagraph B(9), means an Investment Entity that is regulated as a collective investment vehicle, provided that all of the interests in the collective investment vehicle are held by or through individuals or Entities that are not Reportable Persons (e.g. because they are Financial Institutions), except a Passive NFE with Controlling Persons who are Reportable Persons.

53.   As a practical matter, an Investment Entity all the interests in which are held by or through non-Reportable Persons would generally not have any reporting obligations, irrespective of whether it qualifies as an Exempt Collective Investment Vehicle under subparagraph B(9). However, such qualification may be relevant to other obligations imposed on the Investment Entity, such as filing a nil return in the absence of Reportable Accounts (if provided under domestic law).

54.   A rule to be used where a jurisdiction has previously allowed collective investment vehicles to issue bearer shares, is further provided by subparagraph B(9). An Investment Entity that is regulated as a collective investment vehicle does not fail to qualify as an Exempt Collective Investment Vehicle, solely because the collective investment vehicle has issued physical shares in bearer form, provided that:

a) the collective investment vehicle has not issued, and does not issue, any physical shares in bearer form after [xx/xx/xxxx];

b) the collective investment vehicle retires all such shares upon surrender;

c) the collective investment vehicle performs the due diligence procedures set forth in Sections II through VII and reports any information required to be reported with respect to any such shares when such shares are presented for redemption or other payment; and

d) the collective investment vehicle has in place policies and procedures to ensure that such shares are redeemed or immobilised as soon as possible and in any event prior to [xx/xx/xxxx].

Subparagraph B(1)(e) – Trustee-Documented Trust

55.   A trust that is a Financial Institution (e.g. because it is an Investment Entity) is a Non-Reporting Financial Institution, according to subparagraph B(1)(e), to the extent that the trustee of the trust is a Reporting Financial Institution and reports all information required to be reported pursuant to Section I with respect to all Reportable Accounts of the trust.

56.   This category of Non-Reporting Financial Institution reaches a similar result as that under paragraph D of Section II, according to which Reporting Financial Institutions may be allowed to rely on service providers to fulfil their reporting and due diligence obligations. The only difference between that paragraph and this category is that the reporting and due diligence obligations fulfilled by service providers remain the responsibility of the Reporting Financial Institution, while the responsibility of those fulfilled by the trustee of a Trustee-Documented Trust is transferred by the trust to its trustee. This category does not modify, however, the time and manner of the reporting and due diligence obligations which remain the same as if they still were the responsibility of the trust. For example, the trustee must not report the information with respect to a Reportable Account of the Trustee-Documented Trust as if it were a Reportable Account of the trustee. The trustee must report such information as the Trustee-Documented Trust would have reported (e.g. to the same jurisdiction) and identify the Trustee-Documented Trust with respect to which it fulfils the reporting and due diligence obligations. This category of Non-Reporting Financial Institution may also apply to a legal arrangement that is equivalent or similar to a trust, such as a *fideicomiso.*

Paragraph C – Financial Account

Subparagraph C(1) – In general

57.   Subparagraph C(1) defines the term "Financial Account" as an account maintained by a Financial Institution and further clarifies that this term includes:

- Depository Accounts;

- Custodial Accounts;

- Equity and debt interest in certain Investment Entities;

- Cash Value Insurance Contracts; and

- Annuity Contracts.

58.   The term "Financial Account", however, does not include any account that is an Excluded Account and is, thus, not subject to the due diligence procedures that apply for purposes of identifying Reportable Accounts among Financial Accounts (such as obtaining a self-certification). In addition, the term "Financial Account" does not include certain Annuity Contracts described in subparagraph C(1)(c): a noninvestment-linked, non-transferable, immediate life annuity that is issued to an individual and monetises a pension or disability benefit provided under an account that is an Excluded Account. Pension or disability benefits include retirement or death benefits, respectively.

59.   A "noninvestment-linked, non-transferable, immediate life annuity" is a non-transferable Annuity Contract that *(i)* is not an investment-linked annuity contract; *(ii)* is an immediate annuity; and *(iii)* is a life annuity contract. The term "investment-linked annuity contract" means an Annuity Contract under which benefits or premiums are adjusted to reflect the investment return or market value of assets associated with the contract. The term "immediate annuity" means an Annuity Contract that *(i)* is purchased with a single premium or annuity consideration; and *(ii)* no later than one year from the purchase date of the contract commences to pay annually or more frequently substantially equal periodic payments. The term "life annuity contract" means an Annuity Contract that provides for payments over the life or lives of one or more individuals.

60.   According to subparagraph C(1)(a), any equity or debt interest in an Investment Entity is considered a Financial Account. However, equity or debt interests in an Entity that is an Investment Entity solely because it is an investment advisor, or an investment manager, are not Financial Accounts. Thus, equity or debt interests that would generally be considered Financial Accounts include equity or debt interests in an Investment Entity *(i)* that is a professionally managed investment entity, or *(ii)* that functions or holds itself

out as a collective investment vehicle, mutual fund, exchange traded fund, private equity fund, hedge fund, venture capital fund, leveraged buyout fund, or any similar investment vehicle established with an investment strategy of investing, reinvesting, or trading in Financial Assets.

61.   According to subparagraph C(1)(b), an equity or debt interest in a Financial Institution other than those described in subparagraph C(1)(a) is considered a Financial Account only if the class of interests was established with a purpose of avoiding reporting in accordance with Section I. Thus, equity or debt interests in a Custodial Institution, Depository Institution, Investment Entity other than an investment advisor or an investment manager described in subparagraph C(1)(a), or Specified Insurance Company, that were established with a purpose of avoiding reporting will be Financial Accounts.

62.   In general, an account would be considered to be maintained by a Financial Institution as follows:

- in the case of a Custodial Account, by the Financial Institution that holds custody over the assets in the account (including a Financial Institution that holds assets in street name for an Account Holder in such institution).

- in case of a Depository Account, by the Financial Institution that is obligated to make payments with respect to the account (excluding an agent of a Financial Institution regardless of whether such agent is a Financial Institution).

- in the case of any equity or debt interest in a Financial Institution that constitutes a Financial Account, by such Financial Institution.

- in the case of a Cash Value Insurance Contract or an Annuity Contract, by the Financial Institution that is obligated to make payments with respect to the contract.

63.   However, jurisdictions have diverse legal, administrative and operational frameworks and different financial systems, and the meaning of "maintaining an account" may vary among jurisdictions depending on how a particular financial industry is structured. In some cases, a Reporting Financial Institution may not possess all the information to be reported with respect to an account and domestic guidance may be needed in such regard. In adopting such guidance, care should be taken to address any inconsistencies that may arise in a cross-border context, in particular with respect to jurisdictions that are not Participating Jurisdictions or to Financial Institutions that are not Participating Jurisdiction Financial Institutions, so that the guidance does not frustrate the purposes of the Common Reporting Standard (see paragraph 5 of the Commentary on Section IX).

64.   For example, in some Participating Jurisdictions securities may be held in owner-registered accounts that are maintained by a central securities depository and operated by other Financial Institutions. In principle, the central securities depository would be treated as the Reporting Financial Institution with respect to the accounts and, thus, responsible for fulfilling all due diligence and reporting obligations. However, since the client relationships are managed and the due diligence procedures are applied by the other Financial Institutions in their capacity of account operators, the central securities depository may not be in a position to comply with such obligations. Participating Jurisdictions may address such a case, for example, by treating the relevant Custodial Accounts as held by such other Financial Institutions, and such other Financial Institutions as responsible for any reporting required with respect to such Custodial Accounts. However, where the relevant Custodial Accounts are treated as held by such other Financial Institutions, in accordance with paragraph D of Section II, a central securities depository may report on behalf of such other Financial Institutions.

65.   A similar case may occur in some Participating Jurisdictions where trades of equity interests in an exchange traded fund are effected, and the due diligence procedures are applied, by brokers, but the end investors are directly registered in the fund's interest register. In principle, the fund would be treated as the Reporting Financial Institution with respect to the equity interests; however, it would not have the information to comply with its reporting obligations. Participating Jurisdictions may address such a case, for example, by requiring the brokers to provide all the necessary information to the fund, so that it may fulfil its reporting obligations.

Subparagraph C(2) – Depository Account

66.   The term "Depository Account", as defined in subparagraph C(2), includes any commercial, checking, savings, time, or thrift account, or an account that is evidenced by a certificate of deposit, thrift certificate, investment certificate, certificate of indebtedness, or other similar instrument maintained by a Financial Institution in the ordinary course of a banking or similar business. A Depository Account also includes an amount held by an insurance company pursuant to a guaranteed investment contract or similar agreement to pay or credit interest thereon.

67.   An account that is evidenced by a passbook would generally be considered a Depository Account. As mentioned in paragraph 25 above, negotiable debt instruments that are traded on a regulated market or over-the-counter market and distributed and held through Financial Institutions would not generally be considered Depository Accounts, but Financial Assets.

Subparagraph C(3) – Custodial Account

68.   Subparagraph C(3) defines the term "Custodial Account" as an account (other than an Insurance Contract or Annuity Contract) for the benefit of another person that holds one or more Financial Assets.

Subparagraph C(4) – Equity Interest

69.   The definition of the term "Equity Interest" specifically addresses interests in partnerships and trusts. In the case of a partnership that is a Financial Institution, the term "Equity Interest" means a capital or profits interest in the partnership. In the case of a trust that is a Financial Institution, an "Equity Interest" is considered to be held by any person treated as a settlor or beneficiary of all or a portion of the trust, or any other natural person exercising ultimate effective control over the trust. The same as for a trust that is a Financial Institution is applicable for a legal arrangement that is equivalent or similar to a trust, or foundation that is a Financial Institution.

70.   Under subparagraph C(4), a Reportable Person will be treated as being a beneficiary of a trust if such Reportable Person has the right to receive, directly or indirectly (for example, through a nominee), a mandatory distribution or may receive, directly or indirectly, a discretionary distribution from the trust. For these purposes, a beneficiary who may receive a discretionary distribution from the trust only will be treated as a beneficiary of a trust if such person receives a distribution in the calendar year or other appropriate reporting period (i.e. either the distribution has been paid or made payable). The same is applicable with respect to the treatment of a Reportable Person as a beneficiary of a legal arrangement that is equivalent or similar to a trust, or foundation.

71.   Where Equity Interests are held through a Custodial Institution, the Custodial Institution is responsible for reporting, not the Investment Entity. The following example illustrates how such reporting must be done: Reportable Person A holds shares in investment fund L. A holds the shares in custody with custodian Y. Investment fund L is an Investment Entity and, from its perspective, its shares are Financial Accounts (i.e. Equity Interests in an Investment Entity). L must treat custodian Y as its Account Holder. As Y is a Financial Institution (i.e. a Custodial Institution) and Financial Institutions are not Reportable Persons, such shares are not object of reporting by investment fund L. For custodian Y, the shares held for A are Financial Assets held in a Custodial Account. As a Custodial Institution, Y is responsible for reporting the shares it is holding on behalf of A.

Subparagraphs C(5) through (8) – Insurance and Annuity Contracts

72.   Subparagraphs C(5) through (8) contain the various definitions related to insurance products: "Insurance Contract", "Annuity Contract", "Cash Value Insurance Contract" and "Cash Value". While the terms "Insurance Contract" and "Cash Value" are needed to define the scope of the term "Cash Value Insurance Contract", only a contract that is a Cash Value Insurance Contract or an Annuity Contact can be a Financial Account.

73.   The term "Annuity Contract", as defined in subparagraph C(6), means a contract under which the issuer agrees to make payments for a period of time determined in whole or in part by reference to the life expectancy of one or more individuals. The term also includes a contract that is considered to be an Annuity Contract in accordance with the law, regulation, or practice of the jurisdiction in which the contract was issued, and under which the issuer agrees to make payments for a term of years.

74.   According to subparagraph C(5), the term "Insurance Contract" means a contract (other than an Annuity Contract) under which the issuer agrees to pay an amount upon the occurrence of a specified contingency involving mortality, morbidity, accident, liability, or property risk. The term "Cash Value Insurance Contract", as further defined in subparagraph C(7), means an Insurance Contract (other than an indemnity reinsurance contract between two insurance companies) that has a Cash Value.

75.   Subparagraph C(8) defines the term "Cash Value" as the greater of *(i)* the amount that the policyholder is entitled to receive upon surrender or termination of the contract (determined without reduction for any surrender charge or policy loan), and *(ii)* the amount the policyholder can borrow under or with regard to (for example, pledging as collateral) the contract. However, the term "Cash Value" does not include an amount payable under an Insurance Contract:

a) solely by reason of the death of an individual insured under a life insurance contract;

b) as a personal injury or sickness benefit or other benefit providing indemnification of an economic loss incurred upon the occurrence of the event insured against;

c) as a refund of a previously paid premium (less cost of insurance charges whether or not actually imposed) under an Insurance Contract (other than an investment-linked life insurance or annuity contract) due to cancellation or termination of the contract, decrease in risk exposure during the effective period of the contract, or arising from the correction of a posting or similar error with regard to the premium for the contract;

d) as a policyholder dividend (other than a termination dividend) provided that the dividend relates to an Insurance Contract under which the only benefits payable are described in subparagraph C(8)(b); or

e) as a return of an advance premium or premium deposit for an Insurance Contract for which the premium is payable at least annually if the amount of the advance premium or premium deposit does not exceed the next annual premium that will be payable under the contract.

76.   Subparagraph C(8)(b) excludes from the term "Cash Value" an amount payable under an Insurance Contract as a personal injury or sickness benefit or other benefit providing indemnification of an economic loss incurred upon the occurrence of the event insured against. Such "other benefit" does not include any benefit payable under an investment-linked insurance contract. An "investment-linked insurance contract" means an insurance contract under which benefits, premiums, or the period of coverage, are adjusted to reflect the investment return or market value of assets associated with the contract.

77.   The exclusions described in subparagraphs C(8)(a) and (c) are amounts payable in connection with an investment-linked life insurance contract and, in subparagraph C(8)(c), also an investment-linked life annuity contract. An "investment-linked life insurance contract" is an Insurance Contract that *(i)* is an investment-liked insurance contract (see paragraph 76 above); and *(ii)* is a life insurance contract (see paragraph 78 below). An "investment-linked life annuity contract" is an Annuity Contract that *(i)* is an investment-linked annuity contract; and *(ii)* is a life annuity contract (see paragraph 59 above).

78.   A "life insurance contract" is an Insurance Contract under which the issuer, in exchange for consideration, agrees to pay an amount upon the death of one or more individuals. That a contract provides one or more payments (for example, for endowment benefits or disability benefits) in addition to a death benefit does not cause the contract to be other than a life insurance contract.

79.   A policyholder dividend that satisfies all the requirements described in subparagraph C(8)(d) is excluded from the term "Cash Value". A "policyholder dividend" is any dividend or similar distribution to policyholders in their capacity as such, including:

a) an amount paid or credited (including as an increase in benefits) if the amount is not fixed in the contract but rather depends on the experience of the insurance company or the discretion of management;

b) a reduction in the premium that, but for the reduction, would have been required to be paid; and

c) an experience rated refund or credit based solely upon the claims experience of the contract or group involved.

A policyholder dividend cannot exceed the premiums previously paid for the contract, less the sum of the cost of insurance and expense changes (whether or not actually imposed) during the contract's existence and the aggregate amount of any prior dividends paid or credited with regard to the contract.

A policyholder dividend does not include any amount that is in the nature of interest that is paid or credited to a contract holder to the extent that such amount exceeds the minimum rate of interest required to be credited with respect to contract values under local law.

80.   Micro insurance contracts that do not have a Cash Value (including a Cash Value equal to zero) will not be considered Cash Value Insurance Contracts. Insurance wrapper products, such as private placement life insurance contracts, would generally be considered Cash Value Insurance Contracts. An "insurance wrapper product" includes an insurance contract the assets of which are *(i)* held in an account maintained by a financial institution, and *(ii)* managed in accordance with a personalised investment strategy or under the control or influence of the policyholder, owner or beneficiary of the contract.

Subparagraphs C(9) through (16) – Preexisting and New, Individual and Entity Accounts

81.   Subparagraphs C(9) through (16) contain the various categories of Financial Accounts classified by reference to date of opening, Account Holder and balance or value: "Preexisting Account", "New Account", "Preexisting Individual Account", "New Individual Account", "Preexisting Entity Account", "Lower Value Account", "High Value Account" and "New Entity Account".

82.   First, a Financial Account is classified depending on the date of opening. Thus, a Financial Account can be either a "Preexisting Account" or a "New Account". Subparagraphs C(9) and (10) define those terms as a Financial Account maintained by a Reporting Financial Institution as of [xx/xx/xxxx], and opened on or after [xx/xx/xxxx], respectively. However, when implementing the Common Reporting Standard, jurisdictions are free to modify subparagraph C(9) in order to also include certain new accounts of preexisting customers. In such a case, subparagraph C(9) should be replaced by the following:

9. The term "Preexisting Account" means:

a) a Financial Account maintained by a Reporting Financial Institution as of [xx/xx/xxxx].

b) any Financial Account of an Account Holder, regardless of the date such Financial Account was opened, if:

i) the Account Holder also holds with the Reporting Financial Institution (or with a Related Entity within the same jurisdiction as the Reporting Financial Institution) a Financial Account that is a Preexisting Account under subparagraph C(9)(a);

ii) the Reporting Financial Institution (and, as applicable, the Related Entity within the same jurisdiction as the Reporting Financial Institution) treats both of the aforementioned Financial Accounts, and any other Financial Accounts of the Account Holder that are treated as Preexisting Accounts under this subparagraph C(9)(b), as a single Financial Account for purposes of satisfying the standards of knowledge requirements set forth in paragraph A of Section VII, and for purposes of determining the balance or value of any of the Financial Accounts when applying any of the account thresholds;

iii) with respect to a Financial Account that is subject to AML/KYC Procedures, the Reporting Financial Institution is permitted to satisfy such AML/KYC Procedures for the Financial Account by relying upon the AML/KYC Procedures performed for the Preexisting Account described in subparagraph C(9)(a); and

iv) the opening of the Financial Account does not require the provision of new, additional or amended customer information by the Account Holder other than for purposes of the Common Reporting Standard.

Examples where new, additional or amended customer information is likely to be required would be where an Account Holder that currently holds only a Depository Account opens a Custodial Account (as the Account Holder would often be required to provide information with respect to its risk profile), or an Account Holder concludes a new Insurance Contract. The sole acceptance of terms and conditions, or the sole authorisation of a credit rating, with respect to a Financial Account will not constitute customer information.

With respect to subparagraph C(9)(b)(ii), for example, if a Reporting Financial Institution has reason to know that the status assigned to the Account Holder of one of the Financial Accounts is inaccurate, then it has reason to know that the status assigned for all other Financial Accounts of the Account Holder is inaccurate. Similarly, to the extent that an account balance or value is relevant for purposes of applying any account threshold to one or more of the Financial Accounts, the Reporting Financial Institution must aggregate the balance or value of all such Financial Accounts.

A fund will probably not qualify as a Related Entity of another fund under subparagraph E(4) and, as a consequence, the alternative definition of the term "Preexisting Account" would not be applicable to new equity or debt interests held by end investors that are directly registered in the fund's interest register. Jurisdictions wishing to address with such situation must also replace subparagraph E(4) by the following:

4. An Entity is a "Related Entity" of another Entity if (a) *either Entity controls the other Entity;* (b) *the two Entities are under common control; or* (c) *the two Entities are Investment Entities described in subparagraph A(6)(b), are under common management, and such management fulfils the due diligence obligations of such Investment Entities. For this purpose control includes direct or indirect ownership of more than 50% of the vote and value in an Entity.*

83.   A Preexisting Account and a New Account are classified by reference to the type of Account Holder. Thus, a Preexisting Account can be either a "Preexisting Individual Account" or a "Preexisting Entity Account", and a New Account can be either a "New Individual Account" or a "New Entity Account". Subparagraphs C(11) through (13) and (16) define those terms accordingly.

84.   Finally, a Preexisting Individual Account is classified on the basis of its balance or value exceeding USD 1 000 000. Thus, a Preexisting Individual Account can be either a "Lower Value Account" or a "High Value Account". Subparagraphs C(14) and (15) define those terms as follows:

- the term "Lower Value Account" means a Preexisting Individual Account with a balance or value as of 31 December [xxxx] that does not exceed USD 1 000 000.

- the term "High Value Account" means a Preexisting Individual Account with a balance or value that exceeds USD 1 000 000 as of 31 December [xxxx] or 31 December of any subsequent year.

Once an account becomes a High Value Account, it maintains such status until the date of closure and, therefore, can no longer be considered a Lower Value Account.

85.   While the selection of the dates to classify a Financial Account as either a "Preexisting Account" or a "New Account" is a decision of the jurisdiction implementing the Common Reporting Standard, it is expected that the date for the term "New Account" is the day following the date selected for the term "Preexisting Account" (see Annex 5 – Wider Approach to the Common Reporting Standard). With respect to the selection of the year to classify a Financial Account as either a "Lower Value Account" or a "High Value Account", it is expected that the same year is selected for both terms.

Subparagraph C(17) – Excluded Account

86.   Subparagraph C(17) contains the various categories of Excluded Accounts (i.e. accounts that are not Financial Accounts and are therefore excluded from reporting), which are:

a)   retirement and pension accounts;

b)   non-retirement tax-favoured accounts;

c)   term life insurance contracts;

d)   estate accounts;

e)   escrow accounts;

f)   Depository Accounts due to not-returned overpayments; and

g)   low-risk excluded accounts.

These categories would typically be consistent with the types of accounts excluded from the definition of "Financial Accounts" in the intergovernmental agreement concluded between such jurisdiction and the United States to improve international tax compliance including with respect to FATCA, provided that such types of accounts satisfy all the relevant requirements listed in subparagraph C(17).

87.   For purposes of determining whether an account satisfies all the requirements of a particular category of Excluded Account, a Reporting Financial Institution may rely on information in its possession (including information collected pursuant to AML/KYC Procedures) or that is publicly available, based on which it can reasonably determine that the account is an Excluded Account (see paragraph 12 of the Commentary on Section V). As a practical matter, a Reporting Financial Institution that only maintains accounts that are Excluded Accounts does not have any reporting obligations. However, it may have other obligations imposed on the Reporting Financial Institution, such as filing a nil return in the absence of Reportable Accounts (if provided under domestic law).

Retirement and pension accounts

88.   A retirement or pension account can be an Excluded Account, provided that it satisfies all the requirements listed in subparagraph C(17)(a). Those requirements must be satisfied under the laws of the jurisdiction where the account is maintained. In summary, it is required that:

a)   the account is subject to regulation;

b)   the account is tax-favoured;

c) information reporting is required to the tax authorities with respect to the account;

d) withdrawals are conditioned on reaching a specified retirement age, disability, or death, or penalties apply to withdrawals made before such specified events; and

e) either *(i)* annual contributions are limited to USD 50 000 or less, or *(ii)* there is a maximum lifetime contribution limit to the account of USD 1 000 000 or less, excluding rollovers.

89.   Information reporting required in subparagraph C(17)(a)(iii) may vary among jurisdictions. While one jurisdiction could require annual information with respect to the account, another jurisdiction could require monthly information with respect to contributions to the account and associated tax relief, and annual information with respect to Account Holders and total contributions to the account. Thus, provided there is information reporting required to the relevant tax authorities in the jurisdiction where the account is maintained, the time and manner of such reporting is not determinative of whether the account satisfies the requirement under subparagraph C(17)(a)(iii).

Non-retirement tax-favoured accounts

90.   A non-retirement account can be an Excluded Account, provided that it satisfies all the requirements listed in subparagraph C(17)(b). Those requirements must be satisfied under the laws of the jurisdiction where the account is maintained. In summary, it is required that:

a) the account is subject to regulation, and in the case of an investment vehicle is regularly traded on an established securities market (see paragraph 112 below);

b) the account is tax-favoured;

c) withdrawals are conditioned on meeting specified criteria, or penalties apply to withdrawals made before such criteria are met; and

d) annual contributions are limited to USD 50 000 or less, excluding rollovers.

Term life insurance contracts

91.   A life insurance contract with a coverage period that will end before the insured individual attains age 90, can be an Excluded Account, provided that the contract satisfies all the requirements listed in subparagraph C(17)(c). As mentioned in paragraph 77 above, a "life insurance contract" is an Insurance Contract under which the issuer, in exchange for consideration, agrees to pay an amount upon the death of one or more individuals.

Estate accounts

92. According to subparagraph C(17)(d), an account that is held solely by an estate can be an Excluded Account if the documentation for such account includes a copy of the deceased's will or death certificate. For this purpose, the Reporting Financial Institution must treat the account as having the same status that it had prior to the death of the Account Holder until the date it obtains such copy. In determining what is meant by "estate", reference must be made to each jurisdiction's particular rules on the transfer or inheritance of rights and obligations in the event of death (e.g. the rules on universal succession).

Escrow accounts

93. Subparagraph C(17)(e) generally refers to accounts where money is held by a third party on behalf of transacting parties (i.e. escrow accounts). These accounts can be Excluded Accounts where they are established in connection with any of the following:

   a) a court order or judgment.

   b) a sale, exchange, or lease of real or personal property, provided that the account satisfies all the requirements listed in subparagraph C(17)(e)(ii).

   c) an obligation of a Financial Institution servicing a loan secured by real property to set aside a portion of a payment solely to facilitate the payment of taxes or insurance related to the real property at a later time.

   d) an obligation of a Financial Institution solely to facilitate the payment of taxes at a later time.

94. An Excluded Account, as described in subparagraph C(17)(e)(ii), must be established in connection with a sale, exchange, or lease of real or personal property. Defining the concept of real or personal property by reference to the laws of the jurisdiction where the account is maintained will help to avoid difficulties of interpretation over the question whether an asset or a right is to be regarded as real property (i.e. immovable property), personal property or neither of them.

Depository Accounts due to not-returned overpayments

95. As mentioned in paragraph 44 above, a Reporting Financial Institution that does not satisfy the requirements to be a Qualified Credit Card Issuer, but accepts deposits when a customer makes a payment in excess of a balance due with respect to a credit card or other revolving credit facility,

may still not report a Depository Account that qualifies as an Excluded Account under subparagraph C(17)(f). This subparagraph requires that:

   a) the account exists solely because a customer makes a payment in excess of a balance due with respect to a credit card or other revolving credit facility and the overpayment is not immediately returned to the customer; and

   b) beginning on or before [xx/xx/xxxx], the Financial Institution implements policies and procedures either to prevent a customer from making an overpayment in excess of USD 50 000, or to ensure that any customer overpayment in excess of USD 50 000 (and of the balance due with respect to the card or facility) is refunded to the customer within 60 calendar days, in each case applying the rules set forth in paragraph C of Section VII for currency translation. For this purpose, a customer overpayment does not refer to credit balances to the extent of disputed charges but does include credit balances resulting from merchandise returns.

96.   While the selection of the date referred to in subparagraph C(17)(f)(ii) is a decision of the jurisdiction implementing the Common Reporting Standard, it is expected that the date elected for that purpose is the same date as the date selected for the term "New Account". For this purpose, a Financial Institution that is formed or organised after the selected date must satisfy the requirement described in subparagraph C(17)(f)(ii) within six months after the date such Financial Institution was formed or organised.

Low-risk Excluded Accounts

97.   An account can also be an Excluded Account, according to subparagraph C(17)(g), provided that:

   a) the account presents a low risk of being used to evade tax;

   b) the account has substantially similar characteristics to any of the accounts described in subparagraphs C(17)(a) through (f);

   c) the account is defined in domestic law as an Excluded Account; and

   d) the status of the account as an Excluded Account does not frustrate the purposes of the Common Reporting Standard.

98.   This "open" category of Excluded Accounts is intended to accommodate jurisdiction-specific types of accounts satisfy the requirements listed in subparagraph C(17)(g), and avoids the need to negotiate classes of Excluded Accounts when concluding an agreement on the automatic exchange of financial account information.

99.   The first requirement described in subparagraph C(17)(g) is that the account presents a low risk of being used to evade tax. Factors that may be considered to determine such a risk include:

a)   low-risk factors:

    (1)   the account is subject to regulation.

    (2)   the account is tax-favoured.

    (3)   information reporting to the tax authorities is required with respect to the account.

    (4)   contributions or the associated tax relief are limited.

    (5)   the type of account provides appropriately defined and limited services to certain types of customers, so as to increase access for financial inclusion purposes.

b)   high-risk factors:

    (1)   the type of account is not subject to AML/KYC Procedures.

    (2)   the type of account is promoted as a tax minimisation vehicle.

100.   The second requirement described in subparagraph C(17)(g) is that the account has substantially similar characteristics to any of the accounts described in subparagraphs C(17)(a) through (f). This requirement cannot be used solely to eliminate a specific element of a description. Each jurisdiction may evaluate the application of this requirement to a type of account that does not satisfy all the requirements of a particular description listed in subparagraphs C(17)(a) through (f). As part of such evaluation, a jurisdiction must identify which requirements are satisfied and which are not satisfied, and with respect to the requirements that are not satisfied, must identify the existence of a substitute requirement that provides equivalent assurance that the relevant type of account presents a low-risk of tax evasion.

101.   The third requirement described in subparagraph C(17)(g) is that the account is defined in domestic law as an Excluded Account. This requirement is satisfied where a jurisdiction defines a specific type of account as an Excluded Account, and that definition is contained in domestic law. For such purpose, a jurisdiction would typically be consistent with the types of accounts excluded from the definition of "Financial Accounts" in the intergovernmental agreement concluded between such jurisdiction and the United States to improve international tax compliance including with respect to FATCA (e.g. savings accounts that are not already Excluded Accounts), provided that such types of accounts satisfy all the requirements listed in subparagraph C(17)(g). It is expected that each jurisdiction would have only one single list of domestically-defined Excluded Accounts (as opposed to

different lists for different Participating Jurisdictions) and that it would make such a list publicly available.

102.   The fourth requirement described in subparagraph C(17)(g) is that the status of the account as an Excluded Account does not frustrate the purposes of the Common Reporting Standard. It is expected that this requirement will be monitored, inter alia, through the following:

  a)   the administrative procedures that a jurisdiction must have in place to ensure that the accounts defined in domestic law as Excluded Accounts continue to have a low risk of being used to evade tax (see subparagraph A(4) of Section IX);

  b)   the potential suspension of a Competent Authority Agreement where the other Competent Authority has defined the status of accounts as Excluded Accounts in a manner that frustrates the purposes of the Common Reporting Standard (see paragraph 2 of Section 7 of the Model Competent Authority Agreement); and

  c)   the mechanism to review the implementation of the Common Reporting Standard mandated to the Global Forum on Transparency and Exchange of Information for Tax Purposes by the G20 (see paragraph 51 of the G20 Leaders' Declaration, Saint Petersburg Summit, 5-6 September 2013).[12]

103.   The following examples illustrate the application of subparagraph C(17)(g):

  •   Example 1 (Unlimited Annuity Contract): A type of Annuity Contract satisfies all the requirements listed in subparagraph C(17)(a), apart from the one contained in subparagraph C(17)(a)(v) (i.e. contributions are not limited). However, the applicable penalties apply to all withdrawals made before reaching a specified retirement age and include taxing the contributions that were previously tax-favoured with a high flat-rate surtax (e.g. 60%). Because there is a substitute requirement that provides equivalent assurance that the account presents a low-risk of tax evasion, this type of account could be defined in domestic law as an Excluded Account.

  •   Example 2 (Unlimited savings account): A type of savings account satisfies all the requirements listed in subparagraph C(17)(b), apart from the one contained in subparagraph C(17)(b)(iv) (i.e. contributions are not limited). However, the tax relief associated to the contributions is limited by reference to an indexed amount. Because there is a substitute requirement that provides equivalent assurance that the account presents a low-risk of tax evasion, this type of account could be defined in domestic law as an Excluded Account.

12.   Available on https://www.g20.org/.

- Example 3 (Micro Cash Value Insurance Contract): A type of Cash Value Insurance Contract only satisfies the requirement described in subparagraph C(17)(b)(i) (i.e. it is regulated as a savings vehicle for purposes other than for retirement). However, under the micro insurance regulations of the Participating Jurisdiction, *(i)* it is targeted to individuals (or groups of individuals) that are below the poverty line (e.g. living on less than USD 1.25 per person per day in 2005 US dollars), and *(ii)* the total gross amount payable under the contract cannot exceed USD 7 000. Because there is an overall, substitute requirement that provides equivalent assurance that the account presents a low-risk of tax evasion, this type of account could be defined in domestic law as an Excluded Account.

- Example 4 (Social welfare account): A type of savings account only satisfies the requirement described in subparagraph C(17)(b)*(i)* (i.e. it is regulated as a savings vehicle for purposes other than for retirement). However, under the social welfare regulations of the Participating Jurisdiction, it can solely be held by an individual that *(i)* is below the poverty line (e.g. living on less than USD 1.25 per person per day in 2005 US dollars) or otherwise low-income, and *(ii)* is participating in a social welfare programme. Because there is an overall, substitute requirement that provides equivalent assurance that the account presents a low-risk of tax evasion, this type of account could be defined in domestic law as an Excluded Account.

- Example 5 (Financial inclusion account): A type of Depository Account only satisfies the requirements described in subparagraphs C(17)(b)(i) and (iv) (i.e. it is regulated as a savings vehicle for purposes other than for retirement, and annual contributions are limited). However, under the financial regulations of the Participating Jurisdiction, *(i)* it provides defined and limited services to individuals, so as to increase access for financial inclusion purposes; *(ii)* monthly deposits cannot exceed USD 1 250 (excluding deposits by an authorised government body under a social welfare programme); and *(iii)* financial institutions have been allowed to apply simplified AML/KYC Procedures with respect to this type of account, since it has been regarded as having a lower money laundering and terrorist financing risk in accordance with the FATF Recommendations. Because there are overall, substitute requirements that provide equivalent assurance that the account presents a low-risk of tax evasion, this type of account could be defined in domestic law as an Excluded Account.

- Example 6 (Dormant account): A type of Depository Account *(i)* with an annual balance that does not exceed USD 1 000, *(ii)* that is a dormant account (see paragraph 9 of the Commentary on Section III).

Because there are overall, substitute requirements that provide equivalent assurance that the account presents a low-risk of tax evasion, this type of account could be defined in domestic law as an Excluded Account during the dormancy period.

Paragraph D – Reportable Account

104.   Paragraph D contains the definition of the term "Reportable Account" and all the other defined terms that are relevant for determining whether an account is a Reportable Account.

Subparagraph D(1) – Reportable Account

105.   As defined in subparagraph D(1), the term "Reportable Account" means an account held by one or more Reportable Persons or by a Passive NFE with one or more Controlling Persons that is a Reportable Person, provided it has been identified as such pursuant to the due diligence procedures described in Sections II through VII.

Subparagraphs D(2) and (3) – Reportable Person and Reportable Jurisdiction Person

Reportable Jurisdiction Person

106.   As a general rule, an individual or Entity is a "Reportable Jurisdiction Person" if it is resident in a Reportable Jurisdiction under the tax laws of such jurisdiction. As an exception to this rule, an Entity that has no residence for tax purposes (e.g. because it is treated as fiscally transparent) is considered to be resident in the jurisdiction in which its place of effective management is situated.

107.   Domestic laws differ in the treatment of partnerships (including limited liability partnerships). Some jurisdictions treat partnerships as taxable units (sometimes even as companies) whereas other jurisdictions adopt what may be referred to as the fiscally transparent approach, under which the partnership is disregarded for tax purposes. Where a partnership is treated as a company or taxed in the same way, it would generally be considered to be a resident of the Reportable Jurisdiction that taxes the partnership. Where, however, a partnership is treated as fiscally transparent in a Reportable Jurisdiction, the partnership is not "liable to tax" in that jurisdiction, and so cannot be a resident thereof.

108.   An Entity such as a partnership, limited liability partnership or similar legal arrangement that has no residence for tax purposes, according to

subparagraph D(3), shall be treated as resident in the jurisdiction in which its place of effective management is situated. For these purposes, a legal person or a legal arrangement is considered "similar" to a partnership and a limited liability partnership where it is not treated as a taxable unit in a Reportable Jurisdiction under the tax laws of such jurisdiction. However, in order to avoid duplicate reporting (given the wide scope of the term "Controlling Persons" in the case of trusts), a trust that is a Passive NFE may not be considered a similar legal arrangement.

109.   The "place of effective management" is the place where key management and commercial decisions that are necessary for the conduct of the Entity's business as a whole are in substance made. All relevant facts and circumstances must be examined to determine the place of effective management. An Entity may have more than one place of management, but it can have only one place of effective management at any one time.

110.   The term "Reportable Jurisdiction Person" also includes an estate of a decedent that was a resident of a Reportable Jurisdiction. As mentioned in paragraph 92 above, in determining what is meant by "estate", reference must be made to each jurisdiction's particular rules on the transfer or inheritance of rights and obligations in the event of death (e.g. the rules on universal succession).

Reportable Person

111.   Subparagraph D(2) defines the term "Reportable Person" as a Reportable Jurisdiction Person other than:

   a)   a corporation the stock of which is regularly traded on one or more established securities markets;

   b)   any corporation that is a Related Entity of a corporation described previously;

   c)   a Governmental Entity;

   d)   an International Organisation;

   e)   a Central Bank; or

   f)   a Financial Institution.

112.   Whether a corporation that is Reportable Jurisdiction Person is a Reportable Person, as described in subparagraph D(2)(i), can depend on the stock of that corporation being regularly traded on one or more established securities markets. Stock is "regularly traded" if there is a meaningful volume of trading with respect to the stock on an on-going basis, and an "established securities market" means an exchange that is officially recognised and

supervised by a governmental authority in which the market is located and that has a meaningful annual value of shares traded on the exchange.

113.   With respect to each class of stock of the corporation, there is a "meaningful volume of trading on an on-going basis" if *(i)* trades in each such class are effected, other than in de minimis quantities, on one or more established securities markets on at least 60 business days during the prior calendar year; and *(ii)* the aggregate number of shares in each such class that are traded on such market or markets during the prior year are at least 10% of the average number of shares outstanding in that class during the prior calendar year.

114.   A class of stock would generally be treated as meeting the "regularly traded" requirement for a calendar year if the stock is traded during such year on an established securities market and is regularly quoted by dealers making a market in the stock. A dealer makes a market in a stock only if the dealer regularly and actively offers to, and in fact does, purchase the stock from, and sell the stock to, customers who are not related persons with respect to the dealer in the ordinary course of a business.

115.   An exchange has a "meaningful annual value of shares traded on the exchange" if it has an annual value of shares traded on the exchange (or a predecessor exchange) exceeding USD 1 000 000 000 during each of the three calendar years immediately preceding the calendar year in which the determination is being made. If an exchange has more than one tier of market level on which stock may be separately listed or traded, each such tier must be treated as a separate exchange.

116.   Pursuant to subparagraph D(2)(vi), Financial Institutions are excluded from the term "Reportable Person" as they will do their own reporting or are otherwise considered to present a low risk of being used to evade tax. They are thus excluded from reporting, except for Investment Entities described in subparagraph A(6)(b) that are not Participating Jurisdiction Financial Institutions, which are treated as Passive NFEs and thus reported.

Subparagraphs D(4) and (5) – Reportable and Participating Jurisdictions

117.   Subparagraphs D(4) and (5) define the terms "Reportable Jurisdiction" and "Participating Jurisdiction" as follows:

- the term "Reportable Jurisdiction" means a jurisdiction *(i)* with which an agreement is in place pursuant to which there is an obligation in place to provide the information specified in Section I, and *(ii)* which is identified in a published list.

- the term "Participating Jurisdiction" means a jurisdiction *(i)* with which an agreement is in place pursuant to which it will provide the information specified in Section I, and *(ii)* which is identified in a published list.

118.   Those terms are relevant for the scope of financial institutions required to report and account holders subject to reporting, as well as for the requirement to look-through non-participating professionally managed investment entities. Whilst both terms seem similar, there is a significant difference: the term "Participating Jurisdiction" qualifies a jurisdiction with which an agreement on the automatic exchange of financial account information (i.e. the information specified in Section I) is in place, whilst the term "Reportable Jurisdiction" qualifies a Participating Jurisdiction with which an obligation to provide financial account information is in place.

119.   Subparagraphs D(4) and (5) require that the jurisdiction is identified in a published list as a Reportable Jurisdiction and a Participating Jurisdiction, respectively. Each jurisdiction must make such a list publicly available, and update it as appropriate (e.g. every time the jurisdiction signs an agreement on the automatic exchange of financial account information, or such an agreement enters into force).

120.   The following examples illustrate the application of subparagraphs D(4) and (5):

- Example 1 (Reciprocal exchange): Jurisdiction A and Jurisdiction B have a reciprocal agreement on the automatic exchange of financial account information in place. Pursuant to that agreement, both Jurisdictions are obliged to exchange the information specified in Section I. Because Jurisdiction A has an agreement with Jurisdiction B pursuant to which there is an obligation in place to provide the information specified in Section I, from the perspective of Jurisdiction A, Jurisdiction B is both a Participating Jurisdiction and a Reportable Jurisdiction. The same applies from the perspective of Jurisdiction B with respect to Jurisdiction A.

- Example 2 (Nonreciprocal exchange): Jurisdiction X, which does not have an income tax, and Jurisdiction Y have a nonreciprocal agreement on the automatic exchange of financial account information in place. Pursuant to that agreement, only Jurisdiction X is obliged to exchange the information specified in Section I. Because Jurisdiction X has an agreement with Jurisdiction Y pursuant to which there is an obligation in place to provide the information specified in Section I, from the perspective of Jurisdiction X, Jurisdiction Y is both a Participating Jurisdiction and a Reportable Jurisdiction. However, because Jurisdiction Y has an agreement with Jurisdiction X, but it does not have an obligation in place to provide the information specified in Section I pursuant to that agreement, from the perspective of Jurisdiction Y, Jurisdiction X is a Participating Jurisdiction, but not a Reportable Jurisdiction.

Subparagraphs D(6) through (9) – NFE and Controlling Persons

NFE, Passive NFE and Active NFE

121.   Subparagraphs D(6) through (9) define the terms "NFE", "Passive NFE", "Active NFE" and "Controlling Persons", which are relevant for purposes of determining whether an Entity is a Passive NFE with one or more Controlling Persons who are Reportable Persons. When that is the case, as described in subparagraphs D(2) of Section V and A(2) of Section VI, then the account must be treated as a Reportable Account.

122.   The term "NFE" is an acronym for Non-Financial Entity and it means, according to subparagraph D(7), any Entity that is not a Financial Institution. An NFE can be either a Passive NFE or an Active NFE. Subparagraphs D(8) and (9) set forth the meaning of the terms "Passive NFE" and "Active NFE", respectively.

123.   In principle, a "Passive NFE" means an NFE that is not an Active NFE. However, subparagraph D(8) also includes an Investment Entity described in subparagraph A(6)(b) that is not a Participating Jurisdiction Financial Institution. As a result, Reporting Financial Institutions are required to look-through that type of Investment Entity, as illustrated by the following example: Jurisdiction A has a reciprocal agreement on the automatic exchange of financial account information in place with Jurisdiction B, but has no agreement in place with Jurisdiction C. W, a Jurisdiction A Reporting Financial Institution, maintains Financial Accounts for Entities X and Y, both of which are Investment Entities as described in subparagraph A(6)(b). Entity X is resident in Jurisdiction B and Entity Y is resident in Jurisdiction C. From the perspective of W, Entity X is a Participating Jurisdiction Financial Institution and Entity Y is not a Participating Jurisdiction Financial Institution. As a result, W must treat Entity Y is a Passive NFE pursuant to subparagraph D(8).

124.   Any NFE can be an Active NFE, provided that it meets any of the criteria listed in subparagraph D(9). In summary, those criteria refer to:

a)   active NFEs by reason of income and assets;

b)   publicly traded NFEs;

c)   Governmental Entities, International Organisations, Central Banks, or their wholly owned Entities;

d) holding NFEs that are members of a nonfinancial group;

e) start-up NFEs;

f) NFEs that are liquidating or emerging from bankruptcy;

g) treasury centres that are members of a nonfinancial group; or

h) non-profit NFEs.

125. Subparagraph D(9)(a) describes the criterion to qualify for the Active NFE status for "active NFEs by reason of income and assets" as follows: less than 50% of the NFE's gross income for the preceding calendar year or other appropriate reporting period is passive income and less than 50% of the assets held by the NFE during the preceding calendar year or other appropriate reporting period are assets that produce or are held for the production of passive income.

126. In determining what is meant by "passive income", reference must be made to each jurisdiction's particular rules. Passive income would generally be considered to include the portion of gross income that consists of:

a) dividends;

b) interest;

c) income equivalent to interest;

d) rents and royalties, other than rents and royalties derived in the active conduct of a business conducted, at least in part, by employees of the NFE;

e) annuities;

f) the excess of gains over losses from the sale or exchange of Financial Assets that gives rise to the passive income described previously;

g) the excess of gains over losses from transactions (including futures, forwards, options, and similar transactions) in any Financial Assets;

h) the excess of foreign currency gains over foreign currency losses;

i) net income from swaps; or

j) amounts received under Cash Value Insurance Contracts.

Notwithstanding the foregoing, passive income will not include, in the case of a NFE that regularly acts as a dealer in Financial Assets, any income from any transaction entered into in the ordinary course of such dealer's business as such a dealer.

127.	The value of a NFE's assets is determined based on the fair market value or book value of the assets that is reflected on the NFE's balance sheet.

128.	Subparagraph D(9)(b) describes the criterion to qualify for the Active NFE status for "publicly traded NFEs" as follows: the stock of the NFE is regularly traded on an established securities market or the NFE is a Related Entity of an Entity the stock of which is regularly traded on an established securities market. As mentioned in paragraph 112 above, stock is "regularly traded" if there is a meaningful volume of trading with respect to the stock on an on-going basis, and an "established securities market" means an exchange that is officially recognised and supervised by a governmental authority in which the market is located and that has a meaningful annual value of shares traded on the exchange.

129.	Subparagraph D(9)(d) describes the criterion to qualify for the Active NFE status for "holding NFEs that are members of a nonfinancial group" as follows: substantially all of the activities of the NFE consist of holding (in whole or in part) the outstanding stock of, or providing financing and services to, one or more subsidiaries that engage in trades or businesses other than the business of a Financial Institution, except that an Entity does not qualify for this status if the Entity functions (or holds itself out) as an investment fund, such as a private equity fund, venture capital fund, leveraged buyout fund, or any investment vehicle whose purpose is to acquire or fund companies and then hold interests in those companies as capital assets for investment purposes.

130.	With respect to the activities mentioned in subparagraph D(9)(d), "substantially all" means 80% or more. If, however, the NFE's holding or group finance activities constitute less than 80% of its activities but the NFE receives also active income (i.e. income that is not passive income) otherwise, it qualifies for the Active NFE status, provided that the total sum of activities meets the "substantially all test". For purposes of determining whether the activities other than holding and group finance activities of the NFE qualify it as an Active NFE, the test of subparagraph D(9)(a) can be applied to such other activities. For example, if a holding company has holding or finance and service activities to one or more subsidiaries for 60% and also functions for 40% as a distribution centre for the goods produced by the group it belongs to and the income of its distribution centre activities is active according to subparagraph D(9)(a), it is an Active NFE, irrespective of the fact that less than 80% of its activities consist of holding the outstanding stock of, or providing finance and services to, one or more subsidiaries. The term "substantially all" covers also a combination of holding stock of and providing finance and services to one or more subsidiaries. The term "subsidiary" means any entity whose outstanding stock is either directly or indirectly held (in whole or in part) by the NFE.

131.   One of the requirements listed in subparagraph D(9)(h) for "non-profit NFE" to qualify for the Active NFE status is that the applicable laws of the NFE's jurisdiction of residence or the NFE's formation documents do not permit any income or assets of the NFE to be distributed to, or applied for the benefit of, a private person or non-charitable Entity other than pursuant to the conduct of the NFE's charitable activities, or as payment of reasonable compensation for services rendered, or as payment representing the fair market value of property which the NFE has purchased. In addition, the income or assets of the NFE could be distributed to, or applied for the benefit of, a private person or non-charitable Entity as payment of reasonable compensation for the use of property.

Controlling Persons

132.   Subparagraph D(6) sets forth the definition of the term "Controlling Persons". This term corresponds to the term "beneficial owner" as described in Recommendation 10 and the Interpretative Note on Recommendation 10 of the Financial Action Task Force Recommendations (as adopted in February 2012),[13] and must be interpreted in a manner consistent with such Recommendations, with the aim of protecting the international financial system from misuse including with respect to tax crimes.

133.   For an Entity that is a legal person, the term "Controlling Persons" means the natural person(s) who exercises control over the Entity. "Control" over an Entity is generally exercised by the natural person(s) who ultimately has a controlling ownership interest in the Entity. A "control ownership interest" depends on the ownership structure of the legal person and is usually identified on the basis of a threshold applying a risk-based approach (e.g. any person(s) owning more than a certain percentage of the legal person, such as 25%). Where no natural person(s) exercises control through ownership interests, the Controlling Person(s) of the Entity will be the natural person(s) who exercises control of the Entity through other means. Where no natural person(s) is identified as exercising control of the Entity, the Controlling Person(s) of the Entity will be the natural person(s) who holds the position of senior managing official.

134.   In the case of a trust, the term "Controlling Persons" means the settlor(s), the trustee(s), the protector(s) (if any), the beneficiary(ies) or class(es) of beneficiaries, and any other natural person(s) exercising ultimate effective control over the trust. The settlor(s), the trustee(s), the protector(s) (if any), and the beneficiary(ies) or class(es) of beneficiaries, must always be treated

13.   FATF/OECD (2013), *International Standards on Combating Money Laundering and the Financing of Terrorism and Proliferation*, The FATF Recommendations February 2012, FATF/OECD, Paris, available on www.fatf-gafi.org/media/fatf/documents/recommendations/pdfs/FATF_Recommendations.pdf.

as Controlling Persons of a trust, regardless of whether or not any of them exercises control over the trust. It is for this reason that the second sentence of subparagraph D(6) supplements the first sentence of such subparagraph. In addition, any other natural person(s) exercising ultimate effective control over the trust (including through a chain of control or ownership) must also be treated as a Controlling Person of the trust. With a view to establishing the source of funds in the account(s) held by the trust, where the settlor(s) of a trust is an Entity, Reporting Financial Institutions must also identify the Controlling Person(s) of the settlor(s) and report them as Controlling Person(s) of the trust. For beneficiary(ies) of trusts that are designated by characteristics or by class, Reporting Financial Institutions should obtain sufficient information concerning the beneficiary(ies) to satisfy the Reporting Financial Institution that it will be able to establish the identity of the beneficiary(ies) at the time of the pay-out or when the beneficiary(ies) intends to exercise vested rights. Therefore, that occasion will constitute a change in circumstances and will trigger the relevant procedures. When implementing the Common Reporting Standard, a jurisdiction may allow Reporting Financial Institutions to align the scope of the beneficiary(ies) of a trust treated as Controlling Person(s) of the trust with the scope of the beneficiary(ies) of a trust treated as Reportable Persons of a trust that is a Financial Institution (see paragraphs 69-70 above).

135.   In the case of a legal arrangement other than a trust, the term "Controlling Persons" means persons in equivalent or similar positions as those that are Controlling Persons of a trust. Thus, taking into account the different forms and structures of legal arrangements, Reporting Financial Institutions should identify and report persons in equivalent or similar positions, as those required to be identified and reported for trusts.

136.   In relation to legal persons that are functionally similar to trusts (e.g. foundations), Reporting Financial Institutions should identify Controlling Persons through similar customer due diligence procedures as those required for trusts, with a view to achieving appropriate levels of reporting.

137.   Where a Reporting Financial Institution relies on information collected and maintained pursuant to AML/KYC Procedures for purposes of determining the Controlling Persons of an Account Holder of a New Entity Account (see subparagraph A(2)(b) of Section VI), such AML/KYC Procedures must be consistent with Recommendations 10 and 25 of the FATF Recommendations (as adopted in February 2012), including always treating the settlor(s) of a trust as a Controlling Person of the trust and the founder(s) of a foundation as a Controlling Person of the foundation. For purposes of determining the Controlling Persons of an Account Holder of a Preexisting Entity Account (see subparagraph D(2)(b) of Section V), a Reporting Financial Institution may rely on information collected and maintained pursuant to the Reporting Financial Institution's AML/KYC Procedures.

Paragraph E – Miscellaneous

Subparagraph E(1) – Account Holder

138.   Subparagraph E(1) defines the term "Account Holder" as the person listed or identified as the holder of a Financial Account by the Financial Institution that maintains the account. This is regardless of whether such person is a flow-through Entity. Thus, for example, if a trust or an estate is listed as the holder or owner of a Financial Account, the trust or estate is the Account Holder, rather than its owners or beneficiaries. Similarly, if a partnership is listed as the holder or owner of a Financial Account, the partnership is the Account Holder, rather than the partners in the partnership.

139.   A person, other than a Financial Institution, holding a Financial Account for the benefit or account of another person as agent, custodian, nominee, signatory, investment advisor, intermediary, or legal guardian, is not treated as holding the account according to subparagraph E(1). Instead, such other person is treated as holding the account. For these purposes, a Reporting Financial Institution may rely on information in its possession (including information collected pursuant to AML/KYC Procedures), based on which it can reasonably determine whether a person is acting for the benefit or account of another person.

140.   With respect to a jointly held account, each joint holder is treated as an Account Holder for purposes of determining whether the account is a Reportable Account. Thus, an account is a Reportable Account if any of the Account Holders is a Reportable Person or a Passive NFE with one or more Controlling Persons who are Reportable Persons. When more than one Reportable Person is a joint holder, each Reportable Person is treated as an Account Holder and is attributed the entire balance of the jointly held account, including for purposes of applying the aggregation rules set forth in subparagraphs C(1) through (3) of Section VII.

141.   In the case of a Cash Value Insurance Contract or an Annuity Contract, the Account Holder is any person entitled to access the Cash Value or change the beneficiary of the contract. If no person can access the Cash Value or change the beneficiary, the Account Holder is any person named as the owner in the contract and any person with a vested entitlement to payment under the terms of the contract. Upon the maturity of a Cash Value Insurance Contract or an Annuity Contract (i.e. when obligation to pay an amount under the contract becomes fixed), each person entitled to receive a payment under the contract is treated as an Account Holder.

142.   The following examples illustrate the application of subparagraph E(1):

- Example 1 (Account held by agent): F holds a power of attorney from U, a Reportable Person, that authorises F to open, hold, and make deposits and withdrawals with respect to a Depository Account on behalf of U. The balance of the account for the calendar year is USD 100 000. F is listed as the holder of the Depository Account at a Reporting Financial Institution, but because F holds the account as an agent for the benefit of U, F is not ultimately entitled to the funds in the account. Because the Depository Account is treated as held by U, a Reportable Person, the account is a Reportable Account.

- Example 2 (Jointly held accounts): U, a Reportable Person, holds a Depository Account in a Reporting Financial Institution. The balance of the account for the calendar year is USD 100 000. The account is jointly held with A, an individual who is not a Reportable Person. Because one of the joint holders is a Reportable Person, the account is a Reportable Account.

- Example 3 (Jointly held accounts): U and Q, both Reportable Persons, hold a Depository Account in a Reporting Financial Institution. The balance of the account for the calendar year is USD 100 000. The account is a Reportable Account and both U and Q are treated as Account Holders of the account.

Subparagraph E(2) – AML/KYC Procedures

143.   The term "AML/KYC Procedures", as defined in subparagraph E(2), means the customer due diligence procedures of a Reporting Financial Institution pursuant to the anti-money laundering or similar requirements to which such Reporting Financial Institution is subject (e.g. know your customer provisions). These procedures include identifying and verifying the identity of the customer (including the beneficial owners of the customer), understanding the nature and purpose of the account, and on-going monitoring.

Subparagraphs E(3) and (4) – Entity and Related Entity

144.   Subparagraph E(3) defines the term "Entity" as a legal person or a legal arrangement. This term is intended to cover any person other than an individual (i.e. a natural person), in addition to any legal arrangement. Thus, e.g. a corporation, partnership, trust, *fideicomiso*, foundation (*fondation*, *Stiftung*), company, co-operative, association, or *asociación en participación*, falls within the meaning of the term "Entity".

145.   An Entity is a "Related Entity" of another Entity, as defined in subparagraph E(4), if either Entity controls the other Entity, or the two Entities are under common control. For this purpose control includes direct or indirect ownership of more than 50% of the vote and value in an Entity. Whether an Entity is a Related Entity of another Entity is relevant for the account balance

aggregation rules set forth in paragraph C of Section VII, the scope of the term " Reportable Person" described in subparagraph D(2)(ii), and the criterion described in subparagraph D(9)(b) that an NFE can meet to be an Active NFE.

Subparagraph E(5) – TIN

146.   According to subparagraph E(5), the term "TIN" means Taxpayer Identification Number (or functional equivalent in the absence of a Taxpayer Identification Number). A Taxpayer Identification Number is a unique combination of letters or numbers, however described, assigned by a jurisdiction to an individual or an Entity and used to identify the individual or Entity for purposes of administering the tax laws of such jurisdiction.

147.   TINs are also useful for identifying taxpayers who invest in other jurisdictions. TIN specifications (i.e. structure, syntax, etc.) are set by each jurisdiction's tax administrations. Some jurisdictions even have a different TIN structure for different taxes or different categories of taxpayers (e.g. residents and non-residents).

148.   While many jurisdictions utilise a TIN for personal or corporate taxation purposes, some jurisdictions do not issue a TIN. However, these jurisdictions often utilise some other high integrity number with an equivalent level of identification (a "functional equivalent"). Examples of that type of number include, for individuals, a social security/insurance number, citizen/personal identification/service code/number, and resident registration number; and for Entities, a business/company registration code/number.

149.   Participating Jurisdictions are expected to provide Reporting Financial Institutions with information with respect to the issuance, collection and, to the extent possible and practical, the structure and other specifications of taxpayer identification numbers. The OECD will endeavour to facilitate its dissemination. Such information will facilitate the collection of accurate TINs by Reporting Financial Institutions.

Subparagraph E(6) – Documentary Evidence

150.   Subparagraph E(6) describes what is considered to be "Documentary Evidence" for purposes of the due diligence procedures described in Sections II through VII. It includes any of the following:

   a)   a certificate of residence issued by an authorised government body (for example, a government or agency thereof, or a municipality) of the jurisdiction in which the payee claims to be a resident.

   b)   with respect to an individual, any valid identification issued by an authorised government body (for example, a government or agency thereof, or a municipality), that includes the individual's name and is typically used for identification purposes.

 c) with respect to an Entity, any official documentation issued by an authorised government body (for example, a government or agency thereof, or a municipality) that includes the name of the Entity and either the address of its principal office in the jurisdiction in which it claims to be a resident or the jurisdiction in which the Entity was incorporated or organised.

 d) any audited financial statement, third-party credit report, bankruptcy filing, or securities regulator's report.

151. While a Reporting Financial Institution may rely on Documentary Evidence unless it knows or has reason to know that it is incorrect or unreliable (see paragraphs 2-3 of the Commentary on Section VII), it is expected to give preference to a piece of Documentary Evidence that is more recent, or more specific, than another piece of Documentary Evidence.

152. Subparagraph E(6)(a) refers to a certificate of residence issued by an authorised government body of the jurisdiction in which the payee claims to be a resident. Examples of such a certificate include a certificate of residence for tax purposes (that indicates, e.g. that the account holder has filed its most recent income tax return as a resident of that jurisdiction); residence information published by an authorised government body of a jurisdiction, such as a list published by a tax administration that contains the names and residences of taxpayers; and residence information in a publicly accessible register maintained or authorised by an authorised government body of a jurisdiction, such as a public register maintained by a tax administration.

153. One of the requirements described in subparagraph E(6)(c) is that the official documentation includes either the address of the Entity's principal office in the jurisdiction in which it claims to be a resident or the jurisdiction in which the Entity was incorporated or organised. The address of the Entity's principal office is generally the place in which its place of effective management is situated (see paragraph 109 above). The address of a Financial Institution with which the Entity maintains an account, a post office box, or an address used solely for mailing purposes is not the address of the Entity's principal office unless such address is the only address used by the Entity and appears as the Entity's registered address in the Entity's organisational documents. Further, an address that is provided subject to instructions to hold all mail to that address is not the address of the Entity's principal office.

154. In order to build on existing practices, with respect to a Preexisting Entity Account, each jurisdiction may allow Reporting Financial Institutions to use as Documentary Evidence any classification in the Reporting Financial Institution's records with respect to the Account Holder that was determined

based on a standardised industry coding system, that was recorded by the Reporting Financial Institution consistent with its normal business practices for purposes of AML/KYC Procedures or another regulatory purposes (other than for tax purposes) and that was implemented by the Reporting Financial Institution prior to the date used to classify the Financial Account as a Preexisting Account, provided that the Reporting Financial Institution does not know or has reason to know that such classification is incorrect or unreliable. The term "standardised industry coding system" means a coding system used to classify establishments by business type for purposes other than tax purposes. Examples of a standardised industry coding system include the International Standard Industrial Classification (ISIC) from the United Nations, the Statistical classification of economic activities in the European Community (NACE), and the North American Industry Classification System (NAICS).

Requirements for validity of Documentary Evidence

155.   Documentary Evidence that contains an expiration date may be treated as valid on the later of that expiration date, or the last day of the fifth calendar year following the year in which the Documentary Evidence is provided to the Reporting Financial Institution. However, the following Documentary Evidence is considered to remain valid indefinitely:

*   Documentary Evidence furnished by an authorised government body (such as a passport);

*   Documentary Evidence that is not generally renewed or amended (such as a certificate of incorporation); or

*   Documentary Evidence provided by a Non-Reporting Financial Institution or a Reportable Jurisdiction Person that is not a Reportable Person.

All other Documentary Evidence is valid until the last day of the fifth calendar year following the year in which the Documentary Evidence is provided to the Reporting Financial Institution.

156.   Notwithstanding the validity periods, a Reporting Financial Institution may not rely on Documentary Evidence, according to paragraph A of Section VII, if it knows or has reason to know that the Documentary Evidence is incorrect or unreliable (e.g. because of a change in circumstances that makes the information on the documentation incorrect). Therefore, a Reporting Financial Institution is expected to institute procedures to ensure that any change to the customer master files that constitutes a change in circumstances is identified by the Reporting Financial Institution (see paragraphs 26 of the Commentary on Section I and 17 of the Commentary on Section III). In

addition, a Reporting Financial Institution is expected to notify any person providing documentation of the person's obligation to notify the Reporting Financial Institution of a change in circumstances.

157. A Reporting Financial Institution may retain an original, certified copy, or photocopy (including a microfiche, electronic scan, or similar means of electronic storage) of the Documentary Evidence or, at least, a notation of the type of documentation reviewed, the date the documentation was reviewed, and the document's identification number (if any) (for example, a passport number). Any documentation that is stored electronically must be made available in hard copy form upon request.

158. A Reporting Financial Institution may accept a copy of Documentary Evidence electronically if the electronic system ensures that the information received is the information sent, and documents all occasions of user access that result in the submission, renewal, or modification of the Documentary Evidence. In addition, the design and operation of the electronic system, including access procedures, must ensure that the person accessing the system and furnishing the Documentary Evidence is the person named on such Documentary Evidence.

159. In general, a Reporting Financial Institution with which a customer may open an account must obtain Documentary Evidence on an account-by-account basis. However, a Reporting Financial Institution may rely upon the Documentary Evidence furnished by a customer for another account if both accounts are treated as a single account for purposes of satisfying the standards of knowledge requirements set forth in paragraph A of Section VII.

Documentation collected by other persons

160. As provided in paragraph D of Section II, a Participating Jurisdiction may allow Reporting Financial Institutions to use service providers to fulfil their reporting and due diligence obligations. When that is the case, a Reporting Financial Institution may use the documentation collected by service providers (e.g. data providers, financial advisors, insurance agents), subject to the conditions described in domestic law. The reporting and due diligence obligations remain, however, the responsibility of the Reporting Financial Institution.

161. A Reporting Financial Institution may rely on documentation collected by an agent (including a fund advisor for mutual funds, hedge funds, or a private equity group) of the Reporting Financial Institution. The agent may retain the documentation as part of an information system maintained for a single Reporting Financial Institution or multiple Reporting Financial Institutions provided that under the system, any Reporting Financial Institution on behalf of which the agent retains documentation may easily

access data regarding the nature of the documentation, the information contained in the documentation (including a copy of the documentation itself) and its validity, and must allow such Reporting Financial Institution to easily transmit data, either directly into an electronic system or by providing such information to the agent, regarding any facts of which it becomes aware that may affect the reliability of the documentation. The Reporting Financial Institution must be able to establish, to the extent applicable, how and when it has transmitted data regarding any facts of which it became aware that may affect the reliability of the documentation and must be able to establish that any data it has transmitted has been processed and appropriate due diligence has been exercised regarding the validity of the documentation. The agent must have a system in effect to ensure that any information it receives regarding facts that affect the reliability of the documentation or the status assigned to the customer are provided to all Reporting Financial Institutions for which the agent retains the documentation.

162. A Reporting Financial Institution that acquires an account from a predecessor or transferor in a merger or bulk acquisition of accounts for value would generally be permitted to rely upon valid documentation (or copies of valid documentation) collected by the predecessor or transferor. In addition, a Reporting Financial Institution that acquires an account in a merger or bulk acquisition of accounts for value from another Reporting Financial Institution that has completed all the due diligence required under Sections II through VII with respect to the accounts transferred, would generally be permitted to also rely upon the predecessor's or transferor's determination of status of an Account Holder until the acquirer knows, or has reason to know, that the status is inaccurate or a change in circumstances occurs (see paragraph 17 of the Commentary on Section III).

Commentary on Section IX
concerning Effective Implementation

1. The aim of this Section is to ensure that the Common Reporting Standard is effectively implemented by Participating Jurisdictions, it is complied with and it is not circumvented. This is achieved by requiring that jurisdictions have in place certain rules and administrative procedures. These rules may be in the form of primary legislation or secondary legislation (e.g. regulations) and will often be supplemented by guidance. Administrative procedures may be set out in manuals or other communications provided to auditors or other relevant authorities.

2. Under Section IX, a jurisdiction must have rules and administrative procedures in place to ensure the effective implementation of, and compliance with, the reporting and due diligence procedures set out in the Common Reporting Standard. The Standard will not be considered effectively implemented unless it is adopted in good faith with consideration to its Commentary which seeks to promote its consistent application across jurisdictions. Since the application of the CRS requires that it be translated into domestic law, there may be differences in domestic implementation. Therefore, in the cross-border context, reference needs to be made to the law of the implementing jurisdiction. For example, the question may arise whether a particular Entity that is resident in a Participating Jurisdiction and has a Financial Account in another Participating Jurisdiction, meets the definition of "Financial Institution". The Entity may meet the "substantial portion" test to be a Custodial Institution in one Participating Jurisdiction, but different measurement techniques for gross income may mean that the Entity does not meet such test in another Participating Jurisdiction. In such a case, the classification of the Entity ought to be resolved under the law of the Participating Jurisdiction in which the Entity is resident.

3. Subparagraphs A(1) and (2) provide that a jurisdiction must have the following rules:

- to prevent any Financial Institutions, persons or intermediaries from adopting practices intended to circumvent the Common Reporting Standard;

- requiring Reporting Financial Institutions to keep records of the steps undertaken and any evidence relied upon for the performance of the due diligence procedures set out in the CRS; and

- requiring adequate measures to obtain the records described above.

4.   The first rule described in subparagraph A(1) is what is generally referred to as an anti-avoidance rule. An anti-avoidance rule can take various forms. Many jurisdictions have enacted a general anti-avoidance rule in their tax legislation which may also be supplemented by specific anti-avoidance rules. In other jurisdictions, the legislation may include only specific anti-avoidance rules. How the anti-avoidance rule for the CRS is drafted will depend on the general approach adopted by jurisdictions to addressing avoidance as well as to implementing the Common Reporting Standard. For example, a general anti-avoidance rule may cover reporting and due diligence obligations. The form of the rule itself is not important as long as it is effective to prevent circumvention of the reporting requirements and the due diligence procedures.

5.   The following are examples of situations where it is expected that an anti-avoidance rule would apply:

- Example 1 (Shift Maintenance of an Account): A Reporting Financial Institution advises a customer to maintain an account with a Related Entity in a non-Participating Jurisdiction that enables the Reporting Financial Institution to avoid reporting while offering to provide services and retain customer relations as if the account was maintained by the Reporting Financial Institution itself. In such a case, the Reporting Financial Institution should be considered to maintain the account and have the resulting reporting and due diligence requirements.

- Example 2 (Year-end amounts): Financial Institutions, individuals, Entities or intermediaries manipulate year-end amounts, such as account balances, to avoid reporting or being reported upon.

- Example 3 (Park Money with Qualified Credit Card Issuers): Individuals or Entities park balances from other Reportable Accounts with Qualified Credit Card Issuers for a short period at the end of the year to avoid reporting.

- Example 4 (Electronic records and computerised systems): A Reporting Financial Institution deliberately does not create any electronic records (such that an electronic record search would not yield any results) or maintains computerised systems artificially dissociated (to avoid the account aggregation rules).

6.   To increase the reliability of self-certifications, jurisdictions are expected to include a specific provision in their domestic legislation imposing sanctions for signing (or otherwise positively affirming) a false self-certification.

7.   Subparagraph A(2) requires a jurisdiction to have rules in place requiring Reporting Financial Institutions to keep records of the steps undertaken and any evidence relied upon for the performance of the due diligence procedures set out in the CRS. Such records should be available for a sufficiently long period of time and in any event for a period of not less than 5 years after the end of the period within which the Reporting Financial Institution must report the information required to be reported under the Common Reporting Standard.

8.   Documentary Evidence is defined in subparagraph E(6) of Section VIII and is relevant for applying, e.g. the residence address test set out in subparagraph B(1) of Section III and the curing procedure contained in subparagraph B(6) of Section III. As mentioned in paragraph 157 of the Commentary on Section VIII, the Documentary Evidence retained by a Reporting Financial Institution does not have to be the original and may be a certified copy, a photocopy or, at least, a notation of the type of documentation reviewed, the date the documentation was reviewed, and the document's identification number (if any).

9.   In certain cases, for example as set out in paragraph 13 of the Commentary on Section I regarding reasonable efforts to obtain a TIN with respect to Preexisting Accounts, a procedural manual describing appropriate "reasonable efforts" can be a record describing the steps undertaken provided there is also evidence as to how those policies and procedures are followed. For example, in the case of a mail merge, this would not require a Reporting Financial Institution to keep actual copies of the letters sent, but to provide upon request the document that contains the information that is the same in each version and the data file where the unique information is stored.

10.   Subparagraph A(2) also requires that a jurisdiction have adequate measures to obtain the records from the Reporting Financial Institutions. Most jurisdictions have rules in place to compel the taxpayer or a third party to provide documents that are necessary to apply their domestic tax legislation. These rules generally also apply to obtain information to respond to a request for information from an exchange partner under an exchange of information instrument. Some jurisdictions, especially those without an income tax, may have rules that specifically deal with the procedures to obtain information under an exchange of information instrument.

11.   Subparagraphs A(3) and (4) require that jurisdictions have the following administrative procedures in place to:

- verify the compliance of Reporting Financial Institutions with the reporting and due diligence procedures set out in the CRS;

- follow up with a Reporting Financial Institution when undocumented accounts are reported; and

- ensure that the Entities and accounts defined in domestic law as Non-Reporting Financial Institutions and Excluded Accounts continue to have a low risk of being used to evade tax.

12.   Jurisdictions should have procedures in place to periodically verify the compliance of Reporting Financial Institutions. This may be performed as part of a regular tax audit or as a separate inquiry or review.

13.   A jurisdiction must also have procedures in place to follow up with a Reporting Financial Institution when undocumented accounts are reported. An "undocumented account" generally arises when a Reporting Financial Institution is unable to obtain information from an Account Holder in respect of a Preexisting Account (see paragraphs 28-29, 45 and 48 of the Commentary on Section III). This could either be the result of inadequate procedures being implemented by a Reporting Financial Institution to obtain the necessary information or the Account Holder is non-compliant. Either case is a cause for concern.

14.   It is expected that a jurisdiction would follow up with any Reporting Financial Institution that reports an undocumented account. In the case of a small number of undocumented accounts, a simple inquiry to the Reporting Financial Institution may be sufficient. However, if such a Reporting Financial Institution reports a larger than average number of undocumented accounts in any one year or the number of undocumented accounts reported continues to increase, a full audit of the Reporting Financial Institution's due diligence procedures may be appropriate. In such a case, where possible and where feasible, it may be appropriate for the jurisdiction to advise the AML authorities in accordance with domestic law.

15.   As described above, a jurisdiction must have procedures in place to ensure that Non-Reporting Financial Institutions and Excluded Accounts defined in domestic law continue to have a low risk of being used to evade tax. This could include particular Entities or types of Entities. These procedures should include a periodic review of such status. This review may be performed as part of a regular tax audit or as a separate inquiry or review.

16.   Examples of situations where a jurisdiction should re-evaluate the appropriateness of an Entity or an account being so defined includes a situation where an Entity changes its business or the Financial Account changes its nature.

17.   Once a jurisdiction determines that a type of Entity or an account no longer meets the requirement of posing a low risk for evading tax, it shall take all necessary measures as soon as possible to remove such Entity or account from the list of Non-Reporting Financial Institutions or Excluded Accounts in its domestic legislation. Such jurisdiction should also advise its exchange partners of the change in status of the Entity or account. See also paragraph 2

of Section 7 of the Model CAA where defining the status of Entities or accounts as Non-Reporting Financial Institutions or Excluded Accounts in a manner that frustrates the purposes of the CRS would constitute significant non-compliance which could result in a suspension of the Model CAA by the exchange partner.

18.   Subparagraph A(5) requires that a jurisdiction must have effective enforcement provisions to address non-compliance. In some cases, the anti-avoidance rule described in Subparagraph A(1) may be broad enough to cover enforcement. In other cases, there may be separate or more specific rules that address certain enforcement issues on a narrower basis. For example, a jurisdiction may have rules that provide for the imposition of fines or other penalties where a person does not provide information requested by the tax authority. Further, given that obtaining a self-certification for New Accounts is a critical aspect of ensuring that the CRS is effective, it is expected that jurisdictions have strong measures in place to ensure that valid self-certifications are always obtained for New Accounts. An effective way to achieve this outcome would be to introduce legislation making the opening of a New Account conditional upon the receipt of a valid self-certification in the course of account opening procedures. Other jurisdictions may choose different methods; for example, imposing significant penalties on Account Holders that fail to provide a self-certification, or on Reporting Financial Institutions that do not take appropriate measures to obtain a self-certification upon account opening.

Annexes

Annex 1

Multilateral Model Competent Authority Agreement

1.   This document is a multilateral version of the Model Competent Authority Agreement. The legal basis is Article 6 of the Convention on Mutual Administrative Assistance in Tax Matters which specifically provides that two or more Parties can mutually agree to exchange information automatically. The actual exchange of the information itself will be on a bilateral basis.

2.   The main changes to adapt the bilateral Model CAA to a multilateral model are additions to the preamble, generic definitions for Jurisdiction and the term "Common Reporting Standard", the effective date in paragraph 1 of Section 7 including a procedure for jurisdictions to join after the Agreement is in effect, and sending notices to the Secretariat of the Co-ordinating Body of the Convention. In addition the multilateral model contemplates jurisdictions participating on both a reciprocal and nonreciprocal basis (see paragraph 1 of Section 2). Jurisdictions sending information but not receiving information would be listed in Annex A.

MODEL AGREEMENT ON THE AUTOMATIC EXCHANGE OF FINANCIAL ACCOUNT INFORMATION TO IMPROVE INTERNATIONAL TAX COMPLIANCE

Whereas, the Jurisdictions are Parties of, or territories covered by, the Convention on Mutual Administrative Assistance in Tax Matters (the "Convention") and have a longstanding and close relationship with respect to mutual assistance in tax matters and desire to improve international tax compliance by further building on that relationship;

Whereas, the laws of their respective Jurisdictions [are expected to require]/[require]/require or are expected to require] financial institutions to report information regarding certain accounts and follow related due diligence procedures, consistent with the scope of exchange contemplated by Section 2 of this Agreement and the reporting and due diligence procedures set out in the Common Reporting Standard;

Whereas, it is expected that the laws of the Jurisdictions would be amended from time to time to reflect updates to the Common Reporting Standard and once such changes are enacted by a Jurisdiction the definition of "Common Reporting Standard" would be deemed to refer to the updated version in respect of that Jurisdiction;

Whereas, Chapter III of the Convention authorises the exchange of information for tax purposes, including the exchange of information on an automatic basis, and allows the competent authorities of the Jurisdictions (the "Competent Authorities") to agree the scope and modalities of such automatic exchanges;

Whereas Article 6 of the Convention provides that two or more Parties can mutually agree to exchange information automatically, the actual exchange of the information will be on a bilateral basis;

Whereas the Competent Authorities of Jurisdictions or territories listed in Annex A to this Agreement will send information under Section 2, the Competent Authorities will not receive such information;

Whereas, the Jurisdictions have in place *(i)* appropriate safeguards to ensure that the information received pursuant to this Agreement remains confidential and is used solely for the purposes set out in the Convention, and *(ii)* the infrastructure for an effective exchange relationship (including established processes for ensuring timely, accurate, and confidential information exchanges, effective and reliable communications, and capabilities to promptly resolve questions and concerns about exchanges or requests for exchanges and to administer the provisions of Section 4 of this Agreement);

Whereas, the Competent Authorities of the Jurisdictions desire to conclude an agreement to improve international tax compliance based on automatic exchange pursuant to the Convention, and subject to the confidentiality and other protections provided for therein, including the provisions limiting the use of the information exchanged under the Convention;

Now, therefore, the Competent Authorities have agreed as follows:

SECTION 1

Definitions

1.   For the purposes of this agreement ("Agreement"), the following terms have the following meanings:

a)   the term **"Jurisdiction"** means a jurisdiction that is a Party to, or a territory covered by, the Convention and the Competent Authority of which is a signatory to this Agreement.

b)   the term **"Competent Authority"** means, for each respective Jurisdiction, the persons and authorities listed in Annex B of the Convention.

c)   the term **"Jurisdiction Financial Institution"** means, for each respective Jurisdiction, *(i)* any Financial Institution that is resident in the Jurisdiction, but excludes any branch of that Financial Institution that is located outside the Jurisdiction, and *(ii)* any branch of a Financial Institution that is not resident in the Jurisdiction, if that branch is located in the Jurisdiction.

d)   the term **"Reporting Financial Institution"** means any Jurisdiction Financial Institution that is not a Non-Reporting Financial Institution.

e)   the term **"Reportable Account"** means a Financial Account that is maintained by a Reporting Financial Institution and that, pursuant to due diligence procedures consistent with the Common Reporting Standard, has been identified as an account that is held by one or more persons that are Reportable Persons with respect to another Jurisdiction or by a Passive NFE with one or more Controlling Persons that are Reportable Persons with respect to another Jurisdiction.

f)   the term **"Common Reporting Standard"** means the standard for automatic exchange of financial account information developed by the OECD, with G20 countries, presented to the G20 in 2014 and published on the OECD website.

g)   the term **"CB Secretariat"** means the OECD Secretariat that, pursuant to paragraph 3 of Article 24 of the Convention, provides support to the co-ordinating body that is composed of representatives of the competent authorities of the Parties to the Convention.

2.   Any capitalised term not otherwise defined in this Agreement will have the meaning that it has at that time under the law of the Jurisdiction applying the Agreement, such meaning being consistent with the meaning set

forth in the Common Reporting Standard. Any term not otherwise defined in this Agreement or in the Common Reporting Standard will, unless the context otherwise requires or the Competent Authorities agree to a common meaning (as permitted by domestic law), have the meaning that it has at that time under the law of the Jurisdiction applying this Agreement, any meaning under the applicable tax laws of that Jurisdiction prevailing over a meaning given to the term under other laws of that Jurisdiction.

SECTION 2

Exchange of Information with Respect to Reportable Accounts

1. Pursuant to the provisions of Article 6 and 22 of the Convention and subject to the applicable reporting and due diligence rules consistent with the Common Reporting Standard, each Competent Authority will annually exchange with the other Competent Authorities on an automatic basis the information obtained pursuant to such rules and specified in paragraph 2. Notwithstanding the foregoing sentence the Competent Authorities of the Jurisdictions listed in Annex A will exchange, but not receive, the information specified in paragraph 2. Jurisdictions not listed in Annex A will always receive the information specified in paragraph 2 but will not exchange such information with the Jurisdictions listed in Annex A.

2. The information to be exchanged is, with respect to each Reportable Account of another Jurisdiction:

   a) the name, address, TIN(s) and date and place of birth (in the case of an individual) of each Reportable Person that is an Account Holder of the account and, in the case of any Entity that is an Account Holder and that, after application of due diligence procedures consistent with the Common Reporting Standard, is identified as having one or more Controlling Persons that is a Reportable Person, the name, address, and TIN(s) of the Entity and the name, address, TIN(s) and date and place of birth of each Reportable Person;

   b) the account number (or functional equivalent in the absence of an account number);

   c) the name and identifying number (if any) of the Reporting Financial Institution;

   d) the account balance or value (including, in the case of a Cash Value Insurance Contract or Annuity Contract, the Cash Value or surrender value) as of the end of the relevant calendar year or other appropriate reporting period or, if the account was closed during such year or period, the closure of the account;

e) in the case of any Custodial Account:

(1) the total gross amount of interest, the total gross amount of dividends, and the total gross amount of other income generated with respect to the assets held in the account, in each case paid or credited to the account (or with respect to the account) during the calendar year or other appropriate reporting period; and

(2) the total gross proceeds from the sale or redemption of Financial Assets paid or credited to the account during the calendar year or other appropriate reporting period with respect to which the Reporting Financial Institution acted as a custodian, broker, nominee, or otherwise as an agent for the Account Holder;

f) in the case of any Depository Account, the total gross amount of interest paid or credited to the account during the calendar year or other appropriate reporting period; and

g) in the case of any account not described in subparagraph 2(e) or (f), the total gross amount paid or credited to the Account Holder with respect to the account during the calendar year or other appropriate reporting period with respect to which the Reporting Financial Institution is the obligor or debtor, including the aggregate amount of any redemption payments made to the Account Holder during the calendar year or other appropriate reporting period.

SECTION 3

Time and Manner of Exchange of Information

1. For the purposes of the exchange of information in Section 2, the amount and characterisation of payments made with respect to a Reportable Account may be determined in accordance with the principles of the tax laws of the jurisdiction exchanging the information.

2. For the purposes of the exchange of information in Section 2, the information exchanged will identify the currency in which each relevant amount is denominated.

3. With respect to paragraph 2 of Section 2, information is to be exchanged with respect to [xxxx] and all subsequent years and will be exchanged within nine months after the end of the calendar year to which the information relates. Notwithstanding the foregoing sentence information is only required to be exchanged with respect to a calendar year if both Jurisdictions have in effect legislation that requires reporting with respect to such calendar year that is consistent with the scope of exchange provided for

in Section 2 and the reporting and due diligence procedures contained in the Common Reporting Standard.

4.   Notwithstanding paragraph 3, the information to be exchanged with respect to [xxxx] is the information described in paragraph 2 of Section 2, except for gross proceeds described in subparagraph 2(e)(2) of Section 2.

5.   The Competent Authorities will automatically exchange the information described in Section 2 in a common reporting standard schema in Extensible Markup Language.

6.   The Competent Authorities will agree on one or more methods for data transmission including encryption standards.

SECTION 4

Collaboration on Compliance and Enforcement

A Competent Authority will notify the other Competent Authority when the first-mentioned Competent Authority has reason to believe that an error may have led to incorrect or incomplete information reporting or there is non-compliance by a Reporting Financial Institution with the applicable reporting requirements and due diligence procedures consistent with the Common Reporting Standard. The notified Competent Authority will take all appropriate measures available under its domestic law to address the errors or non-compliance described in the notice.

SECTION 5

Confidentiality and Data Safeguards

1.   All information exchanged is subject to the confidentiality rules and other safeguards provided for in the Convention, including the provisions limiting the use of the information exchanged and, to the extent needed to ensure the necessary level of protection of personal data, in accordance with the safeguards which may be specified by the supplying Competent Authority as required under its domestic law.

2.   A Competent Authority will notify the CB Secretariat immediately regarding any breach of confidentiality or failure of safeguards and any sanctions and remedial actions consequently imposed.

SECTION 6

Consultations and Amendments

1.   If any difficulties in the implementation or interpretation of this Agreement arise, a Competent Authority may request consultations with one or more of the Competent Authorities to develop appropriate measures to ensure that this Agreement is fulfilled. The Competent Authority that requested the consultations shall ensure that the CB Secretariat is notified of any appropriate measures that were developed and the CB Secretariat will notify all Competent Authorities, even those that did not participate in the consultations, of any measures that were developed.

2.   This Agreement may be amended by consensus by written agreement of all of the Competent Authorities. Unless otherwise agreed upon, such an amendment is effective on the first day of the month following the expiration of a period of one month after the date of the last signature of such written agreement.

SECTION 7

Term of Agreement

1.   This Agreement will come into effect on the date two or more Competent Authorities have provided notice to, and it has been received by, the CB Secretariat that its Jurisdiction has the necessary laws in place to implement the Agreement. After the effective date a Competent Authority may make a request to sign the Agreement. Notwithstanding the foregoing sentence, a Competent Authority that wants to sign the Agreement before it has come into effect, but after it has been signed by a group of Competent Authorities that are the first signatories to the Agreement, the first-mentioned Competent Authority must make a request to sign the Agreement.

2.   The decision to invite a Competent Authority, and whether the Competent Authority will be listed in Annex A, will be taken by consensus of the Competent Authorities that have signed the Agreement. Following signature the Competent Authority must notify the CB Secretariat that its Jurisdiction has the necessary laws in place to implement the Agreement. The Agreement will become effective with respect to the notifying Competent Authority on the date its notification is received by the CB Secretariat.

3.   A Competent Authority may suspend the exchange of information under this Agreement by giving notice in writing to another Competent Authority that it has determined that there is or has been significant non-compliance by the second-mentioned Competent Authority with this

Agreement. Such suspension will have immediate effect. For the purposes of this paragraph, significant non-compliance includes, but is not limited to, non-compliance with the confidentiality and data safeguard provisions of this Agreement and the Convention, a failure by the Competent Authority to provide timely or adequate information as required under this Agreement or defining the status of Entities or accounts as Non-Reporting Financial Institutions and Excluded Accounts in a manner that frustrates the purposes of the Common Reporting Standard.

4.   A Competent Authority may terminate its participation in this Agreement by giving notice of termination in writing to the CB Secretariat. Such termination will become effective on the first day of the month following the expiration of a period of 12 months after the date of the notice of termination. In the event of termination, all information previously received under this Agreement will remain confidential and subject to the terms of the Convention.

SECTION 8

Notices Received by the CB Secretariat

Unless otherwise provided for in the Agreement, the CB Secretariat will notify all Competent Authorities of any notice that it has received under this Agreement.

Signed in […] on […].   Signed in […] on […].

Competent Authority for   Competent Authority for
[Jurisdiction]:   [Jurisdiction]:

ANNEX A: LIST OF JURISDICTIONS

[Jurisdiction]   [Jurisdiction]

Annex 2

Nonreciprocal Model Competent Authority Agreement

1.   There may be situations where the automatic exchange of financial account information does not need to be reciprocal (e.g. because one of the jurisdictions does not have an income tax). In such cases, the information would be sent only by [Jurisdiction A] to [Jurisdiction B], but not by [Jurisdiction B] to [Jurisdiction A].

2.   While a nonreciprocal agreement could largely be based on the Model Competent Authority Agreement, some changes would be needed in order to reflect its nonreciprocal nature. For example, the definition of the term "Reporting Financial Institution" would need to be modified so that only [Jurisdiction A] Financial Institutions may be Reporting Financial Institutions.

3.   The complete list of provisions that would need to be either modified or removed is the following:

- provisions that would need to be modified: the second, fourth, and fifth clauses of the Preamble; subparagraphs 1(f), (g), and (h) of Section 1; paragraphs 1 and 2 (without its subparagraphs) of Section 2; paragraph 5 of Section 3; Sections 4 and 5; and paragraph 1 of Section 7; and

- provisions that would need to be removed: subparagraphs 1(e), (h), (j), and (m) of Section 1; and the second sentence of paragraph 3 of Section 3.

4.   Those changes have been in incorporated in the following Nonreciprocal Model Competent Authority Agreement:

MODEL AGREEMENT BETWEEN THE COMPETENT AUTHORITIES OF [JURISDICTION A] AND [JURISDICTION B] ON THE AUTOMATIC EXCHANGE OF FINANCIAL ACCOUNT INFORMATION TO IMPROVE INTERNATIONAL TAX COMPLIANCE

Whereas, the Government of [Jurisdiction A] and the Government of [Jurisdiction B] have a longstanding and close relationship with respect to mutual assistance in tax matters and desire to improve international tax compliance by further building on that relationship;

Whereas, the laws of [Jurisdiction A] [are expected to require]/[require] financial institutions to report information regarding certain accounts and follow related due diligence procedures, consistent with the scope of exchange contemplated by Section 2 of this Agreement and the reporting and due diligence procedures contained in the Common Reporting Standard;

Whereas, [Article [...] of the Income Tax Convention between [Jurisdiction A] and [Jurisdiction B]/[Article 6 of the Convention on Mutual Administrative Assistance in Tax Matters] (the "Convention")]/[other applicable legal instrument (the "Instrument")], authorises the exchange of information for tax purposes, including the exchange of information on an automatic basis, and allows the competent authorities of [Jurisdiction A] and [Jurisdiction B] (the "Competent Authorities") to agree the scope and modalities of such automatic exchanges;

Whereas, [Jurisdiction B] has in place *(i)* appropriate safeguards to ensure that the information received pursuant to this Agreement remains confidential and is used solely for the purposes set out in the [Convention]/[Instrument], and *(ii)* the infrastructure for an effective exchange relationship (including established processes for ensuring timely, accurate, and confidential information exchanges, effective and reliable communications, and capabilities to promptly resolve questions and concerns about exchanges or requests for exchanges and to administer the provisions of Section 4 of this Agreement);

Whereas, the Competent Authorities desire to conclude an agreement to improve international tax compliance based on nonreciprocal automatic exchange pursuant to the [Convention]/[Instrument], and subject to the confidentiality and other protections provided for therein, including the provisions limiting the use of the information exchanged under the [Convention]/[Instrument];

Now, therefore, the Competent Authorities have agreed as follows:

SECTION 1

Definitions

1.   For the purposes of this agreement ("Agreement"), the following terms have the following meanings:

a)   the term **"[Jurisdiction A]"** means […].

b)   the term **"[Jurisdiction B]"** means […].

c)   the term **"Competent Authority"** means:

   (1)   in the case of [Jurisdiction A], […]; and

   (2)   in the case of [Jurisdiction B], […].

d)   the term **"[Jurisdiction A] Financial Institution"** means *(i)* any Financial Institution that is resident in [Jurisdiction A], but excludes any branch of that Financial Institution that is located outside [Jurisdiction A], and *(ii)* any branch of a Financial Institution that is not resident in [Jurisdiction A], if that branch is located in [Jurisdiction A].

e)   the term **"Reporting Financial Institution"** means any [Jurisdiction A] Financial Institution that is not a Non-Reporting Financial Institution.

f)   the term **"Reportable Account"** means a [Jurisdiction B] Reportable Account, provided it has been identified as such pursuant to due diligence procedures, consistent with the Common Reporting Standard, in place in [Jurisdiction A].

g)   the term **"[Jurisdiction B] Reportable Account"** means a Financial Account that is maintained by a [Jurisdiction A] Reporting Financial Institution and held by one or more [Jurisdiction B] Persons that are Reportable Persons or by a Passive NFE with one or more Controlling Persons that is a [Jurisdiction B] Reportable Person.

h)   the term **"[Jurisdiction B] Person"** means an individual or Entity that is identified by a [Jurisdiction A] Reporting Financial Institution as resident in [Jurisdiction B] pursuant to due diligence procedures consistent with the Common Reporting Standard, or an estate of a decedent that was a resident of [Jurisdiction B].

i)   the term **"TIN"** means a [Jurisdiction B] TIN.

j)   the term **"[Jurisdiction B] TIN"** means a […].

k)   the term **"Common Reporting Standard"** means the standard for automatic exchange of financial account information developed by the OECD, with G20 countries, presented to the G20 in 2014 and published on the OECD website.

2.   Any capitalised term not otherwise defined in this Agreement will have the meaning that it has at that time under the law of the jurisdiction applying the Agreement, such meaning being consistent with the meaning set forth in the Common Reporting Standard. Any term not otherwise defined in this Agreement or in the Common Reporting Standard will, unless the context otherwise requires or the Competent Authorities agree to a common meaning (as permitted by domestic law), have the meaning that it has at that time under the law of the jurisdiction applying this Agreement, any meaning under the applicable tax laws of that jurisdiction prevailing over a meaning given to the term under other laws of that jurisdiction.

SECTION 2

Exchange of Information with Respect to Reportable Accounts

1.   Pursuant to the provisions of Article [...] of the [Convention]/ [Instrument] and subject to the applicable reporting and due diligence rules consistent with the Common Reporting Standard, [Jurisdiction A] Competent Authority will annually exchange with [Jurisdiction B] Competent Authority on an automatic basis the information obtained pursuant to such rules and specified in paragraph 2.

2.   The information to be exchanged is with respect to each [Jurisdiction B] Reportable Account:

a) the name, address, TIN(s) and date and place of birth (in the case of an individual) of each Reportable Person that is an Account Holder of the account and, in the case of any Entity that is an Account Holder and that, after application of due diligence procedures consistent with the Common Reporting Standard, is identified as having one or more Controlling Persons that is a Reportable Person, the name, address, and TIN(s) of the Entity and the name, address, TIN(s) and date and place of birth of each Reportable Person;

b) the account number (or functional equivalent in the absence of an account number);

c) the name and identifying number (if any) of the Reporting Financial Institution;

d) the account balance or value (including, in the case of a Cash Value Insurance Contract or Annuity Contract, the Cash Value or surrender value) as of the end of the relevant calendar year or other appropriate reporting period or, if the account was closed during such year or period, the closure of the account;

e) in the case of any Custodial Account:

(1) the total gross amount of interest, the total gross amount of dividends, and the total gross amount of other income generated with respect to the assets held in the account, in each case paid or credited to the account (or with respect to the account) during the calendar year or other appropriate reporting period; and

(2) the total gross proceeds from the sale or redemption of Financial Assets paid or credited to the account during the calendar year or other appropriate reporting period with respect to which the Reporting Financial Institution acted as a custodian, broker, nominee, or otherwise as an agent for the Account Holder;

f) in the case of any Depository Account, the total gross amount of interest paid or credited to the account during the calendar year or other appropriate reporting period; and

g) in the case of any account not described in subparagraph 2(e) or (f), the total gross amount paid or credited to the Account Holder with respect to the account during the calendar year or other appropriate reporting period with respect to which the Reporting Financial Institution is the obligor or debtor, including the aggregate amount of any redemption payments made to the Account Holder during the calendar year or other appropriate reporting period.

SECTION 3

Time and Manner of Exchange of Information

1. For the purposes of the exchange of information in Section 2, the amount and characterisation of payments made with respect to a Reportable Account may be determined in accordance with the principles of the tax laws of the jurisdiction exchanging the information.

2. For the purposes of the exchange of information in Section 2, the information exchanged will identify the currency in which each relevant amount is denominated.

3. With respect to paragraph 2 of Section 2, information is to be exchanged with respect to [xxxx] and all subsequent years and will be exchanged within nine months after the end of the calendar year to which the information relates.

4. Notwithstanding paragraph 3, the information to be exchanged with respect to [xxxx] is the information described in paragraph 2 of Section 2, except for gross proceeds described in subparagraph 2(e)(2) of Section 2.

5.   [Jurisdiction A] Competent Authority will automatically exchange the information described in Section 2 in a common reporting standard schema in Extensible Markup Language.

6.   The Competent Authorities will agree on one or more methods for data transmission including encryption standards.

SECTION 4

Collaboration on Compliance and Enforcement

[Jurisdiction B] Competent Authority will notify [Jurisdiction A] Competent Authority when the first-mentioned Competent Authority has reason to believe that an error may have led to incorrect or incomplete information reporting or there is non-compliance by a Reporting Financial Institution with the applicable reporting requirements and due diligence procedures consistent with the Common Reporting Standard. [Jurisdiction A] Competent Authority will take all appropriate measures available under its domestic law to address the errors or non-compliance described in the notice.

SECTION 5

Confidentiality and Data Safeguards

1.   All information exchanged is subject to the confidentiality rules and other safeguards provided for in the [Convention]/[Instrument], including the provisions limiting the use of the information exchanged and, to the extent needed to ensure the necessary level of protection of personal data, in accordance with the safeguards which may be specified by [Jurisdiction A] Competent Authority as required under its domestic law.

2.   [Jurisdiction B] Competent Authority will notify [Jurisdiction A] Competent Authority immediately regarding any breach of confidentiality or failure of safeguards and any sanctions and remedial actions consequently imposed.

SECTION 6

Consultations and Amendments

1.   If any difficulties in the implementation or interpretation of this Agreement arise, either Competent Authority may request consultations to develop appropriate measures to ensure that this Agreement is fulfilled.

2.   This Agreement may be amended by written agreement of the Competent Authorities. Unless otherwise agreed upon, such an amendment is effective on the first day of the month following the expiration of a period of one month after the date of the later of the signatures of such written agreement or the date of the later of the notifications exchanged for purposes of such written agreement.

SECTION 7

Term of Agreement

1.   This Agreement will come into effect […]/[on the date of the notification provided by [Jurisdiction A] Competent Authority that its jurisdiction has the necessary laws in place to implement the Agreement].

2.   A Competent Authority may suspend the exchange of information under this Agreement by giving notice in writing to the other Competent Authority that it has determined that there is or has been significant non-compliance by the other Competent Authority with this Agreement. Such suspension will have immediate effect. For the purposes of this paragraph, significant non-compliance includes, but is not limited to, non-compliance with the confidentiality and data safeguard provisions of this Agreement and the [Convention]/[Instrument], a failure by the Competent Authority to provide timely or adequate information as required under this Agreement or defining the status of Entities or accounts as Non-Reporting Financial Institutions and Excluded Accounts in a manner that frustrates the purposes of the Common Reporting Standard.

3.   Either Competent Authority may terminate this Agreement by giving notice of termination in writing to the other Competent Authority. Such termination will become effective on the first day of the month following the expiration of a period of 12 months after the date of the notice of termination. In the event of termination, all information previously received under this Agreement will remain confidential and subject to the terms of the [Convention/Instrument].

Signed in duplicate in […] on […].

| Competent Authority for [Jurisdiction A]: | Competent Authority for [Jurisdiction B]: |

Annex 3

Common Reporting Standard User Guide

Version 1.0

Introduction

The OECD working with G20 countries has developed a common standard on reporting, due diligence and exchange of financial account information. Under this common standard, jurisdictions obtain from reporting financial institutions and automatically exchange with exchange partners, as appropriate, on an annual basis financial information with respect to all reportable accounts, identified by financial institutions on the basis of common reporting and due diligence rules.

Part of the technical solution to support this common standard is a schema and related instructions.

A schema is a data structure for holding and transmitting information electronically and in bulk. XML "extensible markup language" is commonly used for this purpose. Examples are the OECD's Standard Transmission Format "STF" or the Fisc 153 format used for information exchange for the European Savings Directive.

This User Guide explains the information required to be included in each CRS data element to be reported in the CRS XML Schema v. 1.0. It also contains guidance on how to make corrections of data items within a file that can be processed automatically.

How the CRS User Guide links to the CRS Schema

This User Guide is divided into logical sections based on the schema and provides information on specific data elements and any attributes that describe that data element.

The CRS Schema Information sections are

I   Message Header with the sender, recipient, message type, reporting period

II   Controlling Person or Account Holder details if an individual

III   Account Holder if an entity

IV CRS Body; Reporting FI and Reporting Group and Account details

The numbers of the sections are reflected in the numbering of the diagrams in Appendix A.

The CRS XML Schema is designed to be used for the automatic exchange of financial account information between Competent Authorities ("CAs"). In addition the CRS could also be used for domestic reporting by Financial Institutions ("FIs") to domestic tax authorities under the CRS. Items relevant for domestic reporting only are shown in [*brackets*].

The CRS schema is re-using the FATCA schema and elements of STF, so there are some elements in the CRS schema that are not required for purposes of reporting and exchange under the CRS (e.g. Pool Report and Nationality). These elements are shown in the User Guide as optional, followed by "*non-CRS*".

The comment "*non-CRS*" is also shown on the Appendix A diagrams where relevant.

The CRS XML Schema and its User Guide provide for elements that are unique to CRS e.g. undocumented and closed accounts.

The requirement field for each data element and its attribute indicates whether the element is validation or optional in the schema. Every element is one or the other in the schema.

"Validation" elements MUST be present for ALL data records in a file and an automated validation check can be undertaken. The Sender should do a technical check of the data file content using XML tools to make sure all "Validation" elements are present and if they are not, correct the file. The Receiver may also do so and if incorrect, may reject the file. Where there is a choice between 2 validation elements under a validation parent and only one is needed, this is shown as "Validation (choice)". If the elements are under an optional parent, they are shown as optional.

There may be different business rules for elements that are optional in the schema:

- Some optional fields are shown as "(Optional) Mandatory" – an optional element that is required for CRS reporting as specified in CRS reporting requirements depending on availability of information or legal factors. Mandatory elements may be present in most (but not all) circumstances, so there cannot be a simple IT validation process to check these. (E.g. the CRS provides that a reporting FI is required to report the TIN of an Account Holder only if issued by his jurisdiction of residence / place of birth only if otherwise required to retain and report and is held in electronically searchable records).

- Optional elements may represent a choice between one type or another, where one of them must be used (e.g. choice between address fix or address free). Shown as "Optional" requirement.

- The element may not be required for either schema validation or CRS. It should not be reported in a CRS only file as indicated by "Optional (non CRS)".

Appendix A to the CRS User Guide shows a diagrammatic representation of the CRS XML Schema with all its elements. The numbers next to the headings are the corresponding section numbers in the User Guide text. The comment boxes include both explanations, and changes from the previous version of the CRS schema which will be removed when the draft is agreed.

Appendix B to the CRS User Guide contains a Glossary of namespaces for the CRS XML Schema.

Common Reporting Standard Schema Information

I. Message Header

Information in the message header identifies the tax administration that is sending the message. It specifies when the message was created, what period (normally a year) the report is for, and the nature of the report (original, corrected, supplemental, etc.).

Element	Attribute	Size	Input Type	Requirement
SendingCompanyIN		Unlimited	xsd:string	Optional

[Although not used for exchange between Competent Authorities under CRS, for domestic reporting the Sending Company Identification Number element would be Mandatory and would identify the Financial Institution reporting to the Sending tax authority by domestic TIN (or IN).]

Element	Attribute	Size	Input Type	Requirement
TransmittingCountry		2-character	iso:CountryCode_Type	Validation

This data element identifies the jurisdiction where the reported financial account is maintained or where the reported payment is made by the reporting FI. If the sender is a tax administration, the transmitting country is the jurisdiction of the tax administration. This data element uses the 2-character alphabetic country code and country name list[1] based on the ISO 3166-1 Alpha 2 standard.

[For domestic reporting this element would be the domestic Country Code.]

Element	Attribute	Size	Input Type	Requirement
ReceivingCountry		2-character	iso:CountryCode_Type	Validation

This data element identifies the jurisdiction of the tax administration (the Competent Authority) that is the intended recipient of the message. This data element uses the 2-character alphabetic country code based on the ISO 3166-1 Alpha 2 standard.

[For domestic reporting this element would be the domestic Country Code.]

Element	Attribute	Size	Input Type	Requirement
MessageType			crs:MessageType_EnumType	Validation

This data element specifies the type of message being sent. The only allowable entry in this field for CRS AEOI is "CRS".

Element	Attribute	Size	Input Type	Requirement
Warning			xsd:string	Optional

This data element is a free text field allowing input of specific cautionary instructions about use of the CRS message content, for example terms of the Instrument or Convention under which the data is exchanged. If the reported

---

1. The following disclaimer refers to all uses of the ISO country code list in the CRS schema: *For practical reasons, the list is based on the ISO 3166-1 country list which is currently used by banks and other financial institutions, and hence by tax administrations. The use of this list does not imply the expression by the OECD of any opinion whatsoever concerning the legal status of the territories listed. Its content is without prejudice to the status of or sovereignty over any territory, to the delimitation of international frontiers and boundaries and to the name of any territory, city or area.*

data is for a period other than for a full reporting year this information can be given here as narrative e.g. "ten month period".

Element	Attribute	Size	Input Type	Requirement
Contact			xsd:string	Optional

This data element is a free text field allowing input of specific contact information for the sender of the message. [*May give FI or third party contact for domestic reporting only.*]

Element	Attribute	Size	Input Type	Requirement
MessageRefID			xsd:string	Validation

This data element is a free text field capturing the sender's unique identifying number (created by the sender) that identifies the particular message being sent. The identifier allows both the sender and receiver to identify the specific message later if questions or corrections arise. For exchanges between Competent Authorities, the first part should be the country code of the sending jurisdiction, the second part the year to which the data relates and the third part the receiving country code, before a unique identifier created by the sending jurisdiction (the "national part").

[*If the CRS schema is used for domestic reporting, the FI could include an FI Identification Number in the MessageRefID at the start of the unique identifier created by the FI which is recommended as good practice.*]

Element	Attribute	Size	Input Type	Requirement
MessageTypeIndic			crs:CrsMessageTypeIndic_EnumType	Optional

This data element allows the sender to define the type of message sent. This is an optional element as the DocTypeIndic also identifies whether data is new or corrected (see Guidance on the Correction Process below). Messages must contain all new or all corrected data, [*or advise domestically that there is no data to report*].

[*The MessageTypeIndic can be used domestically to indicate that the Financial Institution has carried out the appropriate checks of its client data but there is no data to report (a "nil return" in effect). In this instance only, Account Report IVc need not be completed.*]

The possible values are:

CRS701= The message contains new information

CRS702= The message contains corrections for previously sent information

CRS703= *The message advises there is no data to report*

Element	Attribute	Size	Input Type	Requirement
CorrMessageRefID			xsd:string	Optional

This data element is a free text field capturing the unique identifying number (as determined by the sender) that identifies a corrected message being sent. This data element MUST reference the original Message Reference ID created for the original message. Guidance on the Correction Process is given below, to explain that this is only used in CRS to cancel a previous message.

Element	Attribute	Size	Input Type	Requirement
ReportingPeriod			xsd:date	Validation

This data element identifies the last day of the reporting period (normally a tax year) to which the message relates in YYYY-MM-DD format. For example, if reporting information for the accounts or payments made in calendar year 2014, the field would read, "2014-12-31". If exceptionally the reporting period is not a year then show the length of the reporting period in Warning.

Element	Attribute	Size	Input Type	Requirement
Timestamp			xsd:dateTime	Validation

This data element identifies the date and time when the message was compiled. It is anticipated this element will be automatically populated by the host system. The format for use is YYYY-MM-DD'T'hh:mm:ss. Fractions of seconds are not used. Example: 2015-03-15T09:45:30.

II. PersonParty_Type

The data elements in this section are used for Individual Account Holders or Controlling Persons of Passive NFEs. This complex type is comprised of the following data elements:

Element	Attribute	Size	Input Type	Requirement
ResCountryCode		2-character	iso:CountryCode_Type	Validation

Element	Attribute	Size	Input Type	Requirement
TIN			cfc:TIN_Type	(Optional) Mandatory

Element	Attribute	Size	Input Type	Requirement
Name			crs:NamePerson_Type	Validation

Element	Attribute	Size	Input Type	Requirement
Address			cfc:Address_Type	Validation

Element	Attribute	Size	Input Type	Requirement
Nationality			iso:CountryCode_Type	Optional (Non CRS)

Element	Attribute	Size	Input Type	Requirement
BirthInfo				(Optional) Mandatory

IIa. ResCountryCode

Element	Attribute	Size	Input Type	Requirement
ResCountryCode		2-character	iso:CountryCode_Type	Validation

This data element describes the tax residence country code(s) for the individual being reported upon and must be present in all data records for CRS AEOI between Competent Authorities.

A separate report for each residence jurisdiction of the Reportable Person including Controlling Persons who are Reportable Persons is required, along with details of the Entity, if there is more than one jurisdiction of residence.

[*For domestic reporting, if the individual is certified or treated as tax resident in more than one jurisdiction then this element may be repeated and the data should be sent to the tax authority. It would also be advisable to mandate the use of the domestic country code for undocumented accounts, which will not be exchanged between Competent Authorities.*]

The complete information including all residence country codes that have been identified as applicable to the Reportable Person may be sent to every Competent Authority of a jurisdiction of residence so that there is an awareness of the possible need to resolve dual residence status or other issues attached to multiple reporting. It is recommended that the Competent Authority send a data record to each of the residence jurisdictions showing all reportable residence jurisdictions.

Alternatively, in certain circumstances the sending jurisdiction may choose to send data with only the residence country code of the receiving jurisdiction to each and may use a different method to exchange information relevant to multiple residence jurisdictions in accordance with the applicable legal instrument(s) if and when required.

IIb. TIN Type

Element	Attribute	Size	Input Type	Requirement
TIN		Min 1 char	cfc:TIN_Type	(Optional) Mandatory

This data element identifies the Tax Identification Number (TIN) used by the receiving tax administration to identify the Individual Account Holder. The TIN (if available) should be supplied as specified in the CRS.

Element	Attribute	Size	Input Type	Requirement
TIN	issuedBy	2-character	iso:CountryCode_Type	(Optional) Mandatory

This attribute identifies the jurisdiction that issued the TIN. If the issuing jurisdiction is not known then this may be left blank.

IIc. NamePerson_Type

Element	Attribute	Size	Input Type	Requirement
NamePerson_Type	nameType		stf:OECDNameType_EnumType	Optional

This data element allows the FI to report both the name at birth and the name after marriage.

OECDNameType_EnumType

It is possible for a CRS individual or entity to have several names. This is a qualifier to indicate the type of a particular name. Such types include nicknames ("nick"), names under which a party does business ("dba" a short name for the entity, or a name that is used for public acquaintance instead of the official business name) etc.

The possible values are:

- OECD201= SMFAliasOrOther (not used for CRS)
- OECD202= indiv
- OECD203= alias
- OECD204= nick
- OECD205= aka
- OECD206= dba
- OECD207= legal
- OECD208= atbirth

Element	Attribute	Size	Input Type	Requirement
PrecedingTitle			xsd:string	Optional

Element	Attribute	Size	Input Type	Requirement
Title			xsd:string	Optional

Element	Attribute	Size	Input Type	Requirement
FirstName			xsd:string	Validation

This data element is required for CRS reporting. If the reporting FI or tax administration transmitting the message does not have a complete first name for an Individual Account Holder or Controlling Person an initial or NFN ("No First Name") may be used here.

Element	Attribute	Size	Input Type	Requirement
FirstName	xnlNameType		xsd:string	Optional

Element	Attribute	Size	Input Type	Requirement
MiddleName			xsd:string	Optional

This data element allows for the Individual's Middle Name. The data is optional for CRS reporting; if the Reporting FI holds a Middle Name or initial it may be included here.

Element	Attribute	Size	Input Type	Requirement
MiddleName	xnlNameType		xsd:string	Optional

Element	Attribute	Size	Input Type	Requirement
NamePrefix			xsd:string	Optional

Element	Attribute	Size	Input Type	Requirement
NamePrefix	xnlNameType		xsd:string	Optional

Element	Attribute	Size	Input Type	Requirement
LastName			xsd:string	Validation

This data element is required for CRS reporting. The reporting FI or tax administration transmitting the message must provide the Individual Account Holder's last name. This field can include any prefix or suffix legally used by the Account Holder.

As the element is a string it is possible to use this for a free format name or two last names although wherever possible the structured first name and last name should be used.

Element	Attribute	Size	Input Type	Requirement
LastName	xnlNameType		xsd:string	Optional

Element	Attribute	Size	Input Type	Requirement
GenerationIdentifier			xsd:string	Optional

Element	Attribute	Size	Input Type	Requirement
Suffix			xsd:string	Optional

Element	Attribute	Size	Input Type	Requirement
GeneralSuffix			xsd:string	Optional

IId. Address_Type

There are two options for Address type in the schema – AddressFix and AddressFree. AddressFix should be used for all CRS reporting unless the reporting FI or tax administration transmitting the message cannot define the various parts of the account holder's address.

This data element is the permanent residence address e.g. of the individual account holder. If the reporting FI or tax administration does not have a permanent residence address on file for the individual, then the address is the mailing address used by the financial institution to contact the individual account holder when the report is compiled.

Element	Attribute	Size	Input Type	Requirement
CountryCode		2-character	iso:CountryCode_Type	Validation

This data element provides the country code associated with the account holder's address. [*For undocumented accounts the domestic country code will be used as no address is available. As the address requires another data item to be completed then "undocumented" could be used instead of an actual address.*]

Element	Attribute	Size	Input Type	Requirement
AddressFree			xsd:string	Optional*

This data element allows input of address information in free text. If the user chooses the option to enter the data required in a less structured way in

"AddressFree" all available address details shall be presented as one string of bytes, blank or "/" (slash) or carriage return-line feed used as a delimiter between parts of the address. *This option should only be used if the data cannot be presented in the AddressFix format.

NOTE: If the reporting FI or tax administration transmitting the message selects AddressFix, it will have the option of inputting the full street address of the account holder in the AddressFree element rather than using the related fixed elements. In this case, the city, subentity, and postal code information should still be entered in the appropriate fixed elements.

Element	Attribute	Size	Input Type	Requirement
AddressType	legalAddressType		stf:OECDLegalAddressType_EnumType	Optional

OECDLegalAddressType_EnumType

This is a datatype for an attribute to an address. It serves to indicate the legal character of that address (residential, business etc.)

The possible values are:

- OECD301= residentialOrBusiness
- OECD302= residential
- OECD303= business
- OECD304= registeredOffice
- OECD305= unspecified

Element	Attribute	Size	Input Type	Requirement
Street			xsd:string	Optional

Element	Attribute	Size	Input Type	Requirement
BuildingIdentifier			xsd:string	Optional

Element	Attribute	Size	Input Type	Requirement
SuiteIdentifier			xsd:string	Optional

Element	Attribute	Size	Input Type	Requirement
FloorIdentifier			xsd:string	Optional

Element	Attribute	Size	Input Type	Requirement
DistrictName			xsd:string	Optional

Element	Attribute	Size	Input Type	Requirement
POB			xsd:string	Optional

Element	Attribute	Size	Input Type	Requirement
PostCode			xsd:string	Optional

Element	Attribute	Size	Input Type	Requirement
City			xsd:string	Validation

Element	Attribute	Size	Input Type	Requirement
CountrySubentity			xsd:string	Optional

The above data elements comprise the AddressFix type. The "City" data element is required for schema validation. The PostCode should always be included where it exists. Information pertaining to the account holder's street address may be entered here or in the AddressFree data element.

IIe. Nationality

Element	Attribute	Size	Input Type	Requirement
Nationality		2-character	iso:CountryCode_Type	Optional (non-CRS)

This data element is not required for CRS and should not be completed.

IIf. BirthInfo

Element	Attribute	Size	Input Type	Requirement
BirthDate			xsd:date	(Optional) Mandatory

This data element identifies the date of birth of the Individual Account Holder. The date of birth may be left empty when it is not required to be reported under the CRS (this may occur for Pre-existing Accounts if the date of birth is not available in the records of the Reporting Financial Institution and is not otherwise required to be collected by such Reporting Financial Institution under domestic law).

The data format is YYYY-MM-DD.

The three data elements below apply specifically to the place of birth and may be provided in accordance with CRS guidance where the financial institution is required to obtain and report the information under domestic law, and it is available in its electronically searchable records.

Element	Attribute	Size	Input Type	Requirement
City			xsd:string	Optional

Element	Attribute	Size	Input Type	Requirement
CitySubentity			xsd:string	Optional

Element	Attribute	Size	Input Type	Requirement
CountryInfo				Optional

This data element gives a choice between a current jurisdiction (identified by 2-character country code) or a former jurisdiction (identified by name). One or other should be supplied if place of birth is reported, together with City or City and CitySubentity.

Element	Attribute	Size	Input Type	Requirement
CountryCode		2-character	iso:CountryCode_Type	Optional

Element	Attribute	Size	Input Type	Requirement
FormerCountryName			xsd:string	Optional

III. OrganisationParty_Type

This complex type identifies the name of an Account Holder that is an Entity as opposed to an Individual.

It is comprised of the following four data elements:

Element	Attribute	Size	Input Type	Requirement
ResCountryCode		2-character	iso:CountryCode_Type	(Optional) Mandatory

Element	Attribute	Size	Input Type	Requirement
IN		Min 1 char	crs: OrganisationIN_Type	(Optional) Mandatory

Element	Attribute	Size	Input Type	Requirement
Name			cfc:NameOrganisation_Type	Validation

Element	Attribute	Size	Input Type	Requirement
Address			cfc:Address_Type	Validation

IIIa. ResCountryCode

Element	Attribute	Size	Input Type	Requirement
ResCountryCode		2-character	iso:CountryCode_Type	(Optional) Mandatory

This data element describes the tax residence country code for the organisation reporting or being reported upon.

IIIb. Entity IN (OrganisationIN_Type)

Element	Attribute	Size	Input Type	Requirement
IN		Min 1 char	crs: OrganisationIN_Type	(Optional) Mandatory

This data element provides the identification number (IN) used by the sending and/or receiving tax administration to identify the Entity Account Holder. For CRS this may be the US GIIN, a TIN, company registration number, Global Entity Identification Number (EIN) or other similar identifying number specified by the tax administration.

This data element can be repeated if a second IN is present.

Element	Attribute	Size	Input Type	Requirement
IN	issuedBy	2-character	iso:CountryCode_Type	Optional

This attribute describes the jurisdiction that issued the IN. If the issuing jurisdiction is not known then this may be left blank.

Element	Attribute	Size	Input Type	Requirement
IN	INType		xsd:string	Optional

This Attribute defines the type of identification number being sent (e.g. US GIIN, EIN, TIN). Possible values should normally be agreed between Competent Authorities.

IIIc. Organisation Name

Element	Attribute	Size	Input Type	Requirement
Name			cfc:NameOrganisation_Type	Validation

Legal name of the entity that is reporting or being reported on.

Element	Attribute	Size	Input Type	Requirement
Name	nameType		stf:OECDNameType_EnumType	Optional

IV. CRS Body

The CRS body comprises the Reporting FI and Reporting Group elements.

IVa. Reporting FI

Identifies the financial institution that maintains the reported financial account or that makes the reported payment.

Reporting FI or tax administration uses the OrganisationParty_Type to provide identifying information

Element	Attribute	Size	Input Type	Requirement
ReportingFI			crs:CorrectableOrganisationParty_Type	Validation

Element	Attribute	Size	Input Type	Requirement
DocSpec			stf:DocSpec_Type	Validation

DocSpec identifies the particular report within the CRS message being transmitted. It allows for identification of reports requiring correction (see also guidance on Corrections below).

IVb. ReportingGroup

This data element provides specific details about the CRS report being sent by the reporting FI or tax administration transmitting the message.

Although in the schema this element is repeatable, for CRS only one ReportingGroup for each CRSBody is to be provided. The AccountReport should be repeated as required.

Element	Attribute	Size	Input Type	Requirement
ReportingGroup			crs:CorrectableOrganisationParty_Type	Validation

The following four data elements comprise the Reporting Group:

Element	Attribute	Size	Input Type	Requirement
Sponsor			crs:CorrectableOrganisationParty_Type	Optional (non-CRS)

Where a Financial Institution uses a third party to submit information on their behalf for CRS this element is not used but contact details can be given in Element "Contact".

Element	Attribute	Size	Input Type	Requirement
Intermediary			crs:CorrectableOrganisationParty_Type	Optional (non-CRS)

IVc. Account Report

Element	Attribute	Size	Input Type	Requirement
AccountReport			crs:CorrectableOrganisationParty_Type	(Optional) Mandatory

AccountReport is mandatory under CRS *(except where the MessageTypeIndic CRS703 is used domestically to indicate that there is no data to report)*. In all other instances AccountReport must be completed. AccountReport includes the following data elements under CorrectableAccoutReport_Type:

Element	Attribute	Size	Input Type	Requirement
DocSpec			stf:DocSpec_Type	Validation

DocSpec identifies the particular report within the CRS message being transmitted. It allows for identification of reports requiring correction. See guidance on Corrections and a description of DocSpec Type.

IVd. Account Number

Element	Attribute	Size	Input Type	Requirement
AccountNumber			crs:FIAccountNumber_Type	Validation

Provide the account number used by the financial institution to identify the account. If the financial institution does not have an account number then provide the functional equivalent unique identifier used by the financial institution to identify the account.

Mandatory for financial institutions that have an account number (including alpha numeric identifiers).

For example: The account number may be the account number of a Custodial Account or Depository Account; ii) the code (ISIN or other) related to a Debt or Equity Interest (if not held in a custody account); or iii) the identification code of a Cash Value Insurance Contract or Annuity Contract.

If exceptionally there is no account numbering system use NANUM for no account number as this is a Validation element.

This format for account number is the same as FATCA and can be used for structured account numbers as well as free format; a non-standard account identifier or an insurance contract number could be included here.

Element	Attribute	Size	Input Type	Requirement
AccountNumber	AcctNumberType		cfc:AcctNumberType_EnumType	Optional

There is an option to include information about the account number type as an enumeration. The possible values are:

- OECD601= IBAN International Bank Account Number (follows a known structure)

- OECD602= OBAN Other Bank Account Number

- OECD603= ISIN International Securities Information Number (follows a known structure)

- OECD604= OSIN Other Securities Information Number

- OECD605= Other Any other type of account number e.g. insurance contract

Where an IBAN or ISIN is available, it should be provided and the appropriate information about the account number type supplied.

Element	Attribute	Size	Input Type	Requirement
AccountNumber	UndocumentedAccount		xsd:boolean	(Optional) Mandatory

[This attribute is for use in CRS domestic reporting to indicate that the account is undocumented.]

Element	Attribute	Size	Input Type	Requirement
AccountNumber	ClosedAccount		xsd:boolean	(Optional) Mandatory

This attribute is for use in CRS reporting to indicate that the account is closed.

Element	Attribute	Size	Input Type	Requirement
AccountNumber	DormantAccount		xsd:boolean	Optional

This attribute may be used in CRS reporting to indicate that the account is dormant.

IVe. Account Holder

Element	Attribute	Size	Input Type	Requirement
AccountHolder			crs:AccountHolder_Type	Validation

For CRS this data element may identify an entity account holder who is

- a passive NFE with one or more controlling person that is a Reportable Person
- a CRS Reportable Person

As there is a choice of entering an individual, or an organisation plus AcctHolderType, (but one or other must be entered as the account holder), these are shown as Validation (choice) below.

Element	Attribute	Size	Input Type	Requirement
Individual			crs:PersonParty_Type	Validation (choice)

If the Account Holder reported is a natural person, report his/her identifying information here.

Element	Attribute	Size	Input Type	Requirement
Organisation			crs:OrganisationParty_Type	Validation (choice)

If the Account Holder reported is not a natural person, report the entity's identifying information here.

Element	Attribute	Size	Input Type	Requirement
AcctHolderType			crs:CrsAcctHolderType_EnumType	Validation (choice)

This data element identifies an entity account holder that is

- a passive NFE with one or more controlling person that is a Reportable Person
- a CRS Reportable Person
- a passive NFE that is a CRS Reportable Person

Complete only if the reported financial account is held by an entity or the reported payment is made to an entity described-above. Allowable entries for CRS:

- CRS101= Passive Non-Financial Entity with – one or more controlling person that is a Reportable Person
- CRS102= CRS Reportable Person
- CRS103= Passive Non-Financial Entity that is a CRS Reportable Person

IVf. Controlling Person

Element	Attribute	Size	Input Type	Requirement
ControllingPerson			crs:ControllingPerson_Type	(Optional) Mandatory

Provide the name of any Controlling Person of a Passive NFE that is a Reportable Person. Mandatory only if the entity Account Holder is a Passive NFE with one or more Controlling Persons who is are Reportable Persons. If the Passive NFE has more than one Controlling Person that is a Reportable Person, then the name of all such Reportable Persons must be reported.

A separate report should be created with respect to each Reportable Jurisdiction that has been identified as a jurisdiction of residence of the Controlling Persons who are Reportable Persons. However, only information of the Reportable Persons of each Reportable Jurisdiction (including information of the Passive NFE and other associated data) should be included in the report.

Where an Entity Account Holder is a Reportable Person and is also a Passive NFE with one or more Controlling Persons that is a Reportable Person, and both the Entity and any of such Controlling Persons are resident in the same Reportable Jurisdiction, the information with respect to the account may be reported *(i)* as an account of an Entity that is a Passive NFE with a Controlling Person that is a Reportable Person, or *(ii)* as such and as an account of an Entity that is a Reportable Person (i.e. as if were information with respect to two accounts).

Where none of such Controlling Persons is resident in the same Reportable Jurisdiction as the Entity, the information with respect to the account must nevertheless be reported as an account of an Entity that is a Reportable Person.

Element	Attribute	Size	Input Type	Requirement
Individual			crs:PersonParty_Type	Validation

Defines a Controlling Person with its Name, Address, Country of Residence.

Element	Attribute	Size	Input Type	Requirement
CtrlgPersonType			crs:CrsCtrlgPersonType_EnumType	(Optional) Mandatory

This data element allows the identification of the type of each Controlling Person ("CP") when available, by use of the attribute "ControllingPersonType" with the following options:

a) CP of legal person – ownership

b) CP of legal person – other means

c) CP of legal person – senior managing official

d) CP of legal arrangement – trust – settlor

e) CP of legal arrangement – trust – trustee

f) CP of legal arrangement – trust – protector

g) CP of legal arrangement – trust – beneficiary

h) CP of legal arrangement – trust – other

i) CP of legal arrangement – other – settlor-equivalent

j) CP of legal arrangement – other – trustee-equivalent

k) CP of legal arrangement – other – protector-equivalent

l) CP of legal arrangement – other – beneficiary-equivalent

m) CP of legal arrangement – other – other-equivalent

Allowable entries for CRS:

- CRS801= CP of legal person – ownership
- CRS802= CP of legal person – other means
- CRS803= CP of legal person – senior managing official
- CRS804= CP of legal arrangement – trust – settlor
- CRS805= CP of legal arrangement – trust – trustee
- CRS806= CP of legal arrangement – trust – protector
- CRS807= CP of legal arrangement – trust – beneficiary
- CRS808= CP of legal arrangement – trust – other
- CRS809= CP of legal arrangement – other – settlor-equivalent
- CRS810= CP of legal arrangement – other – trustee-equivalent
- CRS811= CP of legal arrangement – other – protector-equivalent
- CRS812= CP of legal arrangement – other – beneficiary-equivalent
- CRS813= CP of legal arrangement – other – other-equivalent

IVg. Account Balance

Element	Attribute	Size	Input Type	Requirement
AccountBalance			cfc:MonAmnt_Type	Validation

Provide the account balance or value of the reported financial account.

- Depository and custodial accounts. The account balance or value shall be in accordance with CRS guidance.

- Cash value and annuity contracts. The cash value insurance or annuity contract is the balance or value of the account.

- Debt or equity accounts. The account balance is the value of the debt or equity interest that the account holder has in the financial institution.

- Enter Zero if account has been closed, in combination with account closed attribute.

- Numeric characters (digits). Account balance is entered with 2-digit fractional amounts of the currency in question. For example, USD 1 000 would be entered as 1000.00.

Element	Attribute	Size	Input Type	Requirement
AccountBalance	currCode	3 characters	iso:currCode_Type	Validation

All amounts must be accompanied by the appropriate 3 character currency code[2] based on the ISO 4217 Alpha 3 standard.

IVh. Payment

Element	Attribute	Size	Input Type	Requirement
Payment			crs:Payment_Type	Optional

Provide information on payment made to the reported financial account during the reporting period.

---

2. The following disclaimer refers to all uses of the ISO currency code list in the CRS schema: *For practical reasons, the list is based on the ISO 4217 Alpha 3 currency list which is currently used by banks and other financial institutions, and hence by tax administrations. The use of this list does not imply the expression by the OECD of any opinion whatsoever concerning the legal status of the territories listed. Its content is without prejudice to the status of or sovereignty over any territory, to the delimitation of international frontiers and boundaries and to the name of any territory, city or area.*

Payment information is a repeating element, if more than one payment type needs to be reported.

For example payment types may include the following:

Depository accounts:

- The aggregate gross amount of interest paid or credited to the account during the calendar year.

Custodial accounts:

- The aggregate gross amount of dividends paid or credited to the account during the calendar year (or relevant reporting period);

- The aggregate gross amount of interest paid or credited to the account during the calendar year (or relevant reporting period);

- The gross proceeds from the sale or redemption of property paid or credited to the account during the calendar year (or relevant reporting period) with respect to which the FFI acted as a custodian, broker, nominee, or otherwise as an agent for the account holder and;

- The aggregate gross amount of all other income paid or credited to the account during the calendar year (or relevant reporting period).

Debt or equity accounts:

- The aggregate gross amount of payments paid or credited to the account during the calendar year (or relevant reporting period), including redemption payments.

Cash value insurance and annuity contract accounts:

- The aggregate gross amount of payments paid or credited to the account during the calendar year (or relevant reporting period), including redemption payments.

Element	Attribute	Size	Input Type	Requirement
Type			crs:CrsPaymentType_EnumType	Validation

Select the proper code to identify the payment type. Specific payment types listed are:

- CRS501= Dividends

- CRS502= Interest

- CRS503= Gross Proceeds/Redemptions

- CRS504= Other – CRS. (Example: other income generated with respect to the assets held in the account)

Element	Attribute	Size	Input Type	Requirement
PaymentAmnt			cfc:MonAmnt_Type	Validation

Payment Amounts are entered with 2-digit fractional amounts of the currency in question. For example, USD 1 000 would be entered as 1000.00.

Element	Attribute	Size	Input Type	Requirement
PaymentAmnt	currCode	3 characters	iso:currCode_Type	Validation

All payment amounts must be accompanied by the appropriate 3 character currency code based on the ISO 4217 Alpha 3 standard.

IVi. Pool Report

Element	Attribute	Size	Input Type	Requirement
PoolReport			ftc:CorrectablePoolReport_Type	Optional (Non-CRS)

Pool reporting is not applicable to CRS.

Transliteration

Where transliteration is required because sending and receiving jurisdictions do not use a common alphabet, Competent Authorities may agree how they will undertake such transliteration. If there is no such agreement, then the sending jurisdiction should, if so requested, transliterate from its domestic alphabet or literation to a Latin alphabet aligned with international standards for transliteration (for example as specified in ISO 8859). The sending jurisdiction may send designatory data (e.g. name or address) in both domestic alphabet or literation and separately in Latin alphabet within each account record if they so choose. The receiving jurisdiction should also be prepared to transliterate between Latin and its own domestic alphabet or literation.

Guidance on the correction process for Common Reporting Standard

1.   In the course of AEOI, the sending jurisdiction may need to correct some elements of data previously sent. The section below describes how to make automatic corrections by sending a file of corrected data that can be processed in the same systems as the original data that was received. Reference to corrections also includes deletion of data elements in the following section.

2.   If the whole of a data file is to be completely replaced, there can be a cancellation of the first message, then a new message with a file of completely new data can be sent, with no link to the previous records apart from in the message header – "cancel and replace" not "correct".

(The Competent Authority may keep the original file to investigate reasons for the errors in the data that led to cancellation and issue of the replacement file.)

Technical Guidance

3.   In order to identify the elements to correct, the top-level elements Reporting FI or Account Report include an element of type DocSpec_Type, which provides necessary information for corrections.

DocSpec Type

Element	Attribute	Size	Input Type	Requirement
DocSpec			stf:DocSpec_Type	Validation

DocSpec identifies the particular record within the CRS message being transmitted. It allows for identification of records that require correction. DocSpec_Type is comprised of the following elements:

Element	Attribute	Size	Input Type	Requirement
DocTypeIndic			stf:OECDDocTypeIndic_EnumType	Validation

This element specifies the type of data being submitted. Allowable entries are:

- OECD0= Resend Data (not used for CRS reporting)
- OECD1= New Data
- OECD2= Corrected Data
- OECD3= Deletion of Data
- OECD10= Resend Test Data (not used for CRS reporting)
- OECD11= New Test Data
- OECD12= Corrected Test Data
- OECD13= Deletion of Test Data

4.   A message can contain either new records (OECD1) or corrections/ deletions (OECD2 and OECD3), but should not contain a mixture of both. OECD10 – OECD13 should only be used during previously agreed-upon testing periods or after a bilateral discussion where both parties agree to testing. This is to help eliminate the possibility that test data could be co-mingled with "live" data.

Element	Attribute	Size	Input Type	Requirement
DocRefID		Minimum 1 character	xsd:string	Validation

A unique identifier for this document (i.e. one record and all its children data elements).

A correction (or deletion) must have a new unique DocRefID for future reference.

Element	Attribute	Size	Input Type	Requirement
CorrDocRefID		Minimum 1 character	xsd:string	Optional

The CorrDocRefID references the DocRefID of the element to be corrected/deleted. It must always refer to the latest reference of this Account-report (DocRefID) that was sent.

In this way, a series of corrections or amendments can be handled as each correction completely replaces the previous version. The CRS Correction examples below show how this works in practice.

Element	Attribute	Size	Input Type	Requirement
CorrMessageRefID		Minimum 1 character	xsd:string	Optional (Non-CRS)

Since the DocRefID is unique in space and time, this element is not used for CRS at the DocSpec level.

Uniqueness of MessageRefID and DocRefID

5.   In order to ensure that a message and a record can be identified and corrected, the MessageRefID and DocRefID must be unique in space and time (i.e. there must be no other message or record in existence that has the same reference identifier).

6.   The identifier can contain whatever information the sender uses to allow identification of the particular report but should start with the sending country code as the first element for Competent Authority to Competent Authority transmission, then the year to which the data relates, then the receiving country code before a unique identifier.

e.g. FR2013CA123456789

7.   The unique identifier in the DocRefID could be the reference used by the FI to report nationally, or a different unique reference created by the sending tax administration, but should in all cases start with the country code of the sending jurisdiction

e.g. FRFI286abc123xyz

or FRabc123xyz

8.   *[If the CRS schema is used for domestic reporting, the FI may similarly include an FI Identification Number in both MessageRefID and DocRefID which is recommended as good practice to ensure uniqueness in time and space and helps to link queries to source data.]*

MessageSpec and Corrections

9.   Correction messages must have their own unique MessageRefID so they can also be corrected in the future. There is no equivalent for the DocSpecIndic when it comes to messages as a whole.

10.   To cancel a complete message, the MessageSpec.CorrMessageRefID can be used. Please note that the intention would be only to use this where there has been a major error, for example a processing failure. In this instance all documents contained in these messages should be quarantined.

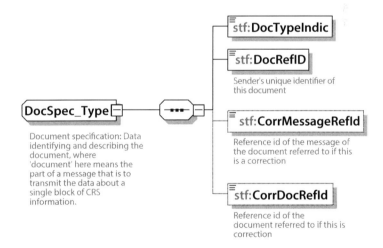

11.   The following three examples show how the DocSpec_Type elements are used to correct one or multiple parts of data previously sent.

Common Reporting Standard Correction examples

First example: a correction is made on the Payment amount.

The correction file is sent from France to Canada (containing only corrections, not a mix of new and corrected data).

MessageRefID: FR2013CAFranceNationalPart00001.

For a Correction, the whole AccountReport must be resent with all its information (AccountNumber, AccountHolder, ControllingPerson, AccountBalance, Payment).

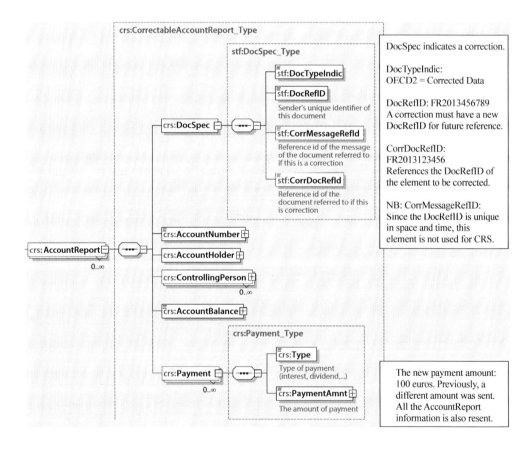

Second example: a correction is made on multiple information: on the name, address and payment amount. The correction is made on the previous correction (so it must reference the latest DocRefID: FR2013456789).

MessageRefID: FR2013CAFranceNationalPart00002.

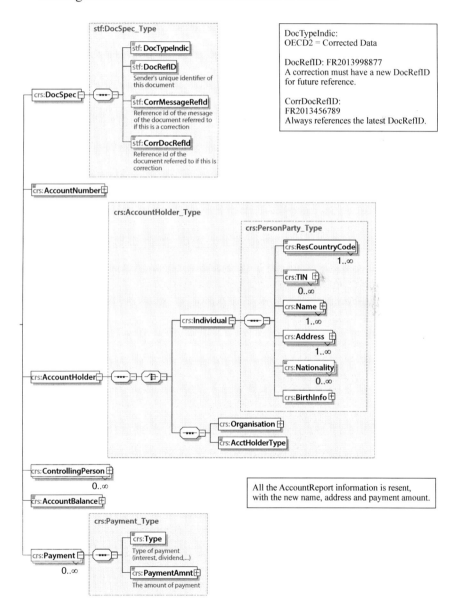

DocTypeIndic:
OECD2 = Corrected Data

DocRefID: FR2013998877
A correction must have a new DocRefID for future reference.

CorrDocRefID:
FR2013456789
Always references the latest DocRefID.

All the AccountReport information is resent, with the new name, address and payment amount.

Third example: a correction is made only on the Reporting FI, no Account Report data needs to be corrected. The correction must reference the ReportingFI to be corrected, via its DocRefID (in this example, assume the previous ReportingFI's DocRefID was FR2013FI007).

MessageRefID: FR2013CAFranceNationalPart00003.

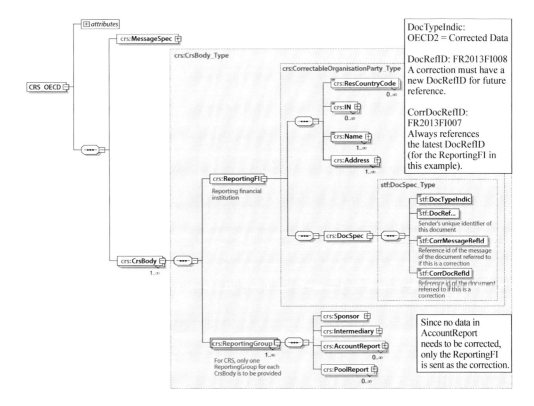

Appendix A

CRS XML Schema v. 1.0 Diagrams

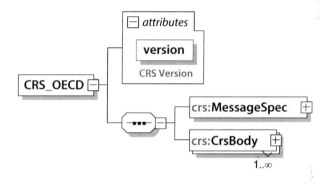

Message Header (Section I)

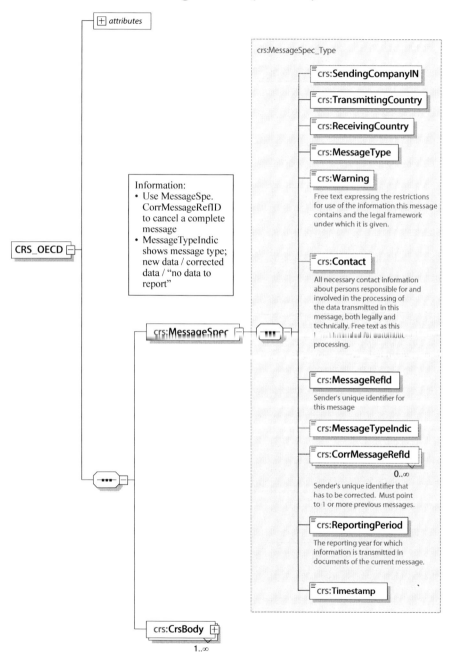

CRS Body (Section IV)

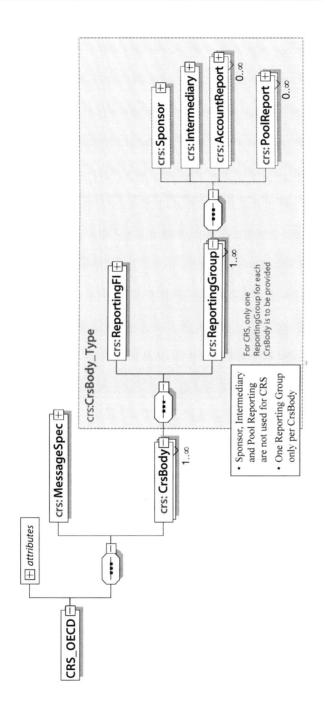

Reporting FI (Section IVa)

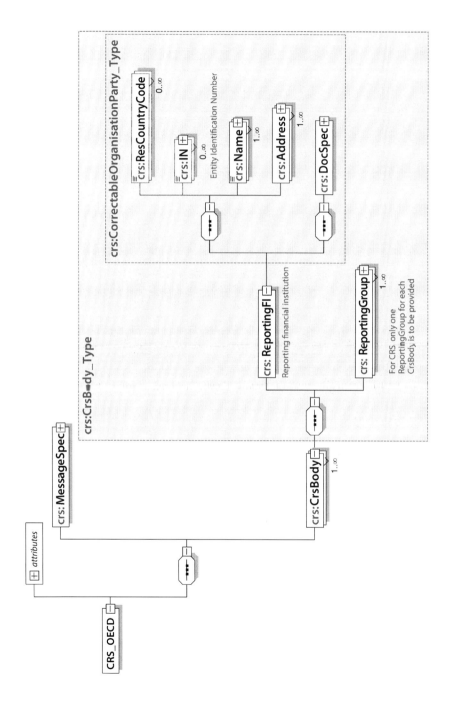

Reporting Group (Section IVb)

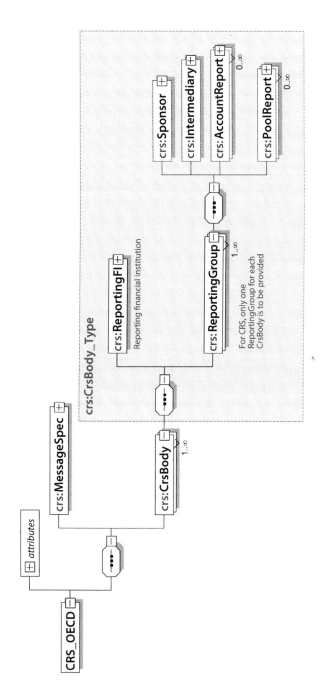

Account Report (Section IVe)

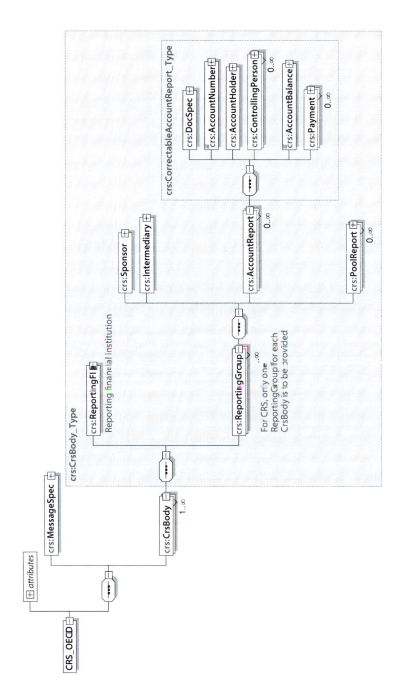

Account Number Type (Section IVd)

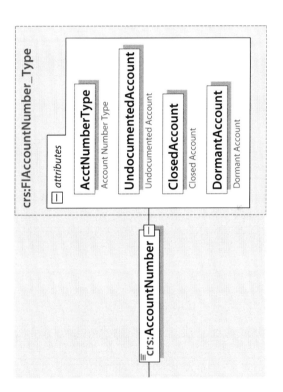

Account Holder (Section IVe)

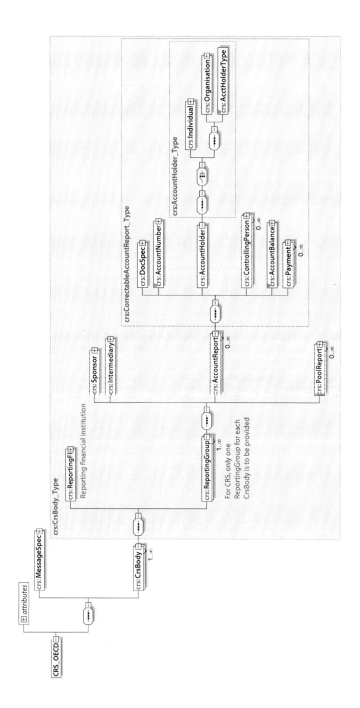

Individual/Organisation Account Holders (Section IVe)

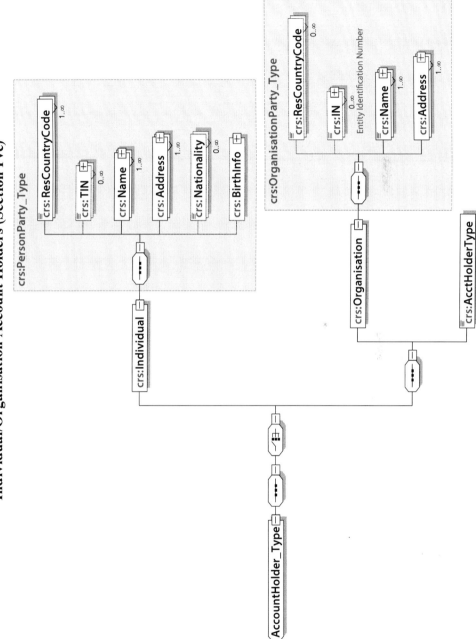

Controlling Person (Section IVf)

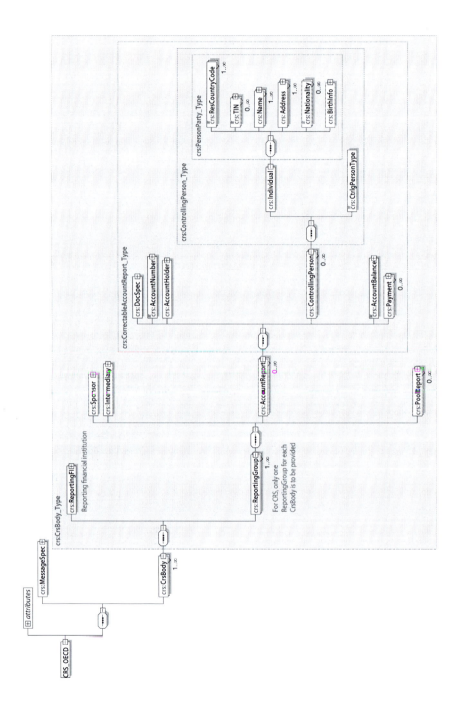

Payment type (Section IVh)

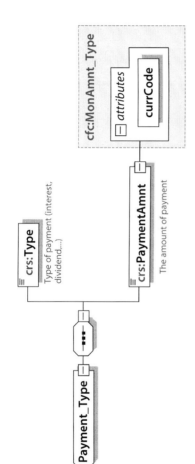

For practical reasons, the CurrencyCode list is based on the ISO 4217 currency code list which is currently used by banks and other financial institutions, and hence by tax administrations. The use of this list does not imply the expression by the OECD of any opinion whatsoever concerning the legal status of the territories listed. Its content is without prejudice to the status of or sovereignty over any territory, to the delimitation of international frontiers and boundaries and to the name of any territory, city or area.

Person Party Type (Section II)

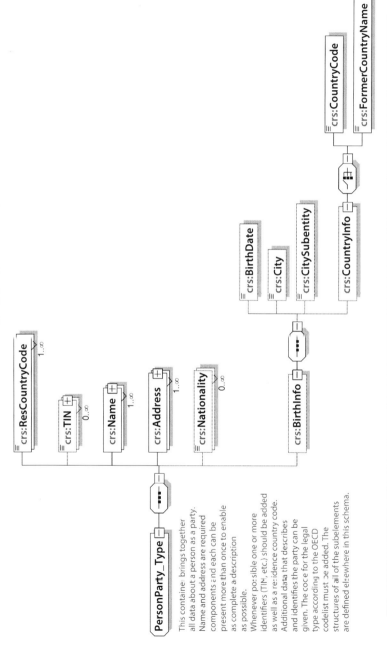

For practical reasons, the ResCountryCode list is based on the ISO 3166-1 country list which is currently used by banks and other financial institutions, and hence by tax administrations. The use of this list does not imply the expression by the OECD of any opinion whatsoever concerning the legal status of the territories listed. Its content is without prejudice to the status of or sovereignty over any territory; to the delimitation of international frontiers and boundaries and to the name of any territory, city or area.

Person Name Type

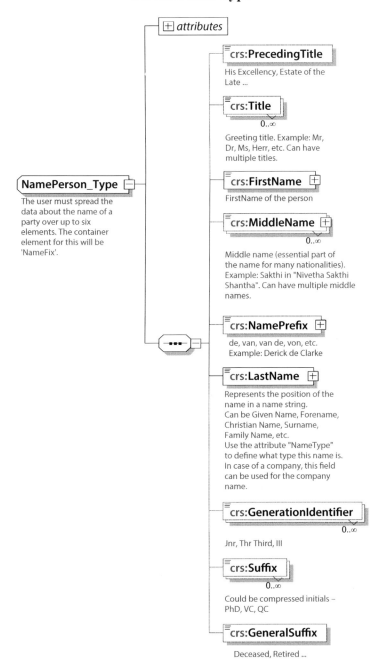

Address Type

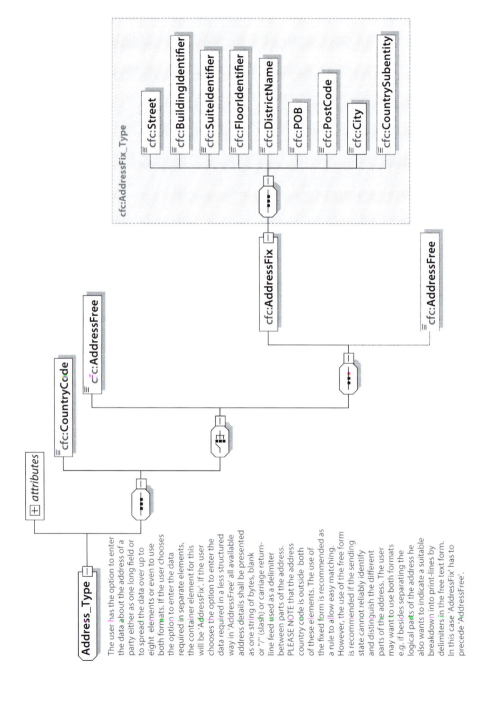

The user has the option to enter the data about the address of a party either as one long field or to spread the data over up to eight elements or even to use both formats. If the user chooses the option to enter the data required in separate elements, the container element for this will be 'AddressFix'. If the user chooses the option to enter the data required in a less structured way in 'AddressFree' all available address details shall be presented as one string of bytes, blank or "/" (slash) or carriage return-line feed used as a delimiter between parts of the address. PLEASE NOTE that the address country code is outside both of these elements. The use of the fixed form is recommended as a rule to allow easy matching. However, the use of the free form is recommended if the sending state cannot reliably identify and distinguish the different parts of the address. The user may want to use both formats e.g. if besides separating the logical parts of the address he also wants to indicate a suitable breakdown into print-lines by delimiters in the free text form. In this case 'AddressFix' has to precede 'AddressFree'.

Organisation Party Type (Section III)

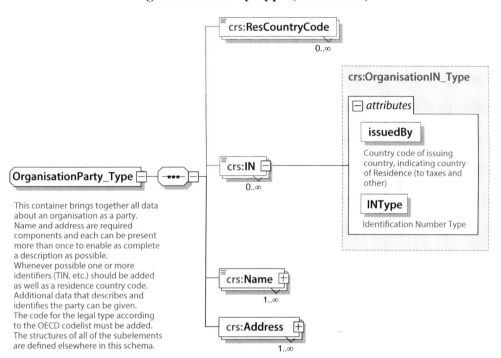

For practical reasons, the ResCountryCode list is based on the ISO 3166-1 country list which is currently used by banks and other financial institutions, and hence by tax administrations. The use of this list does not imply the expression by the OECD of any opinion whatsoever concerning the legal status of the territories listed. Its content is without prejudice to the status of or sovereignty over any territory, to the delimitation of international frontiers and boundaries and to the name of any territory, city or area.

Pool Report (Non-CRS) (Section IVi)

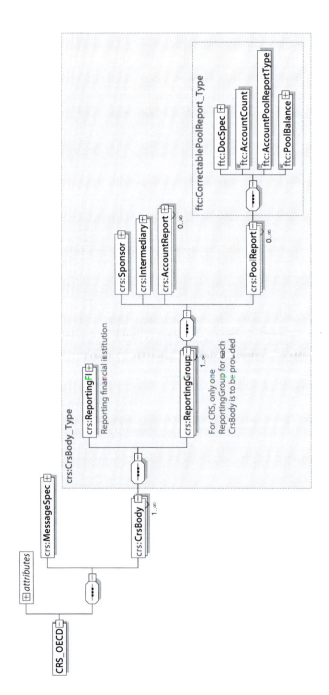

Sponsor & Intermediary (Non-CRS)

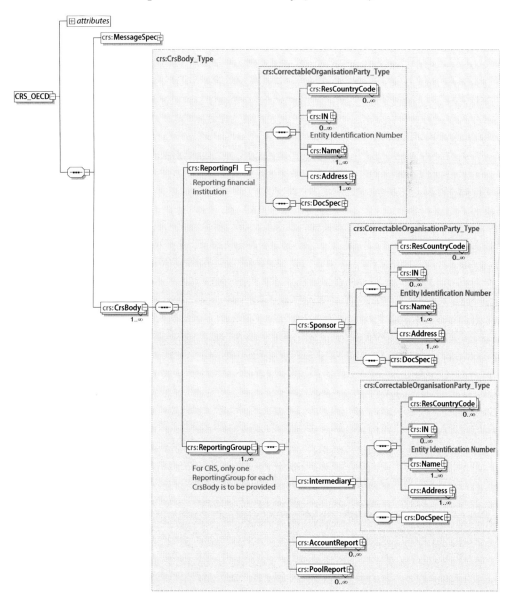

Appendix B

Glossary of Namespaces

CRS Schema Namespaces

Namespace	Description	Filename
crs	CRS specific types	CrsXML_v1.0.xsd
cfc	Common types for FATCA and CRS	CommonTypesFatcaCrs_v1.1.xsd
ftc	FATCA specific types	FatcaTypes_v1.1.xsd
stf	OECD Common Types	OECDTypes_v4.1.xsd
iso	ISO types (Country & Currency codes)	isocrstypes_v1.0.xsd

Annex 4

Example Questionnaire

1. Legal Framework

A legal framework must ensure the confidentiality of exchanged tax information and limit its use to appropriate purposes. The two basic components of such a framework are the terms of the applicable treaty, TIEA or other bilateral agreement for the exchange of information, and a jurisdiction's domestic legislation.

1.1. Tax Conventions, TIEAs & Other Exchange Agreements	
Primary Check-list Areas	• Provisions in tax treaties, TIEAs and international agreements requiring confidentiality of exchanged information and restricting use to intended purposes
How do the exchange of information provisions in your Tax Conventions, TIEAs, or other exchange agreements ensure confidentiality and restrict the use of both outgoing information to other Contracting States and incoming information received in response to a request?	

1.2. Domestic Legislation	
Primary Check-list Areas	• Domestic law must apply safeguards to taxpayer information exchanged pursuant to a treaty, TIEA or other international agreement, and treat those information exchange agreements as binding, restrict data access and use and impose penalties for violations.
How do your domestic laws and regulations safeguard and restrict the use of information exchanged for tax purposes under Tax Conventions, TIEAs, or other exchange instruments? How does the tax administration prevent the misuse of confidential data and prohibit the transfer of tax information from the tax administrative body to non-tax government bodies?	

2. Information Security Management

The information security management systems used by each jurisdiction's tax administration must adhere to standards that ensure the protection of confidential taxpayer data. For example, there must be a screening process for employees handling the information, limits on who can access the information, and systems to detect and trace unauthorised disclosures. The internationally accepted standards for information security are known as the "ISO/IEC 27000-series". As described more fully below, a tax administration should be able to document that it is compliant with the ISO/IEC 27000-series standards or that it has an equivalent information security framework and that taxpayer information obtained under an exchange agreement is protected under that framework.

2.1.1. Background Checks and Contracts	
Primary Check-list Areas	• Screenings and background investigations for employees and contractors • Hiring process and contracts • Responsible Points of Contact
What procedures govern your tax administration's background investigations for employees and contractors who may have access to, use, or are responsible for protecting data received through exchange of information? Is this information publicly available? If so, please provide the reference. If not, please provide a summary of the procedures.	

2.1.2 Training and Awareness	
Primary Check-list Areas	• Initial training and periodic security awareness training based on roles, security risks, and applicable laws
What training does your tax administration provide to employees and contractors regarding confidential information including data received from partners through the Exchange of Information? Does your tax administration maintain a public version of the requirements? If so, please provide the reference. If not, please provide a summary of the requirement.	

2.1.3. Departure Policies	
Primary Check-list Areas	• Departure policies to terminate access to confidential information
What procedures does your tax administration maintain for terminating access to confidential information for departing employees and consultants? Are the procedures publicly available? If so, please provide the reference. If not, please provide a summary of the procedures.	

2.2.1. Physical Security: Access to Premises	
Primary Check-list Areas	• Security measures to restrict entry to premises: security guards, policies, entry access procedures

What procedures does your tax administration maintain to grant employees, consultants, and visitors access to premises where confidential information, paper or electronic, is stored? Are the procedures publicly available? If so, please provide the reference. If not, please provide a summary of the procedures.

2.2.2. Physical Security: Physical Document Storage	
Primary Check-list Areas	• Secure physical storage for confidential documents: policies and procedures

What procedures does your tax administration maintain for receiving, processing, archiving, retrieving and disposing of hard copies of confidential data received from taxpayers or exchange of information partners? Does your tax administration maintain procedures employees must follow when leaving their workspace at the end of the day? Are these procedures publicly available? If yes, please provide the reference. If not, please provide a summary.

Does your tax administration have a data classification policy? If so, please describe how your document storage procedures differ for data at all classification levels. Are these procedures publicly available? If yes, please provide the reference. If not, please provide a summary.

2.3. Planning	
Primary Check-list Areas	• Planning documentation to develop, update, and implement security information systems

What procedures does your tax administration maintain to develop, document, update, and implement security for information systems used to receive, process, archive and retrieve confidential information? Are these procedures publicly available? If yes, please provide the reference. If not, please provide a summary.

What procedures does your tax administration maintain regarding periodic Information Security Plan updates to address changes to the information systems environment, and how are problems and risks identified during the implementation of Information Security Plans resolved? Are these procedures publicly available? If yes, please provide the reference. If not, please provide a summary.

2.4. Configuration Management	
Primary Check-list Areas	• Configuration management and security controls

What policies does your tax administration maintain to regulate system configuration and updates? Are the policies publicly available? If yes, please provide the reference. If not, please provide a summary.

2.5. Access Control	
Primary Check-list Areas	• Access Control Policies and procedures: authorised personnel and international exchange of information

What policies does your tax administration maintain to limit system access to authorised users and safeguard data during transmission when received and stored? Please describe how your tax administration's access authorisation and data transmission policies extend to data received from an exchange of information partner under a Treaty or TIEA or other exchange agreement. Are the policies publicly available? If yes, please provide the reference. If not, please provide a summary.

2.6. Identification and Authentication	
Primary Check-list Areas	• Authenticating the identifying users and devices that require access to information systems

What policies and procedures does your tax administration maintain for each information system connected to confidential data? Are the policies and procedures publicly available? If so, please provide a reference. If not, please provide a summary.

What policies and procedures govern the authentication of authorised tax administration users by systems connected to confidential data? Are the policies and procedures publicly available? If so, please provide a reference. If not, please provide a summary.

2.7. Audit and Accountability	
Primary Check-list Areas	• Traceable electronic actions within systems • System audit procedures: monitoring, analysing, investigating and reporting of unlawful/unauthorised use

What policies and procedures does your tax administration maintain to ensure system audits take place that will detect unauthorised access? Are the policies publicly available? If so, please provide a reference. If not, please provide a summary.

2.8. Maintenance	
Primary Check-list Areas	• Periodic and timely maintenance of systems • Controls over: tools, procedures, and mechanisms for system maintenance and personnel use

What policies govern effective periodic system maintenance by your tax administration? Are these policies publicly available? If so, please provide a reference. If not, please provide a summary.

What procedures govern the resolution of system flaws identified by your tax administration? Are these procedures publicly available? If so, please provide a reference. If not, please provide a summary.

2.9. System and Communications Protection	
Primary Check-list Areas	• Procedures to monitor, control, and protect communications to and from information systems
What policies and procedures does your tax administration maintain for the electronic transmission and receipt of confidential data. Please describe the security and encryption requirements addressed in these policies. Are these policies publicly available? If so, please provide a reference. If not, please provide a summary.	

2.10. System and Information Integrity	
Primary Check-list Areas	• Procedures to identify, report, and correct information system flaws in a timely manner • Protection against malicious code and monitoring system security alerts
What procedures does your tax administration maintain to identify, report, and correct information system flaws in a timely manner? Please describe how these procedures provide for the protection of systems against malicious codes causing harm to data integrity. Are these procedures publicly available? If so, please provide a reference. If not, please provide a summary.	

2.11. Security Assessments	
Primary Check-list Areas	• Processes used to test, validate, and authorise the security controls for protecting data, correcting deficiencies, and reducing vulnerabilities
What policies does your tax administration maintain and regularly update for reviewing the processes used to test, validate, and authorise a security control plan? Is the policy publicly available? If so, please provide a reference. If not, please provide a summary.	

2.12. Contingency Planning	
Primary Check-list Areas	• Plans for emergency response, backup operations, and post-disaster recovery of information systems
What contingency plans and procedures does your tax administration maintain to reduce the impact of improper data disclosure or unrecoverable loss of data? Are the plans and procedures publicly available? If so, please provide a reference. If not, please provide a summary.	

2.13. Risk Assessment	
Primary Check-list Areas	• Potential risk of unauthorised access to taxpayer information • Risk and magnitude of harm from unauthorised use, disclosure, or disruption of the taxpayer information systems • Procedures to update risk assessment methodologies
Does your tax administration conduct risk assessments to identify risks and the potential impact of unauthorised access, use, and disclosure of information, or destruction of information systems? What procedures does your tax administration maintain to update risk assessment methodologies? Are these risk assessments and policies publicly available? If so, please provide a reference. If not, please provide a summary.	

2.14. Systems and Services Acquisition	
Primary Check-list Areas	• Methods and processes to ensure third-party providers of information systems process, store, and transmit confidential information in accordance with computer security requirements
What process does your tax administration maintain to ensure third-party providers are applying appropriate security controls that are consistent with computer security requirements for confidential information? Are the processes publicly available? If so, please provide a reference. If not, please provide a summary.	

2.15. Media Protection	
Primary Check-list Areas	• Processes to protect information in printed or digital form • Security measures used to limit media information access to authorised users only • Methods for sanitising or destroying digital media prior to disposal or reuse
What processes does your tax administration maintain to securely store and limit access to confidential information in printed or digital form upon receipt from any source? How does your tax administration securely destroy confidential media information prior to its disposal? Are the processes available publicly? If so, please provide a reference. If not, please provide a summary.	

2.16. Protection of Treaty-Exchanged data	
Primary Check-list Areas	• Procedures to ensure treaty-exchanged files are safeguarded and clearly labeled • Classification methods of treaty-exchanged files
What policies and processes does your tax administration maintain to store confidential information and clearly label it as treaty-exchanged after receipt from foreign Competent Authorities? Are these policies and processes publicly available? If so, please provide a reference. If not, please provide a summary.	

2.17. Information Disposal Policies	
Primary Check-list Areas	• Procedures for properly disposing paper and electronic files
What procedures does your tax administration maintain for the disposal of confidential information? Do these procedures extend to exchanged information from foreign Competent Authorities? Are the procedures publicly available? If so, please provide a reference. If not, please provide a summary.	

3. Monitoring and Enforcement

In addition to keeping treaty-exchanged information confidential, tax administrations must be able to ensure that its use will be limited to the purposes defined by the applicable information exchange agreement. Thus, compliance with an acceptable information security framework alone is not sufficient to protect treaty-exchanged tax data. In addition, domestic law must impose penalties or sanctions for improper disclosure or use of taxpayer information. To ensure implementation, such laws must be reinforced by adequate administrative resources and procedures.

3.1. Penalties and Sanctions	
Primary Check-list Areas	• Penalties imposed for unauthorised disclosures • Risk mitigation practices
Does your tax administration have the ability to impose penalties for unauthorised disclosures of confidential information? Do the penalties extend to unauthorised disclosure of confidential information exchanged with a treaty or TIEA partner? Are the penalties publicly available? If so, please provide a reference. If not, please provide a summary.	

3.2.1. Policing Unauthorised Access and Disclosure	
Primary Check-list Areas	• Monitoring to detect breaches • Reporting of breaches
What procedures does your tax administration have to monitor confidentiality breaches? What policies and procedures does your tax administration have that require employees and contractors to report actual or potential breaches of confidentiality? What reports does your tax administration prepare when a breach of confidentiality occurs? Are these policies and procedures publicly available? If so, please provide a reference. If not, please provide a summary.	

3.2.2. Sanctions and Prior Experience	
Primary Check-list Areas	• Prior unauthorised disclosures • Policy/process modifications to prevent future breaches
Have there been any cases in your jurisdiction where confidential information has been improperly disclosed? Have there been any cases in your jurisdiction where confidential information received by the Competent Authority from an exchange of information partner has been disclosed other than in accordance with the terms of the instrument under which it was provided? Does your tax administration or Inspector General make available to the public descriptions of any breaches, any penalties/sanctions imposed, and changes put in place to mitigate risk and prevent future breaches? If so, please provide a reference. If not, please provide a summary.	

Annex 5

Wider Approach to the Common Reporting Standard

Introduction

1.   The due diligence procedures in the CRS (in particular the indicia search procedures) are designed to identify Reportable Accounts understood as those of residents in a jurisdiction that is a Reportable Jurisdiction at the moment the due diligence procedures are performed. However, there are good reasons why jurisdictions may wish to go wider and, for instance, extend due diligence procedures to cover all non-residents or residents of jurisdictions with which they have an exchange of information instrument in place. Such an approach could significantly reduce costs for financial institutions because they would not need to perform additional due diligence each time a new jurisdiction joins.

2.   This document contains an extract from the CRS which was amended to provide for such a wider approach. The main changes to the CRS are the following:

- •   Any language suggesting that the procedures are designed to identify accounts that are Reportable Accounts at the moment the due diligence procedures are performed is deleted or amended.

- •   Under the indicia search procedure the Reporting Financial Institution is now required to search for indicia indicating that the Account Holder is resident in a Foreign Jurisdiction and to treat the Account as held by an Account Holder that is resident of each Foreign Jurisdiction for which an indicium is found (unless the FI follows the "curing procedure"). A Foreign Jurisdiction would be defined as any Jurisdiction other than the Jurisdiction of the Reporting Financial Institution. The advantage of this approach is that, if a new jurisdiction joins the system, the Reporting Financial Institution can rely on the results of that indicia search to determine which of its Preexisting Accounts are held by residents of such jurisdiction.

3.   The following examples illustrate the application of this wider approach:

- Example 1: Jurisdiction A decides to implement the Common Reporting Standard effective 1 January 2016, meaning that all accounts opened after that date are considered New Accounts.

  Mr. X is resident of Jurisdiction Z and opens an account with a financial institution in Jurisdiction A on 1 March 2016. At that moment, Jurisdiction Z is not a Reportable Jurisdiction. The financial institution will need to collect a self-certification from Mr. X, which will need to include his jurisdiction of residence for tax purposes but not his TIN or date of birth (as the account is not a Reportable Account at its opening). If Jurisdiction Z becomes a Reportable Jurisdiction in 2017, the financial institution can rely on the self-certification to establish that the account is a Reportable Account and will need to collect the TIN and date of birth from Mr. X by the end of 2019.

- Example 2: The same example, but the account is opened in 2014. If the financial institution has applied the indicia search with respect to Preexisting Accounts in 2016, it may rely on the information collected pursuant to such indicia search to determine the jurisdiction of residence of Mr. X and treat such account as a Reportable Account in 2017.

4.   In the below extract, the Reporting Financial Institution would not be required to report the TIN and date of birth with respect to accounts that were not reportable at the moment it performed the due diligence procedures. However, it would be required to collect such TIN and date of birth by the end of the second calendar year following the year in which such accounts were identified as Reportable Accounts (similar to Preexisting Accounts). To the extent compatible with local data protection rules, jurisdictions may also consider requiring the collection of TIN and/or date of birth for all Account Holders that are identified as foreign upon account opening (and not just those that are identified as resident of a Reportable Jurisdiction). This may possibly further reduce the burden for Financial Institutions as it is easier to collect such information before rather than after account opening. In addition, requiring an Account Holder's TIN would also provide additional assurance of the veracity of its self-certification.

5.   Although not required by the Common Reporting Standard, some jurisdictions may adopt an approach that goes beyond the approach contained in this Annex and, for example, extend the due diligence procedures to cover their own residents that are Controlling Persons of Passive NFEs. Thus, they would also receive information where one of their residents is a Controlling Person of a Passive NFE that holds an account with a Reporting Financial Institution. Such approach would require Reporting Financial Institutions

to report upon residents that, although not Account Holders themselves, are Controlling Persons of a Passive NFE that is an Account Holder. This may be done, e.g. by broadening the scope of the term "Reportable Person".

EXTRACT FROM THE CRS, AS AMENDED TO REQUIRE THE IDENTIFICATION OF THE STATUS OF ALL FOREIGN ACCOUNTS

Section I: General Reporting Requirements

A. Subject to paragraphs C through F, each Reporting Financial Institution must report the following information with respect to each Reportable Account of such Reporting Financial Institution:

1. the name, address, jurisdiction(s) of residence, TIN(s) and date and place of birth (in the case of an individual) of each Reportable Person that is an Account Holder of the account and, in the case of any Entity that is an Account Holder and that, after application of the due diligence procedures consistent with Sections V, VI and VII is identified as having one or more Controlling Persons that is a Reportable Person, the name, address, jurisdiction(s) of residence and TIN(s) of the Entity and the name, address, jurisdiction(s) of residence, TIN(s) and date and place of birth of each Reportable Person;

2. the account number (or functional equivalent in the absence of an account number);

3. the name and identifying number (if any) of the Reporting Financial Institution;

4. the account balance or value (including, in the case of a Cash Value Insurance Contract or Annuity Contract, the Cash Value or surrender value) as of the end of the relevant calendar year or other appropriate reporting period or, if the account was closed during such year or period, the closure of the account;

5. in the case of any Custodial Account:

    a) the total gross amount of interest, the total gross amount of dividends, and the total gross amount of other income generated with respect to the assets held in the account, in each case paid or credited to the account (or with respect to the account) during the calendar year or other appropriate reporting period; and *b)* the total gross proceeds from the sale or redemption of Financial Assets paid or credited to the account during the calendar year or other appropriate reporting period with respect to which the Reporting Financial Institution acted as a custodian, broker, nominee, or otherwise as an agent for the Account Holder;

6. in the case of any Depository Account, the total gross amount of interest paid or credited to the account during the calendar year or other appropriate reporting period; and

7. in the case of any account not described in subparagraph A(5) or A(6), the total gross amount paid or credited to the Account Holder with respect to the account during the calendar year or other appropriate reporting period with respect to which the Reporting Financial Institution is the obligor or debtor, including the aggregate amount of any redemption payments made to the Account Holder during the calendar year or other appropriate reporting period.

B. The information reported must identify the currency in which each amount is denominated.

C. Notwithstanding subparagraph A(1), with respect to each Reportable Account that is a Preexisting Account or with respect to each Financial Account that is opened prior to becoming a Reportable Account, the TIN(s) or date of birth is not required to be reported if such TIN(s) or date of birth is not in the records of the Reporting Financial Institution and is not otherwise required to be collected by such Reporting Financial Institution under domestic law. However, a Reporting Financial Institution is required to use reasonable efforts to obtain the TIN(s) and date of birth with respect to Preexisting Accounts by the end of the second calendar year following the year in which such Accounts were identified as Reportable Accounts.

D. Notwithstanding subparagraph A(1), the TIN is not required to be reported if *(i)* a TIN is not issued by the relevant Reportable Jurisdiction or *(ii)* the domestic law of the relevant Reportable Jurisdiction does not require the collection of the TIN issued by such Reportable Jurisdiction.

E. Notwithstanding subparagraph A(1), the place of birth is not required to be reported unless the Reporting Financial Institution is otherwise required to obtain and report it under domestic law and it is available in the electronically searchable data maintained by the Reporting Financial Institution.

F.   Notwithstanding paragraph A, the information to be reported with respect to [xxxx] is the information described in such paragraph, except for gross proceeds described in subparagraph A(5)(b).

Section II: General Due Diligence Requirements

A.   An account is treated as a Reportable Account beginning as of the date it is identified as such pursuant to the due diligence procedures described in Sections II through VII and, unless otherwise provided, information with respect to a Reportable Account must be reported annually in the calendar year following the year to which the information relates.

B.   A Reporting Financial Institution, which pursuant to the procedures described in Sections II through VII, identifies any account as a Foreign Account that is not a Reportable Account at the time the due diligence is performed, may rely on the outcome of such procedures to comply with future reporting obligations.

C.   The balance or value of an account is determined as of the last day of the calendar year or other appropriate reporting period.

D.   Where a balance or value threshold is to be determined as of the last day of a calendar year, the relevant balance or value must be determined as of the last day of the reporting period that ends with or within that calendar year.

E.   Each Jurisdiction may allow Reporting Financial Institutions to use service providers to fulfil the reporting and due diligence obligations imposed on such Reporting Financial Institutions, as contemplated in domestic law, but these obligations shall remain the responsibility of the Reporting Financial Institutions.

F.   Each Jurisdiction may allow Reporting Financial Institutions to apply the due diligence procedures for New Accounts to Preexisting Accounts, and the due diligence procedures for High value Accounts to Lower Value Accounts. Where a Jurisdiction allows New Account due diligence procedures to be used for Preexisting Accounts, the rules otherwise applicable to Preexisting Accounts continue to apply.

Section III: Due Diligence for Preexisting Individual Accounts

The following procedures apply with respect to Preexisting Individual Accounts.

A. **Accounts Not Required to be Reviewed, Identified, or Reported.** A Preexisting Individual Account that is a Cash Value Insurance Contract or an Annuity Contract is not required to be reviewed, identified or reported, provided the Reporting Financial Institution is effectively prevented by law from selling such Contract to residents of a Reportable Jurisdiction.

B. **Lower Value Accounts.** The following procedures apply with respect to Lower Value Accounts.

1. **Residence Address.** If the Reporting Financial Institution has in its records a current residence address for the individual Account Holder based on Documentary Evidence, the Reporting Financial Institution may treat the individual Account Holder as being a resident for tax purposes of the jurisdiction in which the address is located for purposes of determining whether such individual Account Holder is a Reportable Person.

2. **Electronic Record Search.** If the Reporting Financial Institution does not rely on a current residence address for the individual Account Holder based on Documentary Evidence as set forth in subparagraph B(1), the Reporting Financial Institution must review electronically searchable data maintained by the Reporting Financial Institution for any of the following indicia and apply subparagraphs B(3) through (6):

    a) identification of the Account Holder as a resident of a Foreign Jurisdiction;

    b) current mailing or residence address (including a post office box) in a Foreign Jurisdiction;

    c) one or more telephone numbers in a Foreign Jurisdiction and no telephone number in the jurisdiction of the Reporting Financial Institution;

    d) standing instructions (other than with respect to a Depository Account) to transfer funds to an account maintained in a Foreign Jurisdiction;

    e) currently effective power of attorney or signatory authority granted to a person with an address in a Foreign Jurisdiction; or

    f) a "hold mail" instruction or "in-care-of" address in a Foreign Jurisdiction if the Reporting Financial Institution does not have any other address on file for the Account Holder.

3. If none of the indicia listed in subparagraph B(2) are discovered in the electronic search, then no further action is required until there is a change in circumstances that results in one or more indicia being associated with the account, or the account becomes a High Value Account.

4. If any of the indicia listed in subparagraph B(2)(a) through (e) are discovered in the electronic search, or if there is a change in circumstances that results in one or more indicia being associated with the account, then the Reporting Financial Institution must treat the Account Holder as a resident for tax purposes of each Foreign Jurisdiction for which an indicium is identified, unless it elects to apply subparagraph B(6) and one of the exceptions in such subparagraph applies with respect to that account.

5. If a "hold mail" instruction or "in-care-of" address is discovered in the electronic search and no other address and none of the other indicia listed in subparagraph B(2)(a) through (e) are identified for the Account Holder, the Reporting Financial Institution must, in the order must appropriate to the circumstances, apply the paper record search described in subparagraph C(2), or seek to obtain from the Account Holder a self-certification or Documentary Evidence to establish the residence(s) for tax purposes of such Account Holder. If the paper search fails to establish an indicium and the attempt to obtain the self-certification or Documentary Evidence is not successful, the Reporting Financial Institution must report the account as an undocumented account.

6. Notwithstanding a finding of indicia under subparagraph B(2), a Reporting Financial Institution is not required to treat an Account Holder as a resident of a Foreign Jurisdiction if:

    a) the Account Holder information contains a current mailing or residence address in the Foreign Jurisdiction, one or more telephone numbers in the Foreign Jurisdiction (and no telephone number in the jurisdiction of the Reporting Financial Institution) or standing instructions (with respect to Financial Account other than Depository Accounts) to transfer funds to an account maintained in a Foreign Jurisdiction, the Reporting Financial Institution obtains, or has previously reviewed and maintains a record of:

        i) a self-certification from the Account Holder of the jurisdiction(s) of residence of such Account Holder that does not include such Foreign Jurisdiction; and *ii)* Documentary Evidence establishing the Account Holder's residence for tax purposes other than such Foreign Jurisdiction.

    b) the Account Holder information contains a currently effective power of attorney or signatory authority granted to a person with an address in a Foreign Jurisdiction, the Reporting Financial Institution obtains, or has previously reviewed and maintains a record of:

       i) a self-certification from the Account Holder of the jurisdiction(s) of residence of such Account Holder that does not include such Foreign Jurisdiction; or

       ii) Documentary Evidence establishing the Account Holder's residence for tax purposes other than Foreign Jurisdiction.

C. **Enhanced Review Procedures for High Value Accounts.** The following enhanced review procedures apply with respect to High Value Accounts.

    1. **Electronic Record Search.** With respect to High Value Accounts, the Reporting Financial Institution must review electronically searchable data maintained by the Reporting Financial Institution for any of the indicia described in subparagraph B(2).

    2. **Paper Record Search.** If the Reporting Financial Institution's electronically searchable databases include fields for, and capture all of the information described in, subparagraph C(3), then a further paper record search is no required. If the electronic databases do not capture all of this information, then with respect to a High Value Account, the Reporting Financial Institution must also review the current customer master file and, to the extent not contained in the current customer master file, the following documents associated with the account and obtained by the Reporting Financial Institution within the last five years for any of the indicia described in subparagraph B(2):

       a) the most recent Documentary Evidence collected with respect to the account;

       b) the most recent account opening contract or documentation;

       c) the most recent documentation obtained by the Reporting Financial Institution pursuant to AML/KYC Procedures or for other regulatory purposes;

d) any power of attorney or signature authority forms currently in effect; and

e) any standing instructions (other than with respect to a Depository Account) to transfer funds currently in effect.

3. **Exception To The Extent Databases Contain Sufficient Information.** A Reporting Financial Institution is not required to perform the paper record search described in subparagraph C(2) to the extent the Reporting Financial Institution's electronically searchable information includes the following:

    a) the Account Holder's residence status;

    b) the Account Holder's residence address and mailing address currently on file with the Reporting Financial Institution;

    c) the Account Holder's telephone number(s) currently on file, if any, with the Reporting Financial Institution;

    d) in the case of Financial Accounts other than Depository Accounts, whether there are standing instructions to transfer funds in the account to another account (including an account at another branch of the Reporting Financial Institution or another Financial Institution);

    e) whether there is a current "in care of" address or "hold mail" instruction for the Account Holder; and

    f) whether there is any power of attorney or signatory authority for the account.

4. **Relationship Manager Inquiry for Actual Knowledge.** In addition to the electronic and paper record searches described above, the Reporting Financial Institution must treat as a Reportable Account any High Value Account assigned to a relationship manager (including any Financial Accounts aggregated with that High Value Account) if the relationship manager has actual knowledge that the Account Holder is a Reportable Person.

5. **Effect of Finding Indicia.**

    a) If none of the indicia listed in subparagraph B(2) are discovered in the enhanced review of High Value Accounts described above, and the account is not identified as held by a resident for tax purposes in a Foreign Jurisdiction in subparagraph C(4), then further action is not required until there is a change in circumstances that results in one or more indicia being associated with the account.

b) If any of the indicia listed in subparagraph B(2)(a) through (e) are discovered in the enhanced review of High Value Accounts described above, or if there is a subsequent change in circumstances that results in one or more indicia being associated with the account, then the Reporting Financial Institution must treat the Account Holder as a resident for tax purposes of each Foreign Jurisdiction for which an indicium is identified unless it elects to apply subparagraph B(6) and one of the exceptions in such subparagraph applies with respect to that account.

c) If a "hold mail" instruction or "in-care-of" address is discovered in the enhanced review of High Value Account described above, and no other address and none of the other indicia listed in subparagraph B(2)(a) through (e) are identified for the Account Holder, the Reporting Financial Institution must obtain from such Account Holder a self-certification or Documentary Evidence to establish the residence(s) for tax purposes of the Account Holder. If the Reporting Financial Institution cannot obtain such self-certification or Documentary Evidence, it must report the account as an undocumented account.

6. If a Preexisting Individual Account is not a High Value Account as of 31 December [xxxx], but becomes a High Value Account as of the last day of a subsequent calendar year, the Reporting Financial Institution must complete the enhanced review procedures described in paragraph C with respect to such account within the calendar year following the year in which the account becomes a High Value Account. If based on this review such account is identified as a Reportable Account, the Reporting Financial Institution must report the required information about such account with respect to the year in which it is identified as a Reportable Account and subsequent years on an annual basis, unless the Account Holder ceases to be a Reportable Person.

7. Once a Reporting Financial Institution applies the enhanced review procedures described in paragraph C to a High Value Account, the Reporting Financial Institution is not required to re-apply such procedures, other than the relationship manager inquiry described in subparagraph C(4), to the same High Value Account in any subsequent year unless the account is undocumented where the Reporting Financial Institution should re-apply them annually until such account ceases to be undocumented.

8. If there is a change of circumstances with respect to a High Value Account that results in one or more indicia described in subparagraph B(2) being associated with the account, then the Reporting Financial Institution must treat the account as a Reportable Account with respect to each Foreign Jurisdiction for which an indicium is identified unless it elects to apply subparagraph B(6) and one of the exceptions in such subparagraph applies with respect to that account.

9. A Reporting Financial Institution must implement procedures to ensure that a relationship manager identifies any change in circumstances of an account. For example, if a relationship manager is notified that the Account Holder has a new mailing address in a Foreign Jurisdiction, the Reporting Financial Institution is required to treat the new address as a change in circumstances and, if it elects to apply subparagraph B(6), is required to obtain the appropriate documentation from the Account Holder.

D. Review of Preexisting Individual Accounts must be completed by [xx/xx/xxxx].

Section IV: Due Diligence for New Individual Accounts

The following procedures apply with respect to New Individual Accounts.

A. With respect to New Individual Accounts, upon account opening, a Reporting Financial Institution must obtain a self-certification, which may be part of the account opening documentation, that allows the Reporting Financial Institution to determine the Account Holder's residence(s) for tax purposes and confirm the reasonableness of such self-certification based on the information obtained by the Reporting Financial Institution in connection with the opening of the account, including any documentation collected pursuant to AML/KYC Procedures.

B. If the self-certification establishes that the Account Holder is resident for tax purposes in a Reportable Jurisdiction, the Reporting Financial Institution must treat the account as a Reportable Account and the self-certification must also include the Account Holder's TIN with respect to such Reportable Jurisdiction (subject to paragraph D of Section I) and date of birth.

C. If there is a change of circumstances with respect to a New Individual Account that causes the Reporting Financial Institution to know, or have reason to know, that the original self-certification is incorrect or unreliable, the Reporting Financial Institution cannot rely on the original self-certification and must obtain a valid self-certification that establishes the residence(s) for tax purposes of the Account Holder.

Section V: Due Diligence for Preexisting Entity Accounts

The following procedures apply with respect to Preexisting Entity Accounts.

A. **Entity Accounts Not Required to Be Reviewed, Identified or Reported.** Unless the Reporting Financial Institution elects otherwise, either with respect to all Preexisting Entity Accounts or, separately, with respect to any clearly identified group of such accounts, a Preexisting Entity Account with an aggregate account balance or value that does not exceed USD 250 000 as of 31 December [xxxx], is not required to be reviewed, identified, or reported as a Reportable Account until the aggregate account balance or value exceeds USD 250 000 as of the last day of any subsequent calendar year.

B. **Entity Accounts Subject to Review.** A Preexisting Entity Account that has an aggregate account balance or value that exceeds USD 250 000 as of 31 December [xxxx], and a Preexisting Entity Account that does not exceed USD 250 000 as of 31 December [xxxx] but the aggregate account balance or value of which exceeds USD 250 000 as of the last day of any subsequent calendar year, must be reviewed in accordance with the procedures set forth in paragraph D.

C. **Review Procedures for Identifying Entity Accounts With Respect to Which Reporting may be Required.** For Preexisting Entity Accounts described in paragraph B, a Reporting Financial Institution must apply the following review procedures:

1. **Determine the Residence of the Entity.**

   a) Review information maintained for regulatory or customer relationship purposes (including information collected pursuant to AML/KYC Procedures) to determine the Account Holder's residence. For this purpose, information indicating the Account Holder's residence includes a place of incorporation or organisation, or an address in a Foreign Jurisdiction.

b) If the information indicates that the Account Holder is a Reportable Person, the Reporting Financial Institution must treat the account as a Reportable Account unless it obtains a self-certification from the Account Holder, or reasonably determines based on information in its possession or that is publicly available, that the Account Holder is not a Reportable Person.

2. **Determine the Residence of the Controlling Persons of a Passive NFE.** With respect to an Account Holder of a Preexisting Entity Account (including an Entity that is a Reportable Person), the Reporting Financial Institution must identify whether the Account Holder is a Passive NFE with one or more Controlling Persons and determine the residence of such Controlling Persons. If any of the Controlling Persons of a Passive NFE is a Reportable Person, then the account is treated as a Reportable Account. In making these determinations the Reporting Financial Institution must follow the guidance in subparagraphs C(2)(a) through (c) in the order most appropriate under the circumstances.

a) **Determining whether the Account Holder is a Passive NFE.** For purposes of determining whether the Account Holder is a Passive NFE, the Reporting Financial Institution must obtain a self-certification from the Account Holder to establish its status, unless it has information in its possession or that is publicly available, based on which it can reasonably determine that the Account Holder is an Active NFE or a Financial Institution other than an Investment Entity described in subparagraph A(6)(b) of Section VIII that is not a Participating Jurisdiction Financial Institution.

b) **Determining the Controlling Persons of an Account Holder.** For the purposes of determining the Controlling Persons of an Account Holder, a Reporting Financial Institution may rely on information collected and maintained pursuant to AML/KYC Procedures.

c) **Determining the residence of a Controlling Person of a Passive NFE.** For the purposes of determining the residence of a Controlling Person of a Passive NFE, a Reporting Financial Institution may rely on:

i) information collected and maintained pursuant to AML/ KYC Procedures in the case of a Preexisting Entity Account held by one or more Passive NFEs with an aggregate account balance or value that does not exceed USD 1 000 000; or

ii) a self-certification from the Account Holder or such Controlling Person of the jurisdiction(s) in which the Controlling Person is resident for tax purposes. If a self-certification is not provided, the Reporting Financial Institution will establish such residence(s) by applying the procedures described in paragraph C of Section III.

D. **Timing of Review and Additional Procedures Applicable to Preexisting Entity Accounts.**

1. Review of Preexisting Entity Accounts with an aggregate account balance or value that exceeds USD 250 000 as of 31 December [xxxx] must be completed by 31 December [xxxx].

2. Review of Preexisting Entity Accounts with an aggregate account balance or value that does not exceed USD 250 000 as of 31 December [xxxx], but exceeds USD 250 000 as of 31 December of a subsequent year, must be completed within the calendar year following the year in which the aggregate account balance or value exceeds USD 250 000.

3. If there is a change of circumstances with respect to a Preexisting Entity Account that causes the Reporting Financial Institution to know, or have reason to know, that the self-certification or other documentation associated with an account is incorrect or unreliable, the Reporting Financial Institution must re-determine the status of the account in accordance with the procedures set forth in paragraph C.

Section VI: Due Diligence for New Entity Accounts

The following procedures apply with respect to New Entity Accounts.

A. **Review Procedures for Identifying Entity Accounts With Respect to Which Reporting may be Required.** For New Entity Accounts, a Reporting Financial Institution must apply the following review procedures:

1. **Determine the Residence of the Entity.**

    a) Obtain a self-certification, which may be part of the account opening documentation, that allows the Reporting Financial Institution to determine the Account Holder's residence(s) for tax purposes and confirm the reasonableness of such self-certification based on the information obtained by the Reporting Financial Institution in connection with the opening of the account, including any documentation collected pursuant to AML/KYC Procedures. If the Entity certifies that it has no residence for tax purposes, the Reporting Financial Institution may rely on the address of the principal office of the Entity to determine the residence of the Account Holder.

b) If the self-certification indicates that the Account Holder is resident in a Reportable Jurisdiction, the Reporting Financial Institution must treat the account as a Reportable Account unless it reasonably determines based on information in its possession or that is publicly available, that the Account Holder is not a Reportable Person with respect to such Reportable Jurisdiction.

2. **Determine the Residence of the Controlling Persons of a Passive NFE.** With respect to an Account Holder of a New Entity Account (including an Entity that is a Reportable Person), the Reporting Financial Institution must identify whether the Account Holder is a Passive NFE with one or more Controlling Persons and determine the residence of such Reportable Persons. If any of the Controlling Persons of a Passive NFE is a Reportable Person, then the account must be treated as a Reportable Account. In making these determinations the Reporting Financial Institution must follow the guidance in subparagraphs A(2)(a) through (c) in the order most appropriate under the circumstances.

a) **Determining whether the Account Holder is a Passive NFE.** For purposes of determining whether the Account Holder is a Passive NFE, the Reporting Financial Institution must rely on a self-certification from the Account Holder to establish its status, unless it has information in its possession or that is publicly available, based on which it can reasonably determine that the Account Holder is an Active NFE or a Financial Institution other than an Investment Entity described in subparagraph A(6)(b) of Section VIII that is not a Participating Jurisdiction Financial Institution.

b) **Determining the Controlling Persons of an Account Holder.** For purposes of determining the Controlling Persons of an Account Holder, a Reporting Financial Institution may rely on information collected and maintained pursuant to AML/KYC Procedures.

     c) **Determining the residence of a Controlling Person of a Passive NFE.** For purposes of determining the residence of a Controlling Person of a Passive NFE, a Reporting Financial Institution may rely on a self-certification from the Account Holder or such Controlling Person.

Section VII: Special Due Diligence Rules

     The following additional rules apply in implementing the due diligence procedures described above.

A. **Reliance on Self-Certifications and Documentary Evidence.** A Reporting Financial Institution may not rely on a self-certification or Documentary Evidence if the Reporting Financial Institution knows or has reason to know that the self-certification or Documentary Evidence is incorrect or unreliable.

B. **Alternative Procedures for Financial Accounts Held by Individual Beneficiaries of a Cash Value Insurance Contract or an Annuity Contract.** A Reporting Financial Institution may presume that an individual beneficiary (other than the owner) of a Cash Value Insurance Contract or an Annuity Contract receiving a death benefit is not a Reportable Person and may treat such Financial Account as other than a Reportable Account unless the Reporting Financial Institution has actual knowledge, or reason to know, that the beneficiary is a Reportable Person. A Reporting Financial Institution has reason to know that a beneficiary of a Cash Value Insurance Contract or an Annuity Contract is a Reportable Person if the information collected by the Reporting Financial Institution and associated with the beneficiary contains indicia of residence in a Foreign Jurisdiction as described in paragraph B of Section III. If a Reporting Financial Institution has actual knowledge, or reason to know, that the beneficiary is a Reportable Person, the Reporting Financial Institution must follow the procedures in paragraph B of Section III.

C. **Account Balance Aggregation and Currency Rules.**

    1. **Aggregation of Individual Accounts.** For purposes of determining the aggregate balance or value of Financial Accounts held by an individual, a Reporting Financial Institution is required to aggregate all Financial Accounts maintained by the Reporting Financial Institution, or by a Related Entity, but only to the extent that the Reporting Financial Institution's computerised systems link the Financial Accounts by reference to a data element such as client number or TIN, and allow

account balances or values to be aggregated. Each holder of a jointly held Financial Account shall be attributed the entire balance or value of the jointly held Financial Account for purposes of applying the aggregation requirements described in this subparagraph.

2. **Aggregation of Entity Accounts.** For purposes of determining the aggregate balance or value of Financial Accounts held by an Entity, a Reporting Financial Institution is required to take into account all Financial Accounts that are maintained by the Reporting Financial Institution, or by a Related Entity, but only to the extent that the Reporting Financial Institution's computerised systems link the Financial Accounts by reference to a data element such as client number or TIN, and allow account balances or values to be aggregated. Each holder of a jointly held Financial Account shall be attributed the entire balance or value of the jointly held Financial Account for purposes of applying the aggregation requirements described in this subparagraph.

3. **Special Aggregation Rule Applicable to Relationship Managers.** For purposes of determining the aggregate balance or value of Financial Accounts held by a person to determine whether a Financial Account is a High Value Account, a Reporting Financial Institution is also required, in the case of any Financial Accounts that a relationship manager knows, or has reason to know, are directly or indirectly owned, controlled, or established (other than in a fiduciary capacity) by the same person, to aggregate all such accounts.

4. **Amounts Read to Include Equivalent in Other Currencies.** All dollar amounts are in US dollars and shall be read to include equivalent amounts in other currencies, as determined by domestic law.

Annex 6

Declaration on Automatic Exchange of Information in Tax Matters

(Adopted on 6 May 2014)

WE, THE MINISTERS AND REPRESENTATIVES of Argentina, Australia, Austria, Belgium, Brazil, Canada, the People's Republic of China, Chile, Colombia, Costa Rica, the Czech Republic, Denmark, Estonia, Finland, France, Germany, Greece, Hungary, Iceland, India, Indonesia, Ireland, Israel, Italy, Japan, Korea, Latvia, Lithuania, Luxembourg, Malaysia, Mexico, the Netherlands, New Zealand, Norway, Poland, Portugal, Saudi Arabia, Singapore, the Slovak Republic, Slovenia, South Africa, Spain, Sweden, Switzerland, Turkey, the United Kingdom, the United States and the European Union;

WELCOMING the OECD *Standard for Automatic Exchange of Financial Account Information*, which provides the key elements for establishing a single, common global standard for the automatic exchange of financial account information (hereafter "the new single global standard") thereby affording tax administrations around the world with a very powerful new tool to tackle cross-border tax evasion and non-compliance;

NOTING WITH SATISFACTION its strong endorsement by the G20 Finance Ministers and Central Bank Governors and their commitment to implement it at their meeting on 22-23 February 2014;

CONSIDERING that tax fraud and tax evasion jeopardise citizens' trust in the fairness and integrity of the tax system as a whole, thereby undermining voluntary tax compliance by all taxpayers, which is essential to effective tax administration;

CONSIDERING that the fight against tax fraud and tax evasion will, in turn, increase revenues which will help enable growth-enhancing public investment, restore the health of our public finances and provide the essential public services that our citizens demand;

MINDFUL that as the world becomes increasingly globalised it is becoming easier for all taxpayers to make, hold and manage investments through financial institutions outside of their country of residence, and that investments that are kept offshore by taxpayers may go untaxed to the extent that taxpayers fail to comply with their tax obligations to the detriment of those who pay their taxes;

CONSIDERING that cross-border tax fraud and tax evasion are serious problems for jurisdictions all over the world, small and large, developed and developing;

CONSCIOUS that co-operation between tax administrations is critical in the fight against tax fraud and tax evasion and in promoting international tax compliance, and that a key aspect of such co-operation is effective exchange of information on an automatic basis subject to appropriate safeguards;

RECOGNISING the tremendous progress achieved by the Global Forum on Transparency and Exchange of Information for Tax Purposes (hereafter "Global Forum") in ensuring that international standards of transparency and exchange of information on request are fully implemented around the globe;

NOTING that there is growing interest in many countries in the opportunities provided by reciprocal automatic exchange of information between tax authorities;

WELCOMING the commitments already made for early adoption of the new single global standard by a large number of countries and jurisdictions;

CONSCIOUS that the new single global standard should not impose undue business and administrative costs;

NOTING that although the new single global standard covers financial account information, it does not restrict the ability of countries to exchange financial information under different types of legal arrangements or to exchange other types or categories of information on an automatic basis;

ACKNOWLEDGING the important role that the multilateral Convention on Mutual Administrative Assistance in Tax Matters can play in facilitating rapid implementation of automatic exchange of information and WELCOMING the fact that over 60 countries have already signed the Convention, including almost all OECD countries, all G20 countries, and a growing number of financial centres and developing countries;

WELCOMING the recent establishment by the Global Forum of a Working Group on Automatic Exchange of Information, which will develop a mechanism to monitor and review the implementation of the new single global standard for automatic exchange of information and also a framework to offer technical assistance to developing countries in meeting the standard.

****

1.   DECLARE that we are determined to tackle cross-border tax fraud and tax evasion and to promote international tax compliance through mutual administrative assistance in tax matters and a level playing field;

2.   CONFIRM that automatic exchange of financial account information will further these objectives particularly if the new single global standard, including full transparency on ownership interests, is implemented among all financial centres;

3.   ACKNOWLEDGE that information exchanged on the basis of the new single global standard is subject to appropriate safeguards including certain confidentiality requirements and the requirement that information may be used only for the purposes foreseen by the legal instrument pursuant to which it is exchanged;

4.   ARE DETERMINED to implement the new single global standard swiftly, on a reciprocal basis. We will translate the standard into domestic law, including to ensure that information on beneficial ownership of legal persons and arrangements is effectively collected and exchanged in accordance with the standard;

5.   CALL on all financial centres to implement the new single global standard without delay;

6.   UNDERLINE the need for assistance to be provided to developing countries so that they may be able to reap the benefits of this form of co-operation;

7.   URGE the OECD Committee on Fiscal Affairs, working with G20 members, to proceed rapidly with the elaboration of a) a detailed commentary to help ensure the consistent application of the new single global standard and b) the remaining technical modalities and safeguards including information and guidance on the necessary technical solutions, a standard format for reporting and exchange, and minimum standards on confidentiality;

8.   EXPECT that the remaining elements of the work referred to in paragraph 7 will be finalised and approved by mid-2014;

9.   ENCOURAGE all countries that have not already done so to sign and ratify the multilateral Convention on Mutual Administrative Assistance in Tax Matters without further delay;

10.   EXPECT the swift establishment by the Global Forum of a mechanism to monitor and review the implementation of the new single global standard;

11.   INVITE the Secretary-General of the OECD to report on the Committee on Fiscal Affairs' progress in developing further guidance on the implementation of the new single global standard at the 2015 Meeting of the Council at Ministerial level and at other international fora as appropriate.

Annex 7

Recommendation of the Council on the Standard for Automatic Exchange of Financial Account Information in Tax Matters

(Adopted on 15 July 2014)

THE COUNCIL,

HAVING REGARD to Article 5 b) of the Convention on the Organisation for Economic Co-operation and Development of 14 December 1960;

HAVING REGARD to the Recommendation of the Council on Tax Avoidance and Evasion [C(77)149/FINAL], the Recommendation of the Council on the Use of Tax Identification Numbers in an International Context [C(97)29/FINAL] and the Recommendation of the Council concerning the Model Tax Convention on Income and on Capital [C(97)195/FINAL];

HAVING REGARD to Article 26 of the Model Tax Convention on Income and on Capital;

HAVING REGARD to the Convention on Mutual Administrative Assistance in Tax Matters of 25 January 1988, as amended by the 2010 Protocol [C(2010)10/FINAL], which has a growing number of Parties and signatories, currently totalling over 60 countries;

HAVING REGARD to the significant progress achieved by the Global Forum on Transparency and Exchange of Information for Tax Purposes in ensuring that international standards of transparency and exchange of information on request are fully implemented around the globe;

HAVING REGARD to the Declaration on Automatic Exchange of Information in Tax Matters adopted on 6 May 2014 by 47 countries, including all Members, Argentina, Brazil, the People's Republic of China, Colombia, Costa Rica, India, Indonesia, Latvia, Lithuania, Malaysia, Saudi Arabia, Singapore, South Africa as well as the European Union [C/MIN(2014)5/FINAL];

CONSIDERING that international cooperation is critical in the fight against tax fraud and tax evasion and in ensuring tax compliance, and that a key aspect of such cooperation is effective exchange of information on an automatic basis subject to appropriate safeguards;

CONSIDERING that the adoption of a single standard for automatic exchange of financial account information in tax matters will avoid the proliferation of different standards which would increase complexity and costs for both governments and financial institutions;

CONSIDERING that implementation of a single standard by all financial centres will ensure a level playing field;

CONSIDERING the need to encourage consistent application and interpretation across countries of the single standard;

CONSIDERING the mandate of the Global Forum on Transparency and Exchange of Information for Tax Purposes and the rapid evolution of the standards of transparency and exchange of information for tax purposes;

WELCOMING the Standard for Automatic Exchange of Financial Account Information in Tax Matters which is composed of the Common Reporting Standard and the Model Competent Authority Agreement (hereafter the "Standard"), approved by the Committee on Fiscal Affairs;

TAKING NOTE of the Commentaries to the Common Reporting Standard and the Commentaries to the Model Competent Authority Agreement (hereafter the "Commentaries"), approved by the Committee on Fiscal Affairs [C(2014)81/ADD1];

On the proposal of the Committee on Fiscal Affairs:

I.   RECOMMENDS that Members and non-Members adhering to this Recommendation (hereafter the "Adherents") swiftly implement on a reciprocal basis the Standard set out in the Annex to this Recommendation of which it forms an integral part.

To this effect, Adherents should:

(a) transpose the Standard into domestic law, including to ensure that information on beneficial ownership of legal persons and arrangements is effectively collected and exchanged in accordance with the Standard;

(b) take the necessary measures in compliance with their domestic law to implement any amendments to the Standard; and

(c) ensure that appropriate safeguards are in place to protect the confidentiality of information exchanged and to comply with the requirement that information may be used only for the purposes foreseen by the legal instrument pursuant to which the information is exchanged;

II. RECOMMENDS that Adherents follow the Commentaries when applying and interpreting the relevant domestic law provisions;

III. INVITES Adherents and the Secretary-General to disseminate this Recommendation widely;

IV. INVITES non-Members to implement the Standard and to adhere to this Recommendation;

V. INVITES Adherents to support efforts for capacity building and assistance to developing countries so that they may be able to participate in and reap the benefits of this form of co-operation;

VI. INVITES all countries that have not already done so to sign and ratify the Convention on Mutual Administrative Assistance in Tax Matters as amended by the 2010 Protocol;

VII. INVITES the Global Forum on Transparency and Exchange of Information for Tax Purposes to monitor the implementation of the Standard;

VIII. INSTRUCTS the Committee on Fiscal Affairs to:

(i) monitor the application of the Recommendation and to report thereon to the Council no later than three years following its adoption and regularly thereafter;

(ii) stand ready to review the Standard and Commentaries in the light of experience gained by Adherents and in consultation with stakeholders;

(iii) adopt any required modifications to the Commentaries and make appropriate proposals to Council for modifications to the Standard.

ORGANISATION FOR ECONOMIC CO-OPERATION AND DEVELOPMENT

The OECD is a unique forum where governments work together to address the economic, social and environmental challenges of globalisation. The OECD is also at the forefront of efforts to understand and to help governments respond to new developments and concerns, such as corporate governance, the information economy and the challenges of an ageing population. The Organisation provides a setting where governments can compare policy experiences, seek answers to common problems, identify good practice and work to co-ordinate domestic and international policies.

The OECD member countries are: Australia, Austria, Belgium, Canada, Chile, the Czech Republic, Denmark, Estonia, Finland, France, Germany, Greece, Hungary, Iceland, Ireland, Israel, Italy, Japan, Korea, Luxembourg, Mexico, the Netherlands, New Zealand, Norway, Poland, Portugal, the Slovak Republic, Slovenia, Spain, Sweden, Switzerland, Turkey, the United Kingdom and the United States. The European Union takes part in the work of the OECD.

OECD Publishing disseminates widely the results of the Organisation's statistics gathering and research on economic, social and environmental issues, as well as the conventions, guidelines and standards agreed by its members.

OECD PUBLISHING, 2, rue André-Pascal, 75775 PARIS CEDEX 16
(23 2014 13 1 P) ISBN 978-92-64-21651-8 – 2014